# THE UNBRO

## MARGARET S. MAHLER SERIES

This series of yearly volumes began appearing in 1991 and is based upon the panel discussions presented at the prestigious Annual Margaret Mahler Symposia held in Philadelphia. Each volume consists of three papers and their discussions presented at the most recent Symposium. A thorough introduction and a comprehensive conclusion that pulls all the material together are specially written for the book. Occasionally, one or two papers that were not presented at the meeting but represent the cutting-edge thinking on the topic are also included. While this format and organization gives these books a friendly familiarity, the books' contents vary greatly and are invariably a source of excitement and clinical enthusiasm. Volumes published so far have addressed topics as diverse as hatred and cultural differences in childhood development, extramarital affairs and sibling relationship, mourning and self psychology, and resilience and boundary violations. Among the distinguished psychoanalysts whose work has appeared in this series are Salman Akhtar, Anni Bergman, Harold Blum, Ruth Fischer, Alvin Frank, Dorothy Holmes, Otto Kernberg, Selma Kramer, Peter Neubauer, Henri Parens, Fred Pine, John Munder Ross, and Ernest Wolf, to name a few. The vantage point is always broad-based and includes developmental, clinical, and cultural variables but the end point is consistently an enhancement of the technical armamentarium of the therapist.

## BOOKS BASED UPON THE
## MARGARET S. MAHLER SYMPOSIA

*The Trauma of Transgression* (1991)
*When the Body Speaks* (1992)
*Mahler and Kohut* (1994)
*Prevention in Mental Health* (1993)
*The Birth of Hatred* (1995)
*The Internal Mother* (1995)
*Intimacy and Infidelity* (1996)
*The Seasons of Life* (1997)
*The Colors of Childhood* (1998)
*Thicker Than Blood* (1999)

*Does God Help?* (2000)
*Three Faces of Mourning* (2001)
*Real and Imaginary Fathers*
    (2004)
*The Language of Emotions* (2005)
*Interpersonal Boundaries* (2006)
*Listening to Others* (2007)
*The Unbroken Soul* (2008)
*Lying, Cheating, and Carrying On*
    (2009)

# THE UNBROKEN SOUL

## Tragedy, Trauma, and Human Resilience

*Edited by*
*Henri Parens,*
*Harold P. Blum,*
*and Salman Akhtar*

JASON ARONSON

*Lanham • Boulder • New York • Toronto • Plymouth, UK*

Published in the United States of America
by Jason Aronson
An imprint of Rowman & Littlefield Publishers, Inc.

A wholly owned subsidary of
The Rowman & Littlefield Publishing Group, Inc.
4501 Forbes Boulevard, Suite 200, Lanham, Maryland 20706
www.rowmanlittlefield.com

Estover Road
Plymouth PL6 7PY
United Kingdom

British Library Cataloguing in Publication Information Available

**Library of Congress Cataloging-in-Publication Data**

The unbroken soul : tragedy, trauma, and human resilience / [edited by] Henri Parens, Harold P. Blum, Salman Akhtar.
    p. ; cm.
Includes bibliographical references and index.
ISBN-13: 978-0-7657-0588-4 (cloth : alk. paper)
ISBN-10: 0-7657-0588-5 (cloth : alk. paper)
ISBN-13: 978-0-7657-0589-1 (pbk. : alk. paper)
ISBN-10: 0-7657-0589-3 (pbk. : alk. paper)
    1. Psychic trauma. 2. Post-traumatic stress disorder. 3. Resilience (Personality trait)
I. Parens, Henri, 1928– II. Blum, Harold P., 1929– III. Akhtar, Salman, 1946 July 31–
    [DNLM: 1. Stress, Psychological—psychology. 2. Adaptation, Psychological.
3. Stress Disorders, Post-Traumatic—psychology. WM 172 U54 2008]
RC552.T7U53 2008
    616.85'21—dc22                                                                            2007043651

Printed in the United States of America

# CONTENTS

# ACKNOWLEDGMENTS

The chapters in this volume were presented at two Margaret S. Mahler Symposia on Child Development held annually in Philadelphia that addressed the related topics of trauma and resilience. All but two were part of the Thirty-Eighth Annual Symposium on Resilience held on April 14, 2007, at Jefferson Medical College. The other two were part of the Thirty-Fourth Annual Symposium on Trauma held on May 3, 2003, presentations that were not then published. The editors are indebted to the contributors to this volume. In addition, we are especially indebted to Dr. Michael Vergare, Chairman of the Department of Psychiatry and Human Behavior of Jefferson Medical College, and to Dr. Bernard Friedberg of the Psychoanalytic Center of Philadelphia, Chairman of the Psychoanalytic Foundation, both of whom supported our efforts to effect these symposia along the way. Special appreciation is extended to Melissa Nevin, who, with the help of a number of others from both institutions, contributed time and energy toward their preparation, occurrence, and success. We also thank those members of the Margaret S. Mahler Psychiatric Research Foundation who helped in the planning of these symposia, especially Drs. William Singletary and Jennifer Bonovitz.

# THE BIOPSYCHOSOCIAL MIRACLE OF HUMAN RESILIENCE

## An Overview

*Salman Akhtar, MD*
*and Glenda Wrenn, MD*

The deleterious impact of psychological trauma manifests in symptom clusters that are so diverse as to be practically innumerable. The most commonly seen pathways, however, are (1) phobic withdrawal from specific situations or from life in general, (2) masochistic brooding and "injustice collecting" (Bergler, 1961), (3) chronic anger and revenge seeking, (4) flashbacks, nightmares, startle reactions, and other signs of "post-traumatic stress disorder" (*DSM–IV–TR*, 2000, pp. 463–468), and (5) making narcissistic capital out of misfortune and regarding oneself as an "exception" (Freud, 1916) to the ordinary rules and regulations of the society. All this is well established. It forms the daily staple of clinical practice in the mental health field. Less recognized is the fact that psychological trauma can, at times, have silently positive effects upon the individual's ego functioning and adaptation. These include vigilance, healthy stoicism, enhanced ambition, perseverance, and pursuit of knowledge about self and others. A posttraumatic increase in altruism is also sometimes evident.

Such Janus-faced consequences of trauma give rise to all sorts of questions. For instance, what determines whether positive or negative consequences will be predominant in the aftermath of trauma? What regulates their proportion? Is the outcome of trauma a once-and-for-all occurrence or subject to psychic elaboration, layering, and modification? Do pretraumatic ego assets matter more in governing the outcome of trauma than the ameliorative influences that follow it? What is the role of intelligence, inborn talents, imagination, and fantasy here? How and to what extent do societal institutions (e.g., organizations, museums, memorials) and cultural containers (e.g., theater, cinema, poetry) help transform the impact of individual or group trauma? And, so on.

From this panoply of curiosity, one question stands out for the clinician: why is it that some individuals crumble in the face of trauma while others can withstand any assault on their system? In other words, what are the genesis, dynamics, and epistemology of resilience?

## What Is Resilience?

The major psychoanalytic glossaries (Eidelberg, 1968; Laplanche & Pontalis, 1973; Moore & Fine, 1968, 1990; Rycroft, 1968) do not list *resilience* as a recognized term, and the index to Freud's collected works has no entry on it (*Standard Edition*, Vol. 23). Turning to the English language, one finds *resilience* defined in *Webster's Ninth New Collegiate Dictionary* as "1: the capability of a strained body to recover its size and shape after deformation caused especially by compressive stress, 2: an ability to recover from or adjust easily to misfortune or change" (Mish, 1987, p. 1003). A careful look at this definition reveals that resilience (1) can involve both physical and psychological realms, (2) is not only a response to trauma but to change in general, and (3) consists of either a return to the psychosomatic status quo or to a more or less harmonious adaptation to the altered inner or outer reality.

The last mentioned characteristic brings forth the linguistic conundrum involving the relationship between resilience and flexibility. While occasionally used interchangeably (Kay, 1976, pp. 343, 673), the two denote rather different phenomena. *Flexibility* indicates malleability, compliance, and adjustment to changed situations. *Resilience*, in contrast, puts a premium on return to the original state, defiance, and recovery. In Hartmann's (1939/1958) terms, *flexibility* is closer to *autoplastic* and *resilience* to *alloplastic* adaptation.

This brings us back to psychoanalytic literature pertaining to the forces that lead individuals toward self-protection and recovery from mishaps and hardships. Freud's (1905, 1909, 1915) description of "ego instincts" is a case in point here. These instincts served "self preservative" (1909, p. 44), "self seeking" (1908, p. 212), and "self subsisting" (1930, p. 122) aims. The prefix *self* in this context is usually taken to mean bodily self, and it does have that connotation. However, it also includes the psychic self; thus, the aims of ego instincts were also *psychically* self-preservative and self-seeking. Freud emphasized that self-preservative instincts operate in accord with the reality principle and strive for what is useful to guard against damage to the individual.

A more explicit enunciation of psychological forces that help an individual rebound from suffering is to be found in Nunberg's (1926) paper titled "The Will to Recovery." Nunberg posited that a mind faced with trauma or struggling with neurotic conflict longs for infantile omnipotence. This regressive sleeve of the ego later becomes the source for the energy to overcome the psychic disturbance one is faced with. LaForgue (1929) added that a benevolent superego needs to be in place for this transformation of infantile omnipotence into adaptive energy to take place.

Four years later, Freud (1933) specifically mentioned the "instinct for recovery" (p. 106) and traced its phylogenetic origins to the "power of regenerating lost organs" (p. 106) in lower animals. He acknowledged that this force contributed to the success of psychotherapy and psychoanalysis. Temperamentally given to pessimism, which had steadily increased with old age and illness, Freud, however, did not go deeper into the nature of the "instinct for recovery"; instead, he used the idea to buttress his proposals of repetition-compulsion and death instinct.

The concept of an inner force that propels recovery and, by implication, is responsible for human resilience in the face of trauma remained ill-developed in subsequent years of psychoanalysis. Freud's disinterest contributed to this inattention. The fact that over the years psychoanalytic motivation theory went much farther than its early drive-based model also resulted in the "instinct for recovery" to be left behind.

Three avenues of psychoanalytic observation then led to a rejuvenation of interest in resilience and recovery: (1) the study of the experiences of the Nazi Holocaust survivors (Brenner, 2004; Kestenberg, 1972; Kestenberg & Brenner, 1996; Kogan, 1995, 2007; Valent, 1988), (2) empirical observations of children raised by grossly disturbed (Anthony & Cohler, 1987) or physically impaired (Wagenheim, 1985) parents, and (3) the infant-observational studies (e.g., Edgcumbe & Burgner, 1972; Emde, Graensbauer, & Harmon, 1976; Lichtenberg, 1989; Parens, 1979) that permitted access to the inner motivational systems pertaining to basic human needs of survival and growth, including the human "self righting instinct" (Lichtenberg, 1989). Together these three sources of information shed light upon the multidetermined nature of human resilience. They underscored the complex interplay of constitutional, intrapsychic, and societal factors in the genesis and sustenance of this capacity.

Equipped with this linguistic and psychoanalytic thesaurus, one might define resilience as an ego capacity to metabolize psychological trauma to the extent that resumption of the original level of psychic functioning becomes possible. However, this does not imply a literal return to the original state since the pretrauma innocence is neither recoverable nor desirable anymore. Hence the resumption of functioning typical of resilience is an ego advancement; it assimilates the psychological consequences of trauma and is accompanied by deeper insight into the self and its interpersonal context. Needless to add, such advance is inwardly supported by a strong constitution (Anthony, 1987), unimpeded functioning of ego instincts (Freud, 1905), the achievement of libidinal object constancy (Hartmann, 1952; Mahler, 1968; Mahler, Pine, & Bergman, 1975), a benevolent and kind superego (Nunberg, 1926; LaForgue, 1929) made of good internal objects, and familial and societal support systems.

These complex constituents of resilience will be elucidated in the chapters to follow. However, sensing that the authors of these chapters will focus upon psychological trauma (individual or group), we offer three striking vignettes where the trauma faced by the individual was predominately physical (though, of course, with powerful emotional consequences). We hope that the encounter with their histories will illuminate the mystery of human resilience to some extent.

## Three Exceptional Men

### Stephen Hawking (1942–present)

Professor Stephen Hawking is one of those scientists who truly broadened our understanding of the universe. Explaining the relativity theory and quantum mechanics to lay public in an interesting and comprehensible manner, Hawking has transformed complexities of physics into enlightened living-room conversation. While his intellectual feats are amazing, one is awed by his ability to accomplish his success while battling a degenerative disease; through most of his adult life, he has been confined to a wheelchair.

Hawking does not profess any religious or spiritual sources of encouragement, yet he has transcended a life of suffering. At first glance, the logical thinking that has characterized his professional endeavors would predict a fatalistic and hopeless response to his illness. So what is it about his experiences that allowed him to passionately pursue a scientific career, defy negative prognoses, and captivate us all with his path to find meaning in life? In *Stephen Hawking: A Life in Science*, White and Gribbin (2002) provide a description of both the life and work of Professor Hawking that gives the reader an understanding of his development from a young boy to a world-renowned scientist.

Stephen Hawking was born in London during World War II. His parents were from middle-class families who valued education. His father was a doctor who specialized in tropical diseases. A remote figure in the family, he spent most of his time abroad doing research. He encouraged the young Stephen in his studies and had high expectations that were not always met. For example, when Stephen was eight years old, his father had hoped he would be accepted to the prestigious Westminster school and was greatly disappointed when Stephen failed the entrance exam. As he entered college, his father discouraged Stephen's interest in cosmology as it was not a "respected" field. His relationship with his mother was more supportive. She also studied at Oxford, but was subsequently underemployed as a secretary at a medical research unit. Little is known about their early relationship, but her active role in liberal politics and frequent public rising to Stephen's defense provide some clues that she promoted free thinking and supported Stephen's unconventional choices. Their home was described as clean but cluttered with various things collected from around the world.

As a child, Stephen was eccentric, awkward, skinny, and puny. He was teased and bullied, but formed a small group of friends who were at the "top of the class." His superior intellect was recognized by age 10, but the demands of St. Albans private school left few opportunities to develop interpersonal relationships beyond the classroom. The childhood "war" games he invented had rules and objectives so complex that he and his friends would spend much of their time figuring out the consequence of a single move.

At 17, he began undergraduate studies at Oxford. His father had advocated for his acceptance but did not express great confidence in his son's abilities. A private tutor by the name of Dr. Robert Berman was retained to help Stephen along. Dr. Berman became an important mentor for Stephen during college, although he relied very little on him for academic help. Stephen's innate aptitude and understanding of physics allowed him to work very little, yet win all sorts of awards for academic excellence. He also developed an interest in rowing and transformed into part of an "in crowd" as an aggressive coxswain. His reputation at this time was one of a gritty, ruthless, accomplished but seemingly lazy student. When he scored at the borderline of first and second honors on final exams, it was his hubris that led to a highest-level degree from Oxford and a chance to study under Fred Hoyle (1915–2001), a top astronomer of the time, at Cambridge. He was placed under the lesser-known Dennis Sciama (1926–1999) instead, who turned out to be a highly suitable mentor.

Stephen Hawking was 21 when he was diagnosed with amyotrophic lateral sclerosis (ALS). He had already begun his studies toward a doctorate in cosmology, and the news of his illness caused him deep depression; he was given a two-year life expectancy by his doctors. He became reluctant to proceed with his studies, which were wrought with their own setbacks, but an encounter with a young boy in an adjacent hospital bed helped him shift perspective. As he watched the boy die, he reasoned, "At least my condition doesn't make me feel sick. There are people worse off than me" (White & Gribbin, 2002, p. 63). While in the hospital, he dreamed he was going to be executed. In another recurring dream, he would sacrifice his life to save others. These dreams turned the helplessness of being terminally ill into acts of persecution by others or of altruistic suicide. Either way, they minimized his passivity. He concluded, "If I'm going to die anyway, I might as well do some good" (White & Gribbin, 2002, p. 63).

Another strong influence in his life was a woman he met at a party during the time just prior to his diagnosis, Jane Wilde. She would become his first wife. She restored his will to live and provided the support he needed to complete his doctorate at age 23 despite his rapidly deteriorating health. They decided to start a family quickly, since there was so little time left. Four years after Hawking's diagnosis, the couple had a son. Contrary to all expectations, Hawking did not die. In fact, he strangely blossomed. His scientific career took off, and by age 30 he was an established, world-class physicist. At 36 he received the Albert Einstein Award given by the Lewis and Rosa Strauss Memorial Fund; this is one of the most prestigious prizes in physics. The following year he was appointed as Lucasian Professor of Mathematics at Cambridge University, a chair once held by Sir Issac Newton. He went on to have two other children, and Jane was there to raise them.

His main method of coping with ALS was and has been spending most of his time preoccupied with nature and the origin of the cosmos, what he calls the "game of the Universe" (White & Gribbin, 2002, p. 181). He states that he is not normally depressed about his disability because "I have managed to do what I wanted to do despite it, and that gives me a feeling of achievement" (White & Gribbin, 2002, p. 192). He prefers that others focus on his scientific achievement rather than his physical limitations. In some sense, he has refused to allow ALS to penetrate his psychic structure and define him and his identity. This ego stubbornness in part accounts for his resilience. He has met each challenge to his ability to communicate with others with a creative solution, rejecting the option to remain silent. This has been in the form of technological innovations that allow a computer to speak for him and that allow him to control his own mobility and sometimes express his personality with his computer-guided wheelchair.

The popular success of his books *A Brief History of Time* (1998) and *The Universe in a Nutshell* (2001) demonstrated his ability to relate to a lay audience and helped launch his international fame. He describes his motivation for these projects as simply to meet the exorbitant expenses involved in his daily care. As a public figure he has advocated for people with disabilities to have access to technologies that facilitate mobility and communication. He has not been free of public controversy; most notable was his divorce from his wife of 25 years and subsequent remarriage to his nurse Elaine Mason in 1995. Curiously, Mason's first husband, David, had designed the first version of Hawking's talking computer. This naturally led to some raised eyebrows. Despite such lapses, Stephen Hawking has managed to create an overall life of meaning and purpose. He remains confined to a wheelchair and requires 24-hour care. And yet he continues to contribute to the lives of others, travel extensively for work and pleasure, and passionately pursue scientific inquiry.

## Christopher Reeve (1952–2004)

Widely known for his successful acting career, especially his role as Superman, Christopher Reeve won even greater respect for his response to a horseback-riding accident that left him paralyzed from the neck down. Struggling toward recovery, he gave a voice and a face to those with spinal cord injury. As he regained some function and championed efforts toward stem-cell research, he amazed the world in the process with his heroic efforts and altruism. In his autobiography, *Still Me* (Reeve, 1998), he documented his life prior to the accident and chronicled his experiences afterward. He allowed the reader an intimate witnessing of his journey, revealing his thoughts, feelings, and insights along the way.

Christopher Reeve publicly told a unique story of resilience. He moved beyond the role of survivor and managed to maintain self-esteem, family, and career. His life prior to the accident may hold clues to understanding his internal resources. His story also highlights important external sources of resilience available to him. His way of handling adversity was mediated by both these internal and external factors. It informs a pathway to recovery that does not sidestep one's original goals but allows for overcoming limitations and staying on course.

Christopher Reeve was born in New York, New York, and was four years old when his parents divorced. He grew up in Princeton, New Jersey, mainly with his mother and brother, but had regular contact with his father. His mother, Barbara, was a journalist, and his father, Franklin, was a professor and a writer. This exposed him at an early age to social/societal ideas and the creative arts. He and his father kept regular company with Robert Frost, Robert Penn Warren, and Daniel Patrick Moynihan. His parents greatly valued education; his stepfather funded his tuition at the esteemed Princeton Day School.

His mother was among the first to notice his precocious intellect as well as innate talents, which included sports, theater, and music. By age nine he was performing in professional theater. In his teenage years he balanced a developing career with his schooling. He also had a love for ice hockey and was a leading goalie in high school. He was also a leader among his peers in theater groups and was very active in school organizations. He went on to simultaneously pursue college at Cornell and study/perform in top theaters of Britain and France. In lieu of a final year at Cornell, he accepted a spot at the renowned Julliard School for the Performing Arts in New York; Robin Williams was his roommate, and they were mentored by the best. His talents brought him many opportunities for contact with extraordinary people, most notably Katharine Hepburn, with whom he shared the stage in a Broadway play. Reeve was diligent and committed to his craft, and his hard work was rewarded. He brought a tremendous amount of talent to the opportunities he was presented, and in this sense his success in acting was experienced as effortless. He was confident, handsome, charming, and principled.

In addition to his professional endeavors, Reeve had strong liberal political beliefs. His activism started with opposition to the Vietnam War in high school and continued with his support of environmental protection in college. Reeve addressed the United Nations regarding the pollution of the Hudson River in New York. He also initiated and supported political groups to address the needs of actors and even risked his life to advocate for the Chilean actors persecuted by the Pinochet government. With this background and tenacity, it is not surprising that he would later advocate for all those with spinal cord injury and reject a defeatist position regarding his own medical prognosis.

At 30 years of age, Reeve landed the leading role in the movie *Superman* (Warner Brothers, 1978). It was a risky career move as the childlike and light-hearted nature of the script had the potential of demoting him from the cadre of serious actors. Reeve was, however, not averse to risk taking, and the great success of the movie actually furthered his career. It was during the filming of *Superman* in England that he developed a relationship with modeling executive Gae Exton, which resulted in three children. They separated unmarried four years later but maintained an amicable joint custody arrangement much in the model his parents had demonstrated. Shortly after his separation and return to the United States, he met Dana and fell in love. They married, had a son, and maintained a loving relationship that would later prove able to withstand unthinkable hardship.

Reeve was a sports enthusiast. He was an accomplished pilot, avid sailor, and competitive horseback rider. This is important to understand the tragedy of his riding injury, in that it was not a result of recklessness, but a true accident. Werman's (1979) reminder that subscribing to the principle of psychic determinism must not erase the capacity to believe in the occurrence of random events is pertinent in this context.

Reeve's love of sports and the physical skills nurtured over his lifetime may have translated into the athleticism and competitive intensity he showed in his physical rehabilitation. In the moments and days following his accident, he went through a range of emotions that included depression and suicidal despair. He was quite serious about his desire to end his life, and it was Dana who uttered the words that redeemed him, "You're still you, and I love you" (Reeve, 1998, p. 28). The love of Dana, the nurturance of his family, and the support of an extensive social network became complementary to his own sense of determination. They provided an environment that constantly fueled resilience in the face of setbacks, thick despair, and periods of stagnation.

In the course of his physical rehabilitation, Reeve continued his life as an actor with his starring role in *Rear Window* (ABC, 1998). He also realized a dream as director of the television movie *In the Gloaming* (HBO, 1997), which won an Emmy along with many other awards. He maintained a rigorous commitment to his physical recovery, maintaining the range of motion of his limbs so they would be functional in the event of reinnervation. He used innovative technologies that allowed him to be supported in the upright position and to "walk" on a treadmill using electrical implants to stimulate his muscles.

He spoke to relevant subcommittees of the United States Senate and advocacy groups in support of political steps to remove restrictions on stem-cell research and to increase federal funding for research. In 1996, he created the Christopher Reeve Paralysis Foundation to help raise money for the American Paralysis Association. The Christopher and Dana Reeve Paralysis Resource Center is now the premier resource center for families and patients dealing with paralysis.

Reeve shared his personal story via speaking engagements and his books. He addressed a wide range of audiences with intent to inform and inspire. In his book *Nothing Is Impossible* (2002), Reeve spoke of significant topics such as humor, mind/body, parenting, religion, advocacy, recovery, faith, and hope. In his self-reflection he presented these areas as paramount to his individual healing. He offered an optimistic perspective to his own challenges and suggested that this perspective is available to anyone in any situation.

Christopher Reeve died of complications related to a sacral decubitus ulcer, a common problem in paralyzed individuals as a result of immobility. But it is unlikely he will be remembered for the way he died. His refusal to retreat in the face of a life-altering trauma, all that he lost and all he regained, leaves a legacy of a true Superman who reminds one how to live. He showed that dignity can survive, even triumph over adversity. Reeve was posthumously awarded an honorary Doctorate of Letters degree by Rutgers University in 2005 and a Doctorate of Humane Letters degree by the State University of New York at Stony Brook in the same year. The latter degree was received, on his behalf, by Brooke Ellison, a paralyzed young woman on whose life a television movie had recently been directed by none other than Christopher Reeve.

## Michael J. Fox (1961–present)

In *Lucky Man* (2001), Michael J. Fox, the actor turned activist, chronicles his life and battle with Parkinson's disease. Having burst out on television screens across the nation in the mid-1980s, Fox kept America laughing with his serious comic antics and his boyish charm. His successful career in movies and television sitcoms is how most people remembered him until November of 1998, when he disclosed details of his protracted battle with a relentless, incurable disease. Many shared in the shock of the implications for his future, but most did not understand exactly what it meant. His rise to the role of advocate and fund-raiser for parkinsonism helped educate the general public about the illness and its prognosis. Instead of turning to alcohol or drugs, or self-destructing in some other way, he emerged stronger and more vivacious with renewed fight and purpose. He continued to lead a productive life and gracefully dealt with the loss of his career as an actor.

In the first chapter of his book, Fox notes, "An actor's burning ambition, when you think about it, is to spend as much time as possible pretending to be someone else" (p. 16). He describes self-doubt as a "worm eating away at you that grows in direct proportion to your level of success" (p. 16). It is here that one begins to see how Fox struggled with self-esteem, and his life is revealed as hardly exempt from failures and challenges. One learns that his main struggle was to maintain connection to common human experiences in the midst of an extraordinary life. The narrative Fox provides gives parkinsonism a starring role. As opposed to the role of a career-killing villain, the disease becomes the hero that helps Fox maintain a connection with the soft and vulnerable side of humanity.

Michael's father was an Army soldier, but he spent much of his childhood with his brother and three sisters in Burnaby, British Columbia, after his father's retirement. He enjoyed hockey and was quite good, but his short stature limited any hopes of a professional sports career. He was always the family clown, and his interest in the performing arts was not a surprise to those who knew him during his childhood. His Nana (his caretaker) was one person who took it very seriously and saw something special in his future. It was she who predicted, "He'll probably be famous someday." Her influence on his life was profound, and her death when he was 11 years old, devastating. Her belief in him, however, remained a source of encouragement for him long after her years. His mother was very loving and remains a source of support to him. Fox credits both his parents with enabling him to be psychologically strong and resourceful. This close family network was undoubtedly helpful in nurturing his dreams, but his rise to fame was also facilitated by innate talent, perseverance, and serendipity.

He began to explore the creative arts through writing, art, and playing the guitar in "rock-and-roll garage bands" before realizing his interest in acting. At age 15, he debuted as a professional actor while costarring on a sitcom. At 18 he moved to Los Angeles and after three years of playing small roles landed the part of Alex P. Keaton in the popular television sitcom *Family Ties* (1982–1989). This brought him wide recognition and many professional awards, including three Emmys and a Golden Globe. His subsequent success in *Back to the Future* (Universal Pictures, 1985) made him tremendously wealthy and gave him an enduring sense of achievement. However, fame also brought personal challenges.

A blurred distinction between public and private experience, consequent upon fame, led Fox to feel disoriented and inwardly unanchored. His drinking, already on the brink of being excessive, worsened. While the premise of acting includes a mutual suspension of disbelief and taking on of roles, the "being-famous-in-America's-fun-house" has no guidebook or script to govern one's life. His desperate effort to remain grounded in the real world in the face of being famous was taxed by the complex emotions aroused by learning he was suffering from the serious disease of parkinsonism.

His wife, Tracy Pollan, then became influential in his life. Before their marriage, as his costar on *Family Ties*, she had challenged him to evaluate his drinking habits. Their relationship allowed him to see the importance of creating a sacred space between them that maintained boundaries with the rest of the world, and she encouraged him to discard his "yes-man" persona and made him accountable for his actions. He reduced his drinking, and she stood by his side through the numerous hospital visits his illness dictated.

For the next seven years, Fox kept his diagnosis a secret from the public and the majority of his professional colleagues. During part of this time, he was enduring shock, denial, shame, and fear. The nature of the disease and its available treatment results in oscillations three to four times a day between symptom control and symptom exacerbation. This was a threat to his career; his secrecy kept him further bound. But he also describes his illness as a "gift" that provided him an opportunity to choose between "adopting a siege mentality or embarking upon a journey" (Fox, 2002, p. 5). A "keep-your-head-down-and-keep-moving mentality" (Fox, 2002, p. 17) and frequent reliance on the ability to elude, evade, and anticipate potential obstacles in his way became his self-identified traits of a hearty and adaptive nature.

Fox's personal struggle with Parkinson's disease became public in 1998. Over a series of media disclosures, the news spread, and an unexpected result of this public disclosure was how many other lives were made less shameful by having a connection with him through a shared illness. This observation motivated Fox to begin playing an active role as a public health advocate. In 1999, he addressed the United States Senate Appropriations Committee to seek more federal funding for Parkinson's research. Following his retirement from full-time acting in 2000, he founded the Michael J. Fox Foundation for Parkinson's Research. He now frequently endorses political candidates who support stem-cell research that could lead to a cure for parkinsonism. In this transition, Fox has transformed an impossible personal situation into a societal movement for change while retaining optimism and gratitude for the opportunities life has given him.

## What Does Their Experience Teach Us?

First and foremost, let us acknowledge that the sketches that we have provided here do not constitute psychoanalytic data; gathering that requires consent, cooperation, closeness, confidentiality, and close process monitoring. We do not have that here. What we have is psychodynamically informed ethnography that gives some clues about specific individuals but mostly yields large-scale patterns. Indeed a careful look at the brief histories of these three men does reveal many areas of commonality, which include:

- being born to loving parents (even though Reeve's parents got divorced, they maintained a cordial relationship and cared deeply for their children)
- possessing exceptional inborn talents that were evident from early childhood onward
- encouragement of these talents by loving parents, caretakers (Fox), and mentors (Hawking and Reeve)
- early conviction of bodily strength and integrity, even superiority, via considerable athletic skills (rowing for Hawking, sailing and riding for Reeve, and ice hockey for Fox)
- a supportive and loving spouse
- more than ample "efficacy experiences" (Wolf, 1994) in the form of one's efforts producing desired results and even public recognition
- solid financial resources

These seven factors can be seen as essentially belonging to three categories: (1) *constitutional* (talent, physical prowess, good genes), (2) *familial* (loving parents and spouses), and (3) *societal* (mentors, social success, fame, and money). They constitute what Parens (chapter 6), tipping his hat to the originator of this idea and those who expanded upon it, has termed the "Garmezy-Luthar triadic processes." This refers to the three factors (biological, intrapsychic, and social) proposed by Garmezy (1985) as the fundamental substrate to human resilience.

To belabor the unmistakable presence of this triad in the lives of Hawking, Reeve, and Fox is fruitless. More important is to raise the question of whether all three elements of Garmezy's triad are essential for developing resilience. Can a strong suit in one or the other realm (constitutional, intrapsychic, and societal) render strength in a second or third area unnecessary? Another question involves the "special" status of the three individuals described here. Are these individuals truly exceptional or do they come across as such due to their being world renowned? Christopher Reeve's and Michael J. Fox's preexisting fame certainly has played a role in how awesome their stories appear to us. But what to say of Stephen Hawking, who gained international recognition *after* developing his crippling disease? The answer seems to be that while fame and money can help, it is something internal, some fire within, that pushes through the night of near-surrender. That such "right stuff," to extrapolate from Wolfe's (1979) phrase for the determined nature of Apollo 11 astronauts, is made up of complex biopsychosocial ingredients goes without saying. Hawking might be an "invulnerable child" (Anthony, 1987), but there also seems to be truth in Settlage's (1992) statement that "the predominance of love is the glue of a unified self-representation" (p. 352). If this is correct, then we can add that it is love (from others, for others, for one-self, and for life in general) that ultimately underlies the phenomenon of resilience. At the same time, there seems something elusive here. The need to know more makes itself strongly felt.

## What Else Do We Need to Know?

In this introductory overview of the topic of resilience, we have first high-lighted the difficulties in defining the concept and then offered a tentative psychoanalytic definition of it. We have underscored the multiple and com-plex variables that contribute to human resilience and attempted to demon-strate them with the help of the histories of three distinguished individuals' struggles with devastating physical illness. Having thus set the ground for deeper elucidation of resilience by the contributors to this volume, we wish to conclude by indicating some areas that, in our opinion, strongly require further investigation. We present them in the form of the following questions:

- Does resilience spread evenly across the personality function or exist in combination with brittle islands of rigidity?
- Is resilience after trauma self-limiting or self-perpetuating?
- Do characteristic dreams predict, depict, or accompany resilience after trauma?
- Does the concept of resilience have similar applications in children and adults?
- What is the interplay between resilience and developmental maturation?
- How significant is the cultural context in shaping the resilient outcome of trauma? Harvey and Tummala-Narra's (2007) recent book addresses this issue in depth, leaving one to wonder whether there might be "sub-cultures of flexibility" and "subcultures of resilience" on a large-group-psychology basis.
- What is the role of belief in God vis-à-vis human resilience?
- Is there such a thing as too much resilience?

- At what psychoeconomic point does resilience acquire "as-if" (Deutsch, 1942) qualities?
- Do traumas caused by family members require help from extrafamiliar individuals and vice versa in order to be handled in a resilient manner?
- Does the confluence of constitutional, psychological, and societal factors leading to resilience have a qualitative or quantitative dimension?
- Do creative outlets (e.g., poetry, painting) result from resilience or cause resilience?

As far as this last question is concerned, the answer seems to be "both." In other words, creativity is simultaneously a source and consequence of resilience. This paradox, most likely, is not to be resolved. More important is to recognize what Kogan (2007) has eloquently stated:

By appearing in the transitional space between re-enactment and representation, creative activity ultimately allows the [individual] to be in touch with mourning and enables its working through. It affirms the forces of life, thus overcoming silence and death. As an act of imagination, it is a path to hope and a profound beginning. (p. 122)

## References

American Psychiatric Association. (2000). *Diagnostic and statistical manual of mental disorders* (4th ed., text revision). Washington, DC: Author.

Anthony, E. J. (1987). Risk, vulnerability, and resilience: An overview. In E. J. Anthony & B. J. Cohler (Eds.), *The invulnerable child* (pp. 3–47). New York: Guilford Press.

Anthony, E. J., & Cohler, B. J. (Eds.). (1987). *The invulnerable child.* New York: Guilford Press.

Bergler, E. (1961). *Problems of curable and incurable neurosis: Neurotic versus malignant masochism.* New York: Liveright.

Brenner, I. (2004). *Psychic trauma: Dynamics, symptoms, and treatments.* Lanham, MD: Jason Aronson.

Deutsch, H. (1942). Some forms of emotional disturbance and their relationship to schizophrenia. *Psychiatric Quarterly, 11,* 301–321.

Edgcumbe, R., & Burgner, M. (1972). Some problems in the conceptualization of early object relationships. *Psychoanalytic Study of the Child, 27,* 283–314.

Eidelberg, L. (1968). *The encyclopedia of psychoanalysis.* New York: Free Press.

Emde, R., Graensbauer, T., & Harmon, R. (1976). *Emotional expression in infancy.* New York: International Universities Press.

Fox, M. J. (2002). *Lucky man*. New York: Hyperion Books.

Freud, S. (1905). Three essays on the theory of sexuality. *Standard Edition* 7:135–243.

Freud, S. (1908). On the sexual theories of children. *Standard Edition* 9:209–226.

Freud, S. (1909). Five lectures on psychoanalysis. *Standard Edition* 11:9–55.

Freud, S. (1915). Instincts and their vicissitudes. *Standard Edition* 14:117–140.

Freud, S. (1916). Some character types met with in psychoanalytic work. *Standard Edition* 14:310–333.

Freud, S. (1930). Civilization and its discontents. *Standard Edition* 21:59–145.

Freud, S. (1933). New introductory lectures on psychoanalysis. *Standard Edition* 22:3–82.

Freud, S. (n.d.). General index. *Standard Edition* 23:313–326.

Garmezy, N. (1985). Stress-resistant children: The search for protective factors. In J. E. Stevens (Ed.), *Recent research in developmental psychopathology* (pp. 213–233). Oxford: Pergamon Press.

Hartmann, H. (1939). *Ego psychology and the problem of adaptation* (D. Rapaport, Trans.). New York: International Universities Press [1958].

Hartmann, H. (1952). Mutual influences in the development of the ego and the id: Earliest stages. *Psychoanalytic Study of the Child, 7*, 9–30.

Harvey, M. R., & Tummala-Narra, P. (2007). *Sources and expressions of resiliency in trauma survivors: Ecological theory, multicultural practice*. Binghamton, NY: Haworth Press.

Hawking, S. (1998). *A brief history of time*. New York: Bantam Books.

Hawking, S. (2001). *The universe in a nutshell*. New York: Bantam Books.

Kay, M. W. (Ed.). (1976). *Webster's collegiate thesaurus*. Springfield, MA: G & C Merriam.

Kestenberg, J. S. (1972). Psychoanalytic contributions to the problem of survivors from Nazi persecution. *Israel Annals of Psychiatry and Related Disciplines, 10*, 311–325.

Kestenberg, J. S., & Brenner, I. (1996). *The last witness: The child survivor of the Holocaust*. Washington, DC: American Psychiatric Press.

Kogan, I. (1995). *The cry of mute children: A psychoanalytic perspective of the second generation of the Holocaust*. London: Free Association Books.

Kogan, I. (2007). *The struggle against mourning*. Lanham, MD: Jason Aronson.

LaForgue, R. (1929). 'Active' psychoanalytical technique and the will to recovery. *International Journal of Psychoanalysis, 10*, 411–422.

Laplanche, J., & Pontalis, J. B. (1973). *The language of psychoanalysis* (D. Nicholson-Smith, Trans.). New York: Norton.

Lichtenberg, J. D. (1989). *Psychoanalysis and motivation*. Hillsdale, NJ: Analytic Press.

Mahler, M. S. (1968). *On human symbiosis and the vicissitudes of individuation*. New York: International Universities Press.

Mahler, M. S., Pine, F., & Bergman, A. (1975). *The psychological birth of the human infant*. New York: Basic Books.

Mish, F. C. (Ed.). (1987). *Webster's ninth new collegiate dictionary*. Springfield, MA: G & C Merriam.

Moore, B., & Fine, B. (1968). *A glossary of psychoanalytic terms and concepts*. New York: American Psychoanalytic Association.

Moore, B., & Fine, B. (1990). *Psychoanalytic terms and concepts*. New Haven, CT: Yale University Press.

Nunberg, H. (1926). The will to recovery. *International Journal of Psychoanalysis, 7*, 64–78.

Parens, H. (1979). *The development of aggression in early childhood*. New York: Jason Aronson.

Reeve, C. (1998). *Still me*. New York: Ballantine.

Reeve, C. (2002). *Nothing is impossible*. New York: Random House.

Rycroft, C. (1968). *A critical dictionary of psychoanalysis*. London: Penguin.

Settlage, C. F. (1992). Psychoanalytic observations on adult development in life and in the therapeutic relationship. *Psychoanalysis and Contemporary Thought, 15*, 349–375.

Wagenheim, H. (1985). Aspects of analysis of an adult son of deaf-mute parents. *Journal of the American Psychoanalytic Association, 33*, 413–447.

Werman, D. S. (1979). Chance, ambiguity, and psychological mindedness. *Psychoanalytic Quarterly, 48*, 107–115.

White, M., & Gribbin, J. (2002). *Stephen Hawking: A life in science*. Washington, DC: Joseph Henry Press.

Wolf, E. (1994). Self object experiences: Development, psychopathology, treatment. In S. Kramer & S. Akhtar (Eds.), *Mahler and Kohut: Perspectives on development, psychopathology and technique* (pp. 65–96). Northvale, NJ: Jason Aronson.

Wolfe, T. (1979). *The right stuff*. New York: Penguin Books.

Valent, P. (1988). Resilience in child survivors of the Holocaust. *Psychoanalytic Review, 85*, 517–535.

# 2

# CHILDREN IN WAR AND THEIR RESILIENCES

*Boris Cyrulnik, PR.D., Dr. Hon. Causa*

Since 1980 we talk a lot about post-traumatic stress disorder (PTSD). According to the American Psychiatric Association, 60% of the American people have suffered from a traumatizing event (50% according to the World Health Organization). The problem is, how can one start again on another kind of development after such a psychical death?

## Constellation That Structures Resilience

The main challenge for a child is that a traumatizing event is embedded in his or her development and thus becomes a new part of the child's personality. Specific to human beings is that a mere representation is enough to traumatize a child: a word of course will do it, but also an image, a gesture, a mimic, and, more particularly, a rhetoric. The way a story is structured by the language (body and words) may convey a traumatizing effect.

Following the attack on the twin towers of the World Trade Center, a lot of children were traumatized in France, simply by watching their collapse on TV. What traumatized these children was the emotional reactions and the degree of authenticity attributed to the images stemming from their attachment figure. When the attachment figure was shocked, the sensoriality that enveloped the child was altered by the disturbance of the referring adult. This process is more interactive than private; it is intersubjective and biologically transmitted by the child's sensory environment.

The starting point is in someone else's mind, and the effect goes into the inner world of a child. Someone's expression of emotions is imprinted in someone else's mind. The child traumatized by the Manhattan attack is not empathic with victims, but he or she feels an anxiety response consistent with emotional responses of his or her surroundings. The more a child is attached with a frightened figure, the more he or she is frightened by the "screen" showing the assault (Young, 2006).

The meaning is not in the fact. It is in the affective context of history and in the child's relationships with significant figures.

Three cases can be described.

1. The attachment figure remains a secure base: What is seen on the screen will be a significant event.
2. The attachment figure is frightened: The event on the screen will be frightening.
3. There is no attachment figure near the child: The screen will be empty of meaning.

Hence a child can suffer twice: First, a child can suffer in the reality of his or her perception of what is happening: a broken leg, starvation. That is the trauma.

Second, a child can suffer in the representation of what happened. That is "traumatism"—the internal representation of a traumatizing experience—which depends on a script, like a movie without words, and a narrative, the way this event is translated in words. Therefore, the confluence of witnesses' narratives and family's narratives structure the child's feeling.

The verbal environment gives shape to the emotion imprinted in the child's biological memory. The transaction between who I am and what is around me constitutes the starting point toward either PTSD, with its intrusive remembrances, or its opposite, resilience.

So it is difficult to simply say we will assess the effects of war on children. There are too many variables. It is better to say that we will analyze the constellation of determinants that influence the child's reactions to war in four sections:

1. Acquisition of internal resources of resilience. A secure attachment may predict an easier ability to cope, thus in case of trauma a better adaptive new development.
2. A training to mentalization, which depends on the level of the child's language and on the level of the family's language.

These abilities determine the capability of encountering an attachment figure to speak with and with whom to weave an emotional bond. Hence a new secure base is built, a tutor of resilience.

1. The layout of external resources of resilience: a healthy family, a school, a neighborhood, and the way they envelop the traumatized child with affection, feelings, and narratives.
2. The association between these narratives (their rhetoric, which constitutes a kind of emotional verbal structure) and any social project or daydream gives lots of different meanings to the same event. So, the meaning attributed to the trauma might range from shame to pride consistent with the structure of the constellation around the child.

## Mastering the Meaning We Attribute to the Fact

Even things take their meaning in accordance with the context. If you are given a moldy piece of bread at the family's table, you will be humiliated. On the other hand, if you are given the same piece of moldy bread while in a concentration camp, you will be proud of being capable to eat this disgusting food, which means "I have just succeeded to survive another day. I'm still alive." If you are an adopted child in Liberia (they call it "a given boy" in order to make the grandparents happy), you will be proud to have been adopted. However, if a child is adopted in Japan, it means this child is a less-valued child, deprived of ancestors. This child will be ashamed of having been adopted. "The personal account will derive its meaning from the surrounding historical interpretation" (Ehrensaft & Tousignant, 2006, p. 471).

Refugees from such countries as Argentina, Peru, and various African countries might be perceived as strange people: "Why are they coming here? They are poor, filthy, and culture-deprived." Sometimes a war occurrence constitutes a kind of experiment. The former president of Guatemala organized a political repression against a Mayan village. Its inhabitants had to flee toward Mexico. Some of these villagers were sent north. Cut from their roots and steered by international help organizations, they made up hate discourses that served the purpose of joining the group members together, uniting them in this hatred. Another fraction of that same village was allowed to stay near the border and thus maintain their ritual traditions. Two years later a different government allowed both groups to return to their home. Those who were united in their hatred named their new village "Victoria." However, the hatred that had been an integrating weapon in wartime turned into a poison in peacetime.

On the other hand, upon their return, the group that had been allowed to hold onto traditions called their new village "Esperanza" (Hope) and

became resilient. Fortunate enough to live in peacetime, they were not prisoners of their past and could start a new kind of development. Two external
models, two different situations grounded two different accounts of the same
war episode that "modified the process of facing adversity among members
of the same culture" (Rousseau, Morales, & Foren, 2001, p. 140).

## Making Sense Out of Chaos

One of the main factors of resiliency remains the making of sense out of
chaos.

To admit that we are traumatized is to concede that we are unable to treat
any information or to resolve any problem. Overwhelmed by the trauma, we
are numb, incapable to adapt, to respond to a confusing world. What could
be the possible meaning of witnessing the rape and execution of one's mother?
How could we begin to fathom such a death?

Virtually all Rwandan children were exposed to such scenes during the
genocide in 1994 (Bellamy, 1996). They witnessed murders, rapes, and exe-
cutions and thought they were going to die. How to make meaning of such
senseless atrocities? Knowing that trauma is bound to reality (starvation, torture) and that traumatism is linked to the representation of reality, we can say
it stems from a system of signs, meanings, and expressions of emotion constructed by the group surrounding the child. The meaning ascribed to the
event highlights the critical role of narratives to support resilience or prevent
it. In the wake of trauma, historization of an event—having made it history—
allows a framework toward a vision of the world we perceive (Bruner, 1990).
As soon as the event is framed into a meaning and put toward a direction by
making narratives and daydreams, the wounded child knows how to behave,
how to avoid, how to cajole, and how to attack the stressor or cuddle against
his or her secure base in order to learn to face the danger.

In my opinion, coping is a strategy using every resource to face the danger. But later, in the representation of the painful event, how the child copes
with the attack feeds his or her memory and constitutes the starting point of
his or her internal working model, like a narrative landmark (Neimeyer &
Levitt, 2001).

By structuring his or her story, the narrator enables both self and audience to relate to one another. If the listeners, the family, or the culture express
empathy and endeavor to understand, the wounded doesn't feel lonely
(Bruner, 1990).

Therefore it is not just the way we cope with the trauma that is the starting point of the internal working model (IWM); it is rather the way we remember how we coped, and the way our family or our culture perceives and tells what has happened.

To remain mute or to deny is a way to avoid a painful memory. Being mute or denying is a protective factor but not a resilient one. The resilient narrative of the trauma integrates and reframes the painful past in order to create a shared experience. When young Rwandans emigrated to Brussels (Belgium), those who accepted their parents' values, narratives, beliefs, rituals, and explanations of the genocide made up a more resilient subgroup. On the other hand, those who were isolated and fostered in Catholic or Protestant families started a lesser process of resilience. The feeling of belonging and the meaning attributed to the genocide, the pressing need to understand it, were more protective factors.

The power shaping our feelings is sometimes in the other's eyes. When I work or speak, I am not working or speaking as a blue-eyed man or a dark-skinned one. When suddenly I can see in your eyes that you are thinking that I am a nigger, the way you look at me modifies the way I feel. Aimé Césaire, a poet who served as mayor of Fort-de-France, Martinique, called this process *négritude*, or "niggerness." By creating such a neologism he wanted to emphasize that even a silent insult may modify the way I feel.

I find that the feeling of belonging is more protective than resilient. Algerians during the civil war that followed their independence (1962) were the victims of terrorist attacks that killed 200,000 people the last 10 years of the civil war (Boukhaf, 2007). The feeling of belonging was so effective that it strengthened the clannish groups that fed the civil war. Hatred is a cohesive factor that precludes forgiveness and resilience. The social structure of the persecution against an isolated child or against a gathered group builds different meanings in every individual, each of whom may become ashamed, fearful, proud, or filled with hate.

When we know the structure of an organ, we can predict what effects its function is capable of (Bowlby, 1978, p. 140). When we know the structure of a narrative, we can predict its resulting feeling. The scenario I imagine in my inner world of what happened to me constitutes my narrative identity. The other's account of what happened to me establishes my "niggerness," the way you think of my traumatism. And the history, myth, stereotype, and even prejudice structure the verbal world imprinting in my soul, be it a feeling of shame or of pride, consistent with your rhetoric.

## Reworking Our Internal Working Model

The feeling the wounded child attributes to the traumatizing event depends on the confluence of these three narratives, internal, surrounding, and cultural. There is a huge correlation between a narrative identity and what our family and cultural surrounding think and say about the wounding event. But what we remember depends on the earliest events that built a preferential sensitivity in the child's memory. When he or she grows older, his or her narrative identity evolves and is rebuilt in accordance with new events and changing discourses. Sometimes the narrative identity may collapse when the child is confused or numbed by another trauma.

One might consider the following evolution of a trauma-determined identity narrative: "When I had to face the roar, I was a coward." The trauma was experienced like a black star in a sad story, a conveyor belt to shame. The image I construct of myself is a torn image, breaking down my self-esteem. It is compulsory to become a story teller after a trauma to make sense out of chaos. But nobody wants to hear such a story. It happens that when the culture highlights this story, it may transform the sad story into an interesting one and possibly even a beautiful one, thus changing the feelings of the wounded: "You tell me that I was very brave to cope with such a roar. You are right. I hadn't thought of the trauma that way."

The social support of the community probably constitutes the most important tutor of resilience, thus raising a tricky problem: the main factors of resilience are the affect provided by relatives and friends, as well as the meaning attributed to the fact by the historical and social context. Overall, that is a support network composed of family, peers, and their stories. But what is noteworthy and surprising is that in certain situations, one has fewer peers as a support network and more family, for instance when one is about to emigrate. It seems that such a network is less supportive than peers! In the situation where a posttraumatic disorder occurs, it remains for a longer period of time in one's own family, where the memory of trauma is heavier than among an external group where the emotional weight is slighter. "The peers' resilience factor is more effective than the family's" (Beiser, 1999). Sometimes the family's support is as protective as a jail and as stifling. What's more, in this affectionate jail one will have to live with the memory of the trauma. When one's family is always talking about the past roar, one is restlessly bathing in the evocation of the trauma. And when one's family remains mute, silence subjugates everybody with high anxiety. On the other hand, the peer's protective factor is more open, less suffocating, and thus more socializing. Too often, the otherwise necessary family support network is too tight and too closed, leading to clannish behavior. It depends on the functioning of the family and of the group surrounding the traumatized child.

The most effective network is made up of an emotional constellation in which some stars are close and bright while others are distant, dim, and indistinct. In healthy situations the distant stars constitute tutors of further development. They have separation power that enables the child to weave a bond with somebody heretofore distant. When the predominant close stars are broken down by a trauma, these secondary, heretofore distant stars may become tutors of resilience, offering another opportunity for development. Subsequently the traumatized child has a tricky choice to make: either to evolve toward a close-knit clan or to evolve toward a more open style of attachment, both of which provide for adaptation in the host culture. This follows from the fact that surviving in a ghetto provides a source of security, a sense of cohesiveness that leads to integration within the clan. And when it is a cohesive group, it serves as a secure base that helps with integration into institutions of higher socialization. What works best and supports resilience is an open affective clan constellation as a secure base surrounded by another constellation of peers, each constellation able to rework the meaning of the traumatism. So an integrative process is set up between mother and society, between affectionate jail and the once scary, dark unknown. This process may be shattered by a trauma destroying the secure base (leaving neither family nor peers or friends). Sometimes society pressures the wounded child to remain in a ghetto that is locked from the inside or the outside, thereby interrupting the resilience process.

This explains why resilience was more difficult for young Jewish survivors of the Holocaust who remained in their own traumatized family, a family that had become an insecure base, than for other Jews put into a nontraumatized foster family.

We could observe the same transaction with young Lebanese. After 16 years of civil war in Lebanon, one million emigrants came to France, where their children were not traumatized. Orphans who remained in Beirut in peer groups or who were put in foster families were not much traumatized. However, those who remained in Beirut in their own traumatized family did become traumatized (Gannage, 1999). So it is impossible to say that separation causes a good effect or psychological damage. It depends on the context as well as the existential trajectory. During peacetime, separation allows for evolution. After a trauma, separation may have a good effect if the wounded family has become an insecure base. Sometimes we have to stress that a wounded child grabs at the traumatized mother. In such a situation every separation increases the traumatism, but maintaining the mother-infant tie may imprint a developmental traumatism in the child's mind.

## An Unexpected Finding

An unexpected finding comes from a group of Jewish children I work with who were hidden during the Holocaust.[1] A subgroup of these children were brought up in families composed of two or three survivors. No one in these families spoke about the Shoah.[2] Such a silence hangs over heavily as a dark shadow. These families were depressed, mute; individuals experienced sudden outbursts of anger. In such a context happiness would have been indecent: "How dare you enjoy life when all your family disappeared?" These children were trained, during the war, to be silent, mute, with a secret that had to be kept in order to survive: "If you tell your name, you will be sentenced to death and those who love you will be killed because of you." Most of the time the surviving family was mourning. In such family sadness is contagious. The children adapted to their new family by becoming split: "It is indecent to be happy when your relatives died in agony. If you are happy you are a traitor, you abandon them." Sadness is the only decent feeling. Hidden survivors' children became depressed at home and talkative at school, where they were allowed to be happy.

Children who could remain in their nontraumatized family during the war and during the peace were not traumatized. Another subgroup became resilient because after the war they were placed in nontraumatized foster homes where they could speak bit by bit of their trauma. The more a child could identify with his or her origins, his or her parents' culture, values, and beliefs, the more he or she feels clear, adapted, protected by these real tutors of resilience. Many of the split children overinvested in success in school because it was the only place where they could dig out little bits of happiness (Bailly, 2006). Such a datum is counterintuitive. Maltreated children are almost always weak students, but they are not split. They suffer entirely from their insecure attachment. They become ambivalent, whereas hidden children are split by their secret and their new situation in peacetime: sad at home, happy in school. When I met many of them, I was amazed by their social or academic success contrasting with a hidden part of their mind suffering in silence.

The end of the war is not the end of the problem. With peace, hidden children are still amputated from a part of their family as well as their self-representation. In order to survive they have to accept to be amputated, silent, odd in the eyes of others. In this subgroup I met two Nobel Prize winners (in literature and in physics); many well-known scientists, writers, painters, and actors; and especially many psychoanalysts and psychiatrists, which reveals that there are grave consequences to such traumatism.

I think that many benefited from their split mind: many were all the stronger in social and academic worlds, but they were weaker in affective relationships, still bleeding, long after the war was over. It is less difficult to succeed socially: you need only to be courageous, committing only a part of your personality. But if you want to succeed emotionally, you must resolve relational difficulties every day, committing your whole personality.

## Developing a Representation

"On the level of representations a healthy enough family appears as an anchor of salvation" (Ehrensaft & Tousignant, 2006, p. 474). We have no power over many events and surrounding circumstances such as war, orphanage, or social misery. But the meaning attributed to things or events stems first from our family, its discourses, its nonverbal expressions, its projects, and its remembrances, which structure the surrounding world imprinted in our soul.

When our family is traumatized, the meaning assigned to each current event stems from its personal history. It is the reason why, when the family remained in the country at war, the child was prone to idealize the family. In Lebanon during the civil war, every evening when the father came back home it triggered the signal of joy. But after the war, when reunification was accomplished, problems that had been overlooked sometimes resurfaced. Children had learned to bring about joy when the father came home even though he was unemployed.

The same situation explains the meaning an orphan attributes to his or her foster family. An orphan is the only child who has perfect parents who never grow old and are never tired or unfair, unlike the generous foster family who may be sometimes exhausted, annoyed, and unfair but are quite real. When Corneille, now a Canadian singer, came from Rwanda, where all his family had been slaughtered, he was taken in by a German foster family. The foster parents never pretended to replace his biological parents, and Corneille was grateful for that. When Marcel Desailly, a French soccer player, was accepted into his foster family, it had the same meaning for the orphan. As a little boy Marcel was expelled from Ghana. Surrounding accounts were clear: "You are coming from a dangerous country. Your parents were bold and we are very happy to accept you in our family though we are only your foster family." The family's narrative associated with the cultural one converged on these two teenagers, who became proud of their lost families and attached to their foster parents.

But the truth for a population is not the truth for every individual making up this population. Every child interprets a fact according to the way his or her mind constructs it. When their parents disappeared during World War II, the eldest of three sons became hopeless. The second born thought: "So what? From this day I will have to sort it out by myself." And the third said fifty years later: "I will never forgive my parents for abandoning us." The structure and meaning of a situation has to be dealt with by the dispositions and tendencies of the child's mind. The familial and cultural context of hidden Jewish children converged to give meaning to the situation. After the war, most of the young Jews didn't recover their real parents, and many were adopted by a traumatized surviving family. Knowing that after a sudden death of a newborn, best estimates are that about 50% of bereaved parents divorce within the year, we can understand that for many of them the tragedy turned the spouses' interpersonal difficulties into rationalized, even insane explanations for their misfortune. The same process shaped the meaning of hidden children when after the war they had to survive in a bereaved, traumatized, depressed family where happiness took the meaning of a betrayal.

The representation of time becomes distorted for children in war, whatever their war (soldiers, hidden, persecuted, orphans . . .). People who have to cope with adversity adapt also by splitting their representation of time. When you have to face a deadly danger that makes you numb, your focus is on the immediate necessity of the present rather than digging up the past in order to understand what is happening. In such a situation it is hard to attribute meaning to what is happening. You are simply struggling. But thirty minutes later (or fifty years later), as soon as the family's and cultural context allows you to construct a representation of what you experienced, you'll rework the representation and try to understand what happened.

European Jewish, Rwandan, Tutsi, and Southeast Asian refugees showed similar responses (Beiser, 1999). During the Second World War, an eight-year-old child was arrested by the French Gestapo associated with the German army and put in jail. During this isolation, the benumbed child was somewhat frozen, emotionless. A few weeks later he managed to escape and was helped in the street and then sheltered as a farm boy. Shortly after, he was able to make a representation of the trauma. Suddenly he understood that his parents, who had disappeared two years before, were more than likely dead. Immediately he stopped expecting their return. As he worked on the farm, he came across a Bible and was mesmerized by the biblical story of Lot, which took a special meaning for him because of his special situation. If you want to survive, you must go ahead without looking behind. If you think of your past, you will be turned into a salt statue because of the salt of your tears. Such denial is a protective factor, and such a representation of time is an adaptive response. Numbness is a synchronic response for someone facing a trauma. It prevents suffering. But it is not a resilience factor because the individual does nothing with the event. Years later, when a sense of normality has been reached, the attitude toward time is due to evolve. The wounded soul is due to integrate pieces of memory to build a narrative identity. We are now in a diachronic time of representation.

Therefore, two unhealthy memories are possible.

First, having too much memory makes us remain a prisoner of the past, always thinking about what happened and suffering, as in the case of PTSD, when everything evokes the trauma: nightmares, intrusive images, locations, allusions that call up the devils of the traumatic past.

Second, the other bad memory consists of having no memory, as in the case of repression or denial. We feel better by avoiding remembrances, which, however, prevents us from undergoing a resiliency process. A synchronic protection may hinder the work of constructing a diachronic representation of what happened. Ten years later the rate of depression was higher in the denying subgroup (Lavie, 1998).

## Reminiscence Is Not Reviviscence

Particularly the elderly who practiced trauma denial during their whole life suffered from reviviscence, quite a different matter from reminiscence. With reminiscence, everything one perceives evokes a remembrance that is linked with a meaningful event, whereas with reviviscence there is the sudden coming back of a traumatic event that is imprinted in one's memory. One never suffered from it because one was protected by one's repression and the denial of the culture. After denial, one has to rework what happened in one's representation by a diachronic process.

Toulon is a little town on the Mediterranean Sea. It suffered greatly during the Second World War. There was the destruction by the French of their own French fleet in the harbor, the Italian and then the German occupation, and in 1944 the bombings by the U.S. Air Force, our liberators, that killed numerous people. Fifty years later we made two groups. The first one was made up of communists, who were numerous in the naval shipyard and docks (Delage, 2002). After the war, they protested, made exhibitions of pictures, and wrote in newspapers. The second group was composed of surviving inhabitants who remained silent. The first group remembers clearly what they saw, what was said, and what they suffered. This group was full of reminiscences. The way they developed a resilient process by reworking their representations made them full of memories. Neither prisoners of the past nor without past, they built something with their trauma by protesting, writing, or joining associations in a compelling need to understand.

In the silent group, we could notice a frequent scenario. Suddenly an old woman can hear German soldiers climbing the stairs or the U.S. Air Force bombing the town. In the "Memorial of the Shoah" in Paris,[3] I was able to meet some people who were traumatized and who currently were diving into records of war, pictures, papers, or testimonies about trains that took them where their parents died. A lot of them encounter serious mental health problems by reviving the traumatism without networking it.

Without memory of the trauma, life is meaningless and the past can arise again suddenly. But with only the memory of the trauma, life is unbearable. Luckily it is possible to do something with our wound, to build another narrative by using pieces of memory in order to control our inner world. An individual may change his or her internal working model when he or she grows older and reworks his or her narrative to change the meaning attributed to the fact. A culture may also change its external working model (EWM), such as when politicians adopt another discourse and when story makers invent novels, movies, and essays, whereby they change the narratives surrounding children that make the children able to shift from shame to pride.

## Conclusion

It is impossible to state a definitive conclusion about resilience. It is a lengthy process in need of being attended to and managed. It can last a long time, and yet it may collapse when a meaningful event hits the person at a point of vulnerability. But always, main resources of resilience are feelings provided by the group and meaning transmitted by the narratives.

It is always possible to rework and reframe both, which may be called resiliency.

## References

Bailly, D. (Dir.). (2006). *Enfants cachés: Analyses et débats.* Paris: L'Harmattan.

Beiser, M. (1999). *Strangers at the gate: The "boat people's" first ten years in Canada.* Toronto: University of Toronto Press.

Bellamy, C. (1996). *The state of the world's children* (UNICEF Rep.). Oxford: Oxford University Press.

Boukhaf, M. (2007, June 2). Une adolescente qui revient de loin: Terrorisme en Algérie. *Communication Faculté de Droit.* Toulon, France: Université de Toulon, Faculté de Droit.

Bowlby, J. (1978). *Attachement et perte: La séparation, angoisse et colère.* Paris: Presses Universitaires de France.

Bruner, J. (1990). *Acts of meaning.* Cambridge, MA: Harvard University Press.

Delage, M. (2002). Traumatisme psychique et résilience familiale. *Stress et Trauma, 2*(2), 69–78.

Ehrensaft, E., & Tousignant, M. (2006). Immigration and resilience. In D. L. Sam & J. W. Berry (Eds.), *The Cambridge handbook of acculturation psychology* (pp. 469–483). Cambridge: Cambridge University Press.

Gannage, M. (1999). *L'enfant, les parents et la guerre: Une étude clinique au Liban.* Paris: ESF.

Lavie, P. (1998). *Le monde du sommeil.* Paris: Odile Jacob.

Neimeyer, R. A., & Levitt, H. (2001). Coping and coherences: A narrative perspective on resilience. In C. R. Snyder (Ed.), *Coping with stress: Effective people and processes* (pp. 7–29). New York: Oxford University Press.

Rousseau, C., Morales, M., & Foren, P. (2001). Going home: Giving voice to memory strategies of young Mayan refugees who returned to Guatemala as a community-culture. *Medicine and Psychiatry, 25,* 135–168.

Young, A. (2006). Traumatisme à distance, résilience héroïque et guerre contre le terrorisme. *Contreverses sur le stress. Revue Française de psychanalyse,* 40. Paris: Presses Universitaires de France.

## Notes

1. Bulletin de la Commission Centrale de l'Enfance (CCE), 14 rue de Paradis, 75010 Paris, France.

2. While the World War II Holocaust afflicted Roma (Gypsies), Seventh-Day Adventists, homosexuals, and other "undesirable" minorities, "the Shoah" refers to the mass persecution and murder of the Jews.

3. Musée d'art et d'histoire du judaïsme, Paris, upon my receipt of the Prix du Mémorial de la Shoah (January 21, 2007).

# 3

# Some Thoughts on Psychic Trauma and Its Treatment

*Melvin Singer, MD*

This chapter will deal with the effects of intrapsychic trauma on the internal working model (internal representation), culled from my own experience and a review of the literature. Dr. Cyrulnik has provided us with insights into the external working model, from a lifetime of work on the psychosocial and interpersonal sphere. He has recognized the capacity for resilience in children, not just their psychopathology, and has developed techniques to mobilize resilience to aid in their recovery. Hopefully, this will allow the child to start anew after the period of psychic death throe. The question is how much therapy on the internal working model is necessary in severe trauma cases to put the soul back in order and restore the capacity for hope and the willingness to reestablish libidinal connections.

Major combat in the prior world wars required immediate treatment at the trauma site in addition to after the acute episode during what Dr. Cyrulnik calls the stage of traumatism. Thus shell-shock victims of World War I were treated immediately, and according to a 1917 book, *The Care and Treatment of Mental Disease and the War Neurosis (Shell Shock) in the British Army*, the Salmon four principles applied: immediacy, proximity, expectancy, and simplicity. Early in my career, I treated a woman immediately after she was gang-raped. I used a Pentothal interview equating her psychic trauma to a war neurosis. Using abreaction to eliminate her flashbacks, repetitive dreams, and state of hyperarousal, I achieved surprisingly excellent results. I assumed I used the four principles.

The large-scale wars noted above have now been replaced by regional conflicts and international terrorism. Civilian populations are now disproportionately targeted compared to the past. Tragically, this is especially true for children. According to the United Nations Children's Fund, the proportion of civilian war casualties has increased in the past twenty years from 5%

to 90%, a twentyfold increase. Of those casualties, 50% are children, with 1.5 million dead from 1990 thru 2003 (Wexler, Branski, & Kerem, 2006).

Short of death, the risks of behavior and emotional problems are enormous from direct and indirect traumas resulting from terrorism (Fayyod et al., 2004). Four basic points will be enumerated at first:

1. Traumatized children who are also orphaned during war are doubly traumatized, and this interplay of personal grief and external trauma complicates the picture tragically (Blum, 2003; Joshi & Lewin, 2004).

2. Acute stress or shock trauma can be accompanied by cumulative trauma compounding the "traumatism" (chapter 2) and consequent psychopathology.

3. Symptoms may arise directly from the war trauma; they do not require prior formative-years predispositions or traumatizations that are now reactivated by a current resonating trauma. Contrary to my prior training and experience, I was stunned by the realization that a patient's long-standing agoraphobia was resolved by recovery, abreaction, and an interpretation, indeed a mutative interpretation, of the meaning of a specific past war trauma—which was not achieved during his previous analysis of years before, which emphasized childhood correspondence with current adult life events—but which never broached this earlier adult-years war experience.

4. These traumatic pictures create a differential psychic solution than that seen in neurosis using the classic drive/defense model and compromise formation or even the more severe primitive personalities using object relations models, primitive defenses, and pregenital drives. Instead, severe traumatic states (labeled by Freud "traumatic neuroses") present a picture of an overwhelmed, fractured ego. The protective shield, a term Freud introduced to explain the ego's reactive efforts to protect against the trauma that leads to the war neurosis, has been shattered, leaving the individual with a total inability to master the surge of stimuli. New defenses are called upon to deal with this flooded and overwhelmed ego. Freud (1920, 1926, 1940) thus introduced, starting in the twenties, disavowal, repudiation, primal repression, negation, and splitting of the ego as primitive attempts at mastery along with repression, or in place of it. All these efforts are based on the need to protect the psyche from overwhelming drive derivatives (Freud, 1920). The death instinct was unleashed and unbound from Eros.

Ferenczi (1921) compared this response of the overwhelmed ego state to an epileptic seizure or tic, that is, the continual discharge phenomena seen in reexperiencing the trauma. Kardiner (1932, 1941)—who also noted that Bernheim did the same—followed Ferenczi's lead emphasizing the consequences of this cleavage (splitting or dissociation) of the ego. They also introduced the primary identification into the ego, especially the body ego, not with the object (in typical regression) but with the trauma itself. A body incorporation of the violent intrusion occurred (see Leys, 2000).

Today, the superordinate construct that best captures the survival struggle of the ego is post-traumatic stress disorder and its subsyndromes, characterized by reexperiencing, hyperarousal phenomena, and avoidance techniques. Dissociation, although mentioned but not given special emphasis in *DSM–IV*, is a major defense in severe psychic trauma. Surprisingly, or perhaps not so surprisingly, as Blum (2003) reminds us, the term *dissociation* was never mentioned by Laplanche and Pontalis in their highly regarded 1967 lexicon, or by Moore and Fine in their 1990 *Glossary of Psychoanalytic Terms*. This occurred even though Ferenczi and Kardiner (and Bernheim as well) wrote extensively about it. I presume the term was not conceptualized within the extant canon of classic theory. However, this author remembers trauma-relevant terms like "the release of introjects" used to describe symbolically triggered enactments or the alcoholic-inebriation release of a fully formed, internalized relationship, affect, and behaviors that were totally disjunctive to the usual personality of the patient and were not part of the "developmental identity disorder" group.

In post-traumatic stress disorder, if there is conscious reexperiencing of the trauma in images, thoughts, dreams, and play in children, then we can assume that repression has occurred and declarative memory is available for retrieval. If dissociation has occurred, then cognitive blankness and emotion numbing may exist and then perhaps only nonverbal, encoded body memory is stored. This will be further discussed below.

## Reaction to War Trauma

Many factors have been described to influence the degree and type of reaction to the war trauma, for example, developmental, innate resilience, level and type of exposure, individual vulnerabilities, and protective factors (Fayyod et al., 2004). A few will be discussed:

1. Anna Freud (Freud & Burlingham, 1944) in her classic monograph gave a seminal example of a differential developmental reaction to traumatic violence during the London blitzes. To paraphrase her work, and adding an ego defect model along with her classic one, a child at age two, physically unharmed with an intact family, witnessing violent destructiveness, will experience excitement. He will then play it out on the rubble, since it corresponds to his own age-appropriate destructive fantasies. Unfortunately, this may strengthen and reinforce these drives and associated fantasies, and weaken the ego's reactive tendencies against them, decreasing their later ability to counteract the drives since primitive discharge channels have been permanently opened. The same child, however, at three and a half, witnessing the same event, will react differently—now with terror, castration anxiety, fear of death, and ensuing guilt secondary to retaliatory fantasies.

2. Children's resilience has been measured on many dimensions, and Southwick, Ozbay, and Mayes (chapter 8) add to the literature with their rigorous research. To mention several anecdotal observations culled from the literature, according to Blum, Helene Deutsch (1966) postulated that trauma could possibly strengthen the damaged ego to deal more effectively with future trauma. She called this ego strength "righting reflexes" by their ability to change course and reverse regression (Blum, 2003). Others have described traumatized children as having innate capabilities that precociously develop into survival coping mechanisms. Some were even described as having a "Superman reaction." These children became major caregivers, helpers, and organizers. The "helping professions" certainly have their share of reactive, resilient caretakers with traumatic pasts.

3. Reactions to the level and type of exposure have been placed on a gradient from mild to severe, for both acute stress and post-traumatic stress disorder (PTSD). Mild reactions include generalized apprehension and anxiety. Moderate reactions show more intrusive phenomena producing greater protective and avoidance maneuvers. In severe to most-severe reactions, we observe the full range of PTSD in children. Reexperiencing the trauma in play, visual images, dreams, and behavioral enactments can turn topsy-turvy to manic denial of the trauma and aggression toward the self or others in extreme violent behavior and delinquency.

Psychological numbing may extend to passive, submissive receptivity to suggestion, and further proceed to autohypnotic behavior.

Disturbances in memory and regressive language may lead to an inability to learn.

Regression may occur and extend or delay toilet training and the development of emotional self-regulation as well as intensify and prolong the fear of being alone.

Finally, massive dissociation may lead to blankness and a longing for death.

This totally unconscious dissociation differs from the repression seen in PTSD and neurosis, or the more typical conscious dissociation (or mutual conscious splitting), separated by denial, alternating in gaining conscious access and control, seen in borderline patients (Kernberg, 1967). In unconscious dissociation, the experience may never have been registered in conscious cognition to any significantly retrievable degree but was immediately repudiated by the overwhelmed, fractured ego before associative linkage with thoughts and affects, let alone preconscious words and the chain of symbolic and repressed derivatives. This is Freud's (1920) "primal repression" (no thing or word representation). Encoding takes place in the body ego by forced incorporation as sensory, motor, visceral, and perceptual fragments. Retrieval can only occur by procedural knowledge, which can be enacted within the transference-countertransference and be intersubjectively experienced by a counter projective-identification. Through and within this transitional space, mirroring of the therapist's counter projective-identification becomes an affectocognitive learning experience for the patient. As mentioned, the conscious experience before this enactment is blankness and a possible longing for death.

Segal (1993) explains well the steps in the phenomenon of a longing for death. These woeful survivors turn away from "life-promoting tendencies." The trauma acts as an extreme deprivation of need and all libidinal connection. The survivor then turns toward the aggressive drive to annihilate the need, and then to annihilate the perceiving and experiencing self that carries the need that won't go away, as well as anything that is perceived with it. I presume that the part self carrying the need is viewed as a noxious foreign body to be expelled at all costs (see Laub & Lee, 2003).

Krystal (1997) gives us another explanatory dimension to this death throe. He speaks to the profound state of helplessness and surrender from the effects of the trauma (Freud's definition) as phylogenetically patterned and common to the entire animal kingdom. A state of cataleptic immobility is set in motion. This is the autohypnotic behavior mentioned earlier. A trance-like blind obedience progresses to numbing of all physical and psychological pain. This "closing off" of all mental functioning, in all animals, carries from birth the guarantee of a painless, anesthetized, and dissociated death. This Holocaust-type horror reaction relates to the somewhat milder Borderline variation that Singer (1977) described as the "zombie" state of psychic deadness from intrafamilial trauma and the avoidance of self-responsibility.

## Treatment Considerations

There are a number of principles to the treatment of severe trauma. The therapeutic action requires the safety and security of an empathetic therapist who can, so to speak, "walk with them through the valley of death." Accompanying the victim and providing a protective arm not only symbolically shares this pain but provides for them the courage to face and relive the unspeakable dreaded memory. Abreaction can then accompany recall and, like a surgeon's scalpel, excise the pocket of psychic pus and, by discharging, relieve the pressure and thereby reduce the level of hurt and suffering. This releases the person from this continual torture and sapping of energy.

In repression as well as in dissociation, of course, recall and abreaction of the trauma may not be possible via the route of retrieval from memory storage. Reconstruction becomes imperative (Blum, 2003). The memory, if declarative, can be partially retrieved in words, or if procedural, reconstructed via enactments in the realm of the transference-countertransference. It is never recalled literally; at best, for both declarative and procedural memory, the trauma is recalled inexactly by reconstruction. The internal retrieval pattern and the pathway toward mastery and integration will always be used for defensive and drive purposes, as well as for retribution, restitution, and redemption in compromise formation.

Furthermore, the trauma must not only be faced and relived but concurrently named, and a coherent and historical narrative of the horror must be created. This process is fraught with difficulties. Defensive techniques intervene, for example, obsessive doubting alternating with surety, disbelief alternating with belief, and so forth. A falsification of memory can occur to lessen the unbelievable. Eventually this can lead to blankness or absence of all memory. I encountered a pertinent clinical example many years ago in my practice. An adolescent girl presented with severe psychopathology, accusing her father of sexual abuse by his incestuous behavior. At one session, she presented memory fragments with certainty and appropriate outrage, only to be followed the next day by denial, confusion, and doubt! This cognitive chaos, with alternating belief and disbelief, continued unabated for months. Concurrently, along with the mental health profession's awareness of the actuality of possible incest came the publicizing of the "false memory syndrome." The combination of all the above in time led me to shift from confusion to doubt to disbelief. Unfortunately, the therapy was abruptly terminated by forces outside of my control.

Returning to the value of a coherent narrative, clarifying this chaos in words promotes personality reorganization and a binding of anxiety and impulses. Freud's (1900) trial action in words can now act as a self-regulatory control mechanism, containing and transforming impulsive action into thought-out action. This allows for delay, reality assessment, and then internal judgment and to develop. This taming by naming, as Blum (2003) so aptly put it, can hopefully lead to signal anxiety and then impulse control.

Finally, creating a coherent if only a personal, inexact narrative is "to bear witness," which is fundamental to the survival of meaning, the truth, and even the preservation of life. Here, Dr. Cyrulnik's well-informed, cogent comments on the role of the caregiver to direct the emphasis in the historical narrative, that is, what to say and what not to say, are most poignant.

# References

American Psychiatric Association. (1994). *Diagnostic and statistical manual of mental disorders* (4th ed.). Washington, DC: Author.

Blum, H. (2003). Psychic trauma and traumatic object loss. *Journal of the American Psychoanalytic Association, 51*(2), 415–432.

Deutsch, H. (1966). Absence of grief. *Psychoanalytic Quarterly, 6*, 12–22.

Fayyod, J., Karam, E. J., Karam, A. N., Tabet, C. C., Mneimneh, Z., Ghosn, M. B., et al. (2004). PTSD in children and adolescents following war. In R. R. Silva (Ed.), *Post traumatic stress disorders in children and adolescents: Handbook* (pp. 306–352). New York: Norton.

Ferenczi, S. (1921). Psychoanalytic observations on tic (J. Suttie, Trans.). In J. Richman (Ed.), *Further contributions to the theory and technique of psychoanalysis* (p. 155). London: Hogarth Press.

Freud, S. (1900). The interpretation of dreams. *Standard Edition* 4–5.

Freud, S. (1920). Beyond the pleasure principle. *Standard Edition* 18:7–64.

Freud, S. (1926). Inhibitions, symptoms, and anxiety. *Standard Edition* 20:77–174.

Freud, S. (1940). Splitting the ego in the process of defense. *Standard Edition* 23:271–275.

Freud, A., & Burlingham, D. (1944). *War and children*. New York: International Universities Press.

Joshi, P. T., & Lewin, S. M. (2004). Disaster, terrorism and children. *Psychiatric Annals, 34*(9), 710–719.

Kardiner, A. (1932). Bio-analysis of the epileptic reaction. *Psychoanalytic Quarterly, 2*, 375–483.

Kardiner, A. (1941). *The traumatic neurosis of war*. Washington, DC: National Research Council.

Kernberg, O. (1967). Borderline personality organization. *Journal of the American Psychoanalytic Association, 15*, 641–685.

Krystal, H. (1997). Desomatization and the consequences of infantile psychic trauma. *Psychoanalytic Inquiry, 17*, 126–150.

Laplanche, J., & Pontalis, J. B. (1973). *The language of psychoanalysis* (D. Nicholson-Smith, Trans.). New York: Norton. (Original work published 1967.)

Laub, D., & Lee, S. (2003). Thanatos and massive psychic trauma: The impact of the death instinct on knowing, remembering, and forgetting. *Journal of the American Psychoanalytic Association, 51*, 433–464.

Leys, R. (2000). Death masks: Kardiner and Ferenczi on psychic trauma. In *Trauma: A genealogy* (pp. 44–73). Chicago: University of Chicago Press.

Moore, B., & Fine, B. (Eds.). (1990). *Psychoanalytic terms and concepts*. New Haven, CT: Yale University Press.

Salmon, T. W. (1917). *The care and treatment of mental disease and the war neurosis (shell shock) in the British Army*. New York: The War Work Committee of the National Committee for Mental Hygiene.

Segal, H. (1993). On the clinical usefulness of the death instinct. *International Journal of Psychoanalysis, 74*, 55–61.

Singer, M. (1977). Experience of emptiness in narcissistic and borderline personalities, part II: Loss of the sense of self and the potential for suicide. *International Review of Psychoanalysis, 4*, 471–479.

Wexler, I. D., Branski, D., & Kerem, E. (2006). War and children. *Journal of the American Medical Association, 296*(5), 579–581.

# 4

# RESILIENCE
## Accommodation and Recovery

*Henry Krystal, MD*

The analytic involvement with survivors of the Holocaust started with a number of leading analysts (Niederland, Schur, Eissler, Wangh, and others). We succeeded in establishing in Germany the principles of psychological damages from the persecutions. This became the legal basis for the restitution laws, which made possible psychoanalytic treatment for survivors. The insights derived from this work had widespread effects. Through conferences and joint efforts by analysts, the study of the Holocaust became a major stimulus of generalized research and treatment of post-traumatic stress disorders. Presently, there is worldwide recognition of the pioneering nature of this work.

Much of what we learned in the analytic studies of Holocaust and genocide survivors was applied directly to the treatment of survivors of natural and human-made disasters. The greatest application and further boost to this kind of exploration and care came from extending these views to the treatment of Vietnam War veterans. By now, psychoanalytic insights into trauma and its prevention and treatment have been made available throughout the world and have been applied to all ages and situations.

We are all aware that there are limitations concerning generalizations about the reactions of people during the Holocaust, because even among those who were at the very same place at the same time, each one had a different experience (Sigmund Freud's "Erlebnisse"). The variety of experiences was enormous. Depending on what challenges an individual had to face, the individual's personal traits, assets, and patterns of behavior influenced the success of his or her efforts. Some choices of behaviors favored survival. I will limit my present discussion to one pattern. In some respects, the concentration camps were the epitome of the genocidal war and involved the most terrible and unique stresses. The responses in this situation are, in retrospect, most clearly classifiable. Considering these extreme conditions will illustrate some points relevant to our quest.

I feel that "healthy" infantile omnipotence is the most important asset for dealing with life's stresses and potential trauma (Krystal, 1997a; Ornstein, 1997). It is the emotional mainspring of extraordinary reserves. It provides a profound, unshakable conviction of one's invulnerability, derived in the first place from a fortunate and harmonious pre-object, symbiotic relatedness (Kumin, 1997). The programming of the infant's sense of security is achieved by the empathic care and adoring eye-to-eye (right hemisphere to right hemisphere) communication of the mothering parent in the first three years of life (Schore, 1994).

In an adult, there is hardly any reflective self-awareness of the emotional reserves hidden deep in the soul. The availability of these emotional reserves is recognizable in a special vitality, in an optimistic and adventuresome attitude, and in social and career contacts—conveying the subject's calm conviction that he or she will be welcomed and liked. The foundation of it all is an innate, infantile, magical state, programmed, as it were, for receiving positive mothering care and thriving on it. As the infant establishes a functional self-awareness and discovers the "outside" good object, the mother is watchful for the child's distress and translates it into her affective responses. She strives to attend to the infant's needs immediately and to soothe and restore a state of well-being. Through her behavior, she conveys to the infant the message that he or she is lovable and perfect. Thus is established our sense of omnipotence that is later observed in our belief in the magical power of our wishes.

Individuals who have a healthy dose of the adult residuals of infantile narcissism can preserve their optimism in situations of stress and danger. They are able to retain initiative in their thinking, in their planning, or even just in their fantasy. Even when under severe stress, they manage to recognize the chances of improving the dangerous situation at varying degrees of risk. The ones whose risk taking worked out well treasure the memories of the actions and self-reliance that saved their own or other's lives (Krystal 1997b, 1997c; Ornstein, 1997).

Consider the opposite side of the issue: trauma is an intrapsychic phenomenon. Although certain situations can be assumed to be traumatic to all who experience them, some people can handle situations that overwhelm others. Fear is the signal of impending avoidable, manageable danger. It activates the entire organism including, and especially, the mind. In contrast, when one is confronted with danger that is estimated to be unavoidable and inescapable, one surrenders to it. Based on the subjective evaluation of the situation and with the estimation of one's own helplessness, the affect changes from fear to a catatonoid reaction. This emotion triggers surrender and initiates the traumatic state. The individual gives up all initiative and obeys orders. This state is of a cataleptic nature and has a powerful hypnotic effect. The more one obeys orders, the deeper one goes into the trance. This state starts a progression that cannot be stopped until one reaches a "robot" state. Being able to establish and maintain the constricted state is potentially a lifesaving operation.

If we have a chance to examine an individual in this condition, we find an overwhelmed, immobilized, withdrawn person, often showing derealization and depersonalization. The focus of attention is very narrow. In concentration camps, upon being unloaded from the deadly cattle cars and experiencing the dehumanization, terrorization, and loss of everyone dear, potential survivors had to be able to directly block their affective responses to the fate of their families and to respond only to what needed to be done on a moment-to-moment basis with "Kadaver Gehorchsamkeit" (cadaver-like obedience—Himmler's favorite expression). Failure to achieve this feat resulted in being killed immediately. Zalman Loewenthal, while in the *Sonderkommando* (the group who was isolated from the other prisoners and whose task it was to burn the newly gassed transports in the crematoria of Auschwitz), reported, "They succeeded in blunting all emotion, all thought of any action" (Mark, 1988, p. 219).

Some prisoners instantly identified with the aggressors and imitated their behavior. Commonly, these individuals became kapos. In Auschwitz from 1942 to 1944, they had to become killers of their fellow inmates on a daily quota basis. Eventually, they expressed their sadism constantly, even in encountering newly arriving transports. A note from Zalman Gradowski written while he was in the *Sonderkommando* and buried in a scroll in the ashes around the crematorium describes the experiences of newly arriving transports:

> We endeavor to engage the more senior inmates in conversation, to learn more. But how nasty are those whom we address! How can they be so sadistic to make fun of our miserable people? How lightly, without contorting their faces, they answer questions about our families: "They are in heaven already." Has the camp caused them to lose all feelings, leaving them no better amusement then to take pleasure in the torture and suffering of others? . . . The words of such cruel statements: "Your families are buried!"

Everyone is terrified. The heart recoils from the very sound of the words: "your family is no longer alive." . . . The barrack kapos . . . tell us and instruct us how to behave toward them during working hours: "Remember that you have to become robots and move at our will. Don't take a step without an order from us!" (Mark, 1988, pp. 197–198)

Our reaction to those who so thoroughly identified with the aggressor is to condemn them and to wish we could punish them. However, Lifton (1986, p. 251) reflected about a doctor in Auschwitz who was a collaborator in medical experimentation: "Samuel was a Jew, which meant a person one hundred percent condemned to death in the camp. So he had a right to prolong his life—week by week, month by month."

Returning to the process of trauma, which we left at the robot state: If the effort to arrest the progression of the traumatic state failed, the deepening of it manifested in a growing numbing of pain and painful emotions, followed by a loss of all vestiges of self-reliance, initiative, and agency. The empowerment to say "no" and to carry out self-defense was progressively lost. At a certain point, the traumatic closure reached a malignant state, with the blocking of all mental functions: cognition, registration of perceptions, recall, scanning, information processing in general, planning, and problem solving. Finally, just a vestige of these functions was retained, with some capacity for self-observation. If the traumatic process continued, all vitality was suppressed, and the individual succumbed to psychogenic death, with the heart stopping in diastole.

The following is the description Bomba (1985, p. 49) gives of his first day in Auschwitz:

In the morning when they had the appeal to go out from the barracks, from our group I would say at least four or five were dead. I do not know how it happened—they must have had with them some kind of poison and poisoned themselves. At least two of them were my close friends. They did not say anything. We did not even know they had poison with them.

Indeed, likely, they did not, and their death was psychogenic. Franz Suchomel, an SS man in Treblinka, stated that in a transport of five thousand Jews from France, three thousand were dead on arrival: "Some had slashed their wrists or *just died*" (emphasis mine) (Lanzmann, 1985, p. 53). Even about shorter transports, he said that the people were "half dead and half mad."

After a couple of months of incarceration, a different kind of death made its appearance and grew in frequency: the "Musulman" process. In the early deaths, there was a direct progression of the traumatic process toward death, following a universal pattern common to the entire animal kingdom (Meerloo, 1959; Seligman, 1975). By contrast, the Musulman death pattern followed the exhaustion of all emotional resources and manifested in an observable pattern of ceasing necessary survival behavior. Sometimes, just before death, the Musulman manifested an ineffectual rage, indiscriminately lashing out at anyone who happened to be around him (Krystal, 1988). The inmates' awareness of the danger of the Musulman surrender pattern and the need to guard against it motivated many of the adjustments and behaviors in the concentration camps. For instance, the strong effort to keep the infestation with lice from getting out of hand was directly linked to this danger, because the impending Musulmen were often observed literally crawling with lice.

For those who managed to arrest the traumatic process in the robot state and had to live in this condition for a significant period, there were consequences that were to last the rest of their lives (Krystal, 1988, 1997b). Survival in the face of an impasse, a "no exit" situation, takes place in a state of "psychic closing off." Survivors undergo symbolic death in order to avoid physical or psychic death. Such cataclysms result in a permanent "death imprint," desensitization, and identification with death and with the dead (Lifton, 1976).

Many psychological functions serve the prevention of massive psychic trauma. Examples of such functions are perception, registration, and, most of all, self-evaluation in a given situation. In the past, I have studied the multiplicity of functions, including ego functions, involved in trauma prevention, representing the exploration and elaboration of the idea of the "stimulus barrier," not as a passive bar, but as the totality of potentially mobilizable defenses (Krystal, 1985). Signal affects are the essential sensory, monitoring, and regulatory signals or "switches" in information processing. They determine the choice of behavior in a given situation. They "color" the nature of the constant reinterpretation of self-representations and object representations. Signal affects do not stop totally in the traumatic state. Indeed, as always, we have to create our mental representation of everything we behold. We must maintain our psychic reality, as it is the only knowable reality (Dorsey, 1943, 1965; Krystal 1973, 1988).

Let us consider the application of what we used to call the "stimulus barrier" to the understanding of one's functioning in the traumatic state. In my

1985 article "Trauma and the Stimulus Barrier," I examine many aspects of the perceptive, cognitive, sensorimotor, affective, and consciousness-regulatory functions that operate unceasingly and silently in our orientation and adjustment process. I show how many mental activities serving a variety of functions are simultaneously involved in the organism's self-preservation. An example of a unique defensive operation is presented by a number of Cambodian women, who during the genocidal attack, sometimes at the instant when their loved ones were about to be killed, developed a functional blindness. This is a kind of partial blindness that persisted for years despite treatment (Wilkinson, 1994). It is quite different from conversion reaction, and it illustrates the difference between repression and repudiation (*Verwerfung* versus *Verdrängung*). From this point of view, these defensive aspects of the mind are like immunological and cellular reactions that are quietly involved in the prevention of infection and neoplasia. We become aware of them only when there is a partial failure. What can be learned about these functions from studies of the sequelae of the traumatic state?

We focus on the traumatic state, not the traumatic situation. This is why we have to look beyond ego defenses and venture into an examination of all the information processing. The contributions from experimental psychology, developmental psychology, perceptgenesis, and neuroscience have to be combined and reconciled with psychoanalytic contributions to expose the extreme complexity of factors involving attention, perception, evaluation, recall, and various memory functions. Part of the process consists of multiple "takes" of improving detail and elaboration, ending in creating a stimulus-proximate registration, on which we can obtain intersubjective agreement with others. All these operations are executed on the unconscious level.

Next, we bring in associations. We compare and confront current perceptions with accumulated memories. These memories bring in their own affect qualities that become the signal affects directing further mental element processing (Krystal & Krystal, 1994; Westerlundh & Smith, 1983). This signal determines where and how the percept is registered in the mind. It also determines the kind and degree of consciousness and the accessibility of it for the future.

Returning to the first mental act in the chain, what could be the nature of perception in the traumatic state? From the beginning, there is a blocking of all the functions reviewed—the processes of perception and cognition on the one hand, and the affect signals on the other—that produce the particular self-evaluation in the emergency situation. In the traumatic state, the choices and breadth of references are greatly limited and the scope of attention is severely narrowed, just as in a hypnotic trance. However, some capacity for reflective self-awareness and some recognition of imminent danger may continue. Some individuals remain able to mobilize life-preserving action in dire emergencies. (For example, during "selections," some people managed to run to the "good side.") Occasionally, when they recognize an opportunity, some people in a traumatic state can mobilize themselves and act swiftly and effectively. Those decisions, such as choosing whether to go on an available transport, can have life-or-death consequences.

We can thus distinguish between those individuals who, when confronted with great danger, surrendered to it totally, and those who were able to ward off abject submission. Surrender also had serious consequences for the way the people acted thereafter. Traumatic constriction interfered with taking initiative on the one hand and the capacity to maintain associations and mutual-assistance group formations on the other. In the concentration camps, even though there was significant traumatization, there were individuals who, with luck and health, were able to establish a pattern of living that they accepted as being a greatly abnormal, but temporary, situation. They were able to preserve their intrapsychic resistance and initiative and to nurture the belief that they would survive and return to a condition of normality. In fact, during some temporary respites one could hear some inmates of the camps resting in their cots sharing fantasies that "when this is over" they will just show people their tattoos and receive all kinds of special compensations, favored treatment, and even honors. As long as they maintained such hope, their degree of dehumanization was moderated. Hidden vestigial optimism permitted some limited alertness and initiative, even inventiveness.

A very special combination of favorable personality assets and fortunate circumstances was required for an inmate to conceive a plan to escape and to carry it out successfully, as did Rudolf Vrba. He recounted: "The decision to escape . . . was formed immediately . . . when [he] arrived in Auschwitz" (Lanzmann, 1985, pp. 165–166). In preparing to escape, he dared to find and contact individuals who were part of the Auschwitz Resistance. As it happened, he also had a faithful comrade and collaborator "from home," and together they made preparations to escape. Vrba was dedicated to getting back to Hungary and informing the world about what was going on in Auschwitz, a goal that he was willing to die for. Thus the paralyzing power of the fear of death was suspended by his devoting himself to an objective more valued than his survival.

Members of the Auschwitz *Sonderkommando* struggled with a bitter determination to express their outrage in a suicidal rebellion. Zalman Gradowski
entered in his buried scroll:

> As for us, we have already lost all hope of living to the day of liberation.
> Despite the fact that joyful news reaches us, we have learned that the world
> is letting the barbarian destroy the remnants of the Jewish people. . . . We
> the Sonderkommando have wanted for a long time to put an end to our
> terrible labor, forced on us on the pain of death. We wanted to do a great
> deed. (Mark, 1988, p. 201)

Zalman Loewenthal, a fellow inmate, who was also killed in the uprising,
described the agony of defeat, as one after another of the group members collapsed in their resolve. Some even turned informer, as did one who turned in
the leader who was preparing the rebellion and escape. Still, the preparations
continued for a few months, despite many delays, even when it was clear that
their own group would be liquidated. Two hundred of them were sent to
another camp, and the conspirators learned that they were directly gassed.

The postwar discovery of the Auschwitz scrolls buried by these men gives
us a chance to observe the nature of their cognition directly. Gradowski used
an unnatural, emotional style in a vibrant and literary Yiddish with a tendency toward Germanisms and flowery phrases. He addressed the reader
directly. He sounded as if he were giving his own eulogy. Loewenthal's man-
uscript was written in a nervous, distracted style with no small degree of confusion. It is an affectless communication. There is, in fact, no mention of any
*feelings* about the horrors and his own degradation—from being the head of
a rabbinical court to becoming a desperate, enslaved participant in the genocide (Mark, 1988). Both styles illustrate characteristic traumatic distortions
of memory and oral history (Krystal, 1998).

Contemporary work with survivor testimonies still shows the characteristic cognitive styles that yield clues about the nature of registration in the
traumatic state. The styles of recall and reporting are consistent with those
found in other studies of posttraumatic behavior. The stories are related in a
"facts only," constricted manner. Testimonies are given in a conflictual,
painful way and are spotty and highly distorted. Some recollections are con-
spicuously improbable and show displacements. Some can best be understood as amalgams of dreams and fears. Some of them are screen memories,
and some are found modified in 30-year follow-up reexaminations.

These phenomena illustrate that defensive reprocessing of memory traces from the traumatic state continue to be operational, now serving to protect one from the possibility of retraumatization (Krystal, 1999). Thus, a major lifesaving operation is the creation of traumatic screens and distorted memories that function as a protection against the unthinkable. The catatonoid reaction produces primary repression. Information incompatible with the survival of the self is not registered at all, creating a "black hole" in the information processing system. This reaction is what earlier I called repudiation (Cohen, 1985). It manifests itself in survivor testimonies and is a major problem in attempting to do psychoanalysis with traumatized individuals (Krystal, 1999).

Another universal defensive operation is the traumatic splitting of one's self-representation. There are many splitting patterns residual from the traumatic state (Brenner, 2001). The most conspicuous of these patterns results from a fixation on the past. One has to live in the present but is not able to stop living in the past. Another major dissonance is between believing and not believing what happened—how it could have happened? This demonstrates the continuation of the defensive functions of denial and disavowal.

The splitting of identity common in other posttraumatic states is rare in Holocaust survivors. However, the following pattern is virtually universal: there is a splitting within the individual along the polarization between victim and oppressor representations. These two parasitic self-representations must be kept rigidly apart at almost any cost. Even in some analyses, they cannot be fully or carelessly exposed and discovered by the patient without causing a serious disturbance (Krystal, 1988, 1999; Shaw, 1967). An 80-year-old woman seen recently, who had many different complaints, kept complaining repetitively about pain in her left breast. My records, obtained 30 years earlier, showed that she had been bitten on the left breast by an SS man while he raped her. She was not able to make the connection between the symptom and the assault.

Repression and repudiation keep one attached to one's mental representation of the perpetrator, victim, and the primitive affect precursors generated in the traumatic state. Recall is also disturbed by the fact that in the traumatic state, registration is on a sensorimotor level that is preverbal, and therefore no language is available for the presentation of some memory traces. Recollections are presented in an "understated" way. Memories are related in a staccato, aprosodic manner. The melody is gone out of the speech. Even though statements appear lucid, their heuristic value is like the memory of a nightmare.

Memory is unreliable. In one instance, a survivor was able to recall and retell the death march from Auschwitz westward to the next camp. He could describe the circumstances of the terrible night, the frost, and the killing of everyone who could not keep on marching. There was no doubt in his mind that he recalled the whole experience, but there was never an occasion for him to tell the whole story or an audience to whom to tell it. Recently, through the "testimony" program, he started examining himself to see what he actually recalled. It turned out that he remembered only certain unconnected vignettes, isolated fragments of the event.

One of them was waiting to be marched out from Birkenau. Another was marching in the dark and beginning to hear (and see?) that people were being killed by the side of the road. Next was an image of struggling to keep marching together with two friends. One of them became weak and wanted to give up, sit down, and be killed. The two men held him up and continued marching. He does not remember how long this went on or how it stopped. In his next image he finds himself at dawn marching alone—no columns, no other prisoners. He drags himself onto an empty road and encounters an old German soldier who is leaning against a fence and carrying his rifle. The soldier seems to be in as bad a shape as he is. No dialogue between them is recalled. Next, the two of them are walking through the city in which he visualizes a busy intersection with traffic regulated by military police. Somehow, he finds himself in the camp where the prisoners are "stored." Sometime later in the evening of the same or the next day he is loaded into a cattle car, and with him are the two men with whom he had been marching on the first night. They manage to get to the corner of the wagon that is a defensive position. (Also see Laub, 1995.)

The spottiness of this narrative shows disturbances in registration and recall even 55 years later. I found in the 35 years of therapeutic experience and reexamination follow-ups that unconscious registrations (including repressed ones) do not remain unchanged, but are reworked perpetually (Krystal, 1998a, 1997b). This is especially conspicuous in the aging survivor as the losses of old age necessitate grieving, which in turn brings up the never accomplished or even attempted mourning. The losses occurring in aging require changes in self-representation through grieving. The capacity to grieve successfully, to a point of acceptance and acquiescence to losses, is the prerequisite for harmonious senescence. If the grieving is effective, then one can discover (in analysis) revisions of various mental contents including pathological memory traces of traumatic registrations (Krystal, 1981, 1991, 1995). Dissociation and disavowal were indispensable in unbearable conditions. Denial may have been temporary or lasting, but clearly, in Auschwitz, without that kind of catastrophic reaction one would have been overwhelmed with a flood of emotions, especially grief. Mourning had to be delayed, sometimes forever.

These defenses were necessary because the imprisonment, the isolation, and the experience of sadistic killer kapos of one's own people made it most difficult to maintain loyalty and love. Love represents our life power (Dorsey, 1971; Krystal, 1988, 1999). To put it in a teleological way: in order to improve one's chances of survival, one had to favor the secret preservation of love, hope, and faith under the most difficult circumstances. If one could not help one's fellow prisoners, it was sometimes an expression of love to restrain from hurting or exploiting them. The capacity for loving aided in continuing links with other people struggling for survival and providing a means of preserving hope and faith. Resilience was proportional to an individual's ability to accept unbearable conditions and persevere with at least *intrapsychic* protest, resistance, and the preservation of pre-Holocaust goals and ideals.

The preservation of some ingenuity and alertness to "what worked" in the traumatic state was a special and rare talent. In those situations in which the victims of persecution were not isolated but stayed with a group from home, preserving the capacity for socialization was perhaps the single most important resource favoring survival. In concentration camps and related experiences, no one survived without some help from others. The preservation of some capacity for social interaction was a great aid in maintaining one's own sense of humanity. The ability to form temporary alliances for survival, and, when possible, to help someone, constituted a rare source of restoring a sense of being a "good person" and maintaining some self-respect.

When people were able to stay together with a group from home, they acquired a source of support to their humanity (Ornstein, 1985). The ultimate benefit of these social relations was the preservation of a viable human self-representation with some dignity. Although it was not possible to keep these principles in the forefront, it was essential to preserve the values and ideals built on the foundation of family and community life and traditions. The enduring self-view was built on a deep-seated sense of belonging in the context of a loving, sharing, and supportive family. I found an illustration of the preservation of such inner forces under the most extreme circumstances from a testimony of a *Sonderkommando* survivor: "We used to share everything. . . . When one of us was observed not sharing—we knew that he was on the way to become a Musulman" (Mark, 1988, p. 221). Under those unimaginable conditions of confrontation with death, having surrendered to the genocidal enemies and participated in their murderous design, group loyalty was the last protection against final withdrawal, surrender, and death.

Besides the traits that I have emphasized so far, which were trauma moderating, there were character traits that had survival value, with some variation

according to the nature of the experiences one had. For most people, to survive, it was necessary to be flexible. The world of the Holocaust was ever
changing and unpredictable. The kinds of things that people adjusted to
exceed the power of our imagination. Children were separated from their parents. Those that survived had to be able to adjust to the conditions in which
they found themselves—being kept alive temporarily until it was their turn to
be subjected to "medical" experiments and then "sacrificed" just like laboratory animals. How could these children, who had already lost everyone they
loved, function in the recognition that the doctors were not helpers but tor-
turers and killers? They had to be capable of complete "psychic closing off." As
for the children that had been in the Birkenau experimentation barrack, some
managed to survive. They had bonded to each other and trusted no adults.
This was still their condition after they were rescued and brought to the
Hempstead Nursery (Freud & Dann, 1951). To this day, it is incomprehensible to the world, even though it was exposed and proven at least since
1986, that the entire German genocide program and its operation was the
work of physicians (Lifton, 1986, and a movie based on his work in 1998,
*Healing by Killing*).

The survival in ghettos, in camps, living on false papers—all required an
extraordinary flexibility. With the sudden radical change of circumstances,
one had to land on both feet and forthwith use one's skills and resources. One
had to be able to accept constant changeability and unpredictability, rather
than stability, as the order of life.

An inner resource of enormous power was the ability to maintain some
sense of continuing identification with something transcendental that would
endure: God, the Jewish people—some "higher power." Robbed of their ability to trust God, many people derived emotional support from their internalized parental images or other benign introjects. The psychological
regression in the infantilizing oppression and incarceration necessitated the
evocation of idealized magical objects. In the absence of an actual mental representation of parents to pray to, one survivor used the image of the door handle of his home as his "survival image."

In considering concentration camp survivors' reaction to liberation, it is
relevant to recall that some individuals experienced brief postliberation psy-
choses, for the most part persevering in continuing persecutory states. There
seems to have been a need for a gradual termination of the traumatic state.
Being able to monitor one's status, to regulate the rising complex feelings
attending liberation, and to control the rate of increasing food intake were

talents that had direct survival value. Nelly Sachs pleaded for the rescued, "Show us the sun, but gradually!" (Sachs, 1967, p. 145).

The task of psychological recovery required attaining the capacity to restore a sense of continuity and to return to an ability to anticipate the future with enthusiasm and vitality. Involved in "coming back" was the initiation of reconstruction, "piecing together of reconstructed memories, idealized childhood memories which were going to serve as inspiration, anchors and organizers" (Ornstein, 1985, p. 127). For the great majority of liberated survivors, life was totally disrupted, and all family was lost. As soon as people were well enough and had recovered from the shock of liberation, they became involved, in one form or another, in searching for the remnants of families and for fellow survivors to whom they had become attached. In general, the reestablishment of close groups and the creation of as many joint activities as possible were favorable developments.

Behind this tendency was the need to marry and reestablish families, and this was often experienced as an imperative to save the continuity of the Jewish people. This double motivation produced many hasty marriages based on some commonalities—finding someone with a familiar background, one coming from anywhere close to one's hometown or homeland. However, this behavior was, in part, problematic, because the task of reconstructing an acceptable worldview, the rebuilding of a reasonable and secure world order, had not yet been achieved. Above all, the capacity to love and feel loved was not yet restored. Symptomatic of poorly relieved regression was that inordinately many of the first pregnancies ended in miscarriages, and deliveries were often accompanied by a persecutory panic, sometimes expressed as the dread that the German doctors will kill the baby. When I speak of regression in the camps, one universal symptom of it was the cessation of menstruation by all women. Many of the same people were later in need of intervention and were identified as "numb" or "victim" families (Danieli, 1981).

For survivors, the anxiety was, at the core, derived from the question of how to deal with the (prepersecution) notions of God. How was one to reconcile the idea of a benevolent, omniscient, and omnipotent God with what they had just witnessed? How was it going to be possible to resume a normal life pattern in a world that had betrayed the Jews and abandoned them to their destruction? How was one going to be able to experience love for a new spouse and children when the lost ones could not be mourned? Is it any wonder that so many survivors became obsessed with the missing graves of the lost families?

The problem of survivor guilt was intensified by prewar indoctrination in a religious system that encouraged magical thinking. If neither God nor the survivor was crazy, then there was only one possible answer to the cause of the desolation: the failure of God to rescue His people meant that one's death wishes caused the devastation. To restore his or her fundamentalist belief in God and to avoid becoming overwhelmed with guilt, a rigid person would be driven to the one answer most survivors shunned: that the ones who perished were evil and brought the punishment on themselves. The survivors were brought up on the biblical tradition that explained all calamities that befell the Jews in this way, beginning with the story of the deluge.

Consequently, the generation of survivors who had lost their spouses and children in the Holocaust was condemned to a penitential lifestyle (Krystal, 1981). These were the kinds of emotional and moral dilemmas that plagued the survivors' families. Resilience here permitted a choice of atheism or, more commonly, a slow and gradual return to traditional practices. Doubts and obsessions were often covered up with a driven, never-ending multiplicity of rituals (many minor ones and unrecognized as such) that accompanied every aspect of their lives.

This kind of adjustment permitted fairly good family functioning, albeit with a very common "affective anesthesia" pattern (Minkowski, 1946; Sifneos, 1967) and/or the breakthrough of symptomatic behavior such as mothers being too frightened to let their children out of their sight or vacillating from overprotectiveness to uncontrollable rages in which the children were sometimes called names like "Hitler." It would be unreasonable to expect survivors to be asymptomatic: we have been studying the various "Survivor Syndromes" ever since Niederland named them in 1961. The one thing we have learned and have been able to apply to a worldwide science of posttraumatic disorders is that every symptom and every problem represents creativity, a capacity for adjustment that at its genesis served to avert something worse. Most of all there is the clear indication that one's resilience is proportional to the capacity to mobilize one's love powers. Love outraged is experienced as anger or hate. Love rendered helpless manifests itself as shame. However, love represents the survivor's self-reintegrating and self-healing powers.

## References

The paper on which this chapter is based was read at the 41st International Congress of Psychoanalysis in Santiago, Chile, on July 28, 1999, and was awarded the Elisa M.

Hayman Prize for research in Holocaust and Genocide. It was first published as Krystal, H. (2000). Psychische widerständigkeit: Anpassung und Restitution bei Holocaust-Überlebenden. *Psyche Zeitschrift, 54*(9/10), 839–859. Reprinted with permission from *Psyche Zeitschrift.*

Bomba, A. (1985). *The screenplay of SHOAH* (C. Lanzmann, Ed.). New York: Pantheon Books.

Brenner, I. (2001). *Dissociation of trauma, theory, phenomenology and technique.* Madison, CT: International Universities Press.

Cohen, J. (1985). Trauma and repression. *Psychoanalytic Inquiry, 14*, 163–189.

Danieli, Y. (1981). Differing adaptational styles in families of survivors of the Nazi Holocaust: Some implications for treatment. *Children Today, 10*, 34–35.

Dorsey, J. M. (1943). Some considerations of psychic reality. *International Journal of Psychoanalysis, 29*, 147–151.

Dorsey, J. M. (1965). *Illness or allness: Conversations of a psychiatrist.* Detroit, MI: Wayne State University Press.

Dorsey, J. M. (1971). *Psychology of emotion: Self conscious discipline by conscious emotional continence.* Detroit, MI: Wayne State University Press.

Freud, A., & Dann, S. (1951). An experiment in group upbringing. In R. Eissler, A. Freud, H. Hartmann, & M. Kris (Eds.), *The psychoanalytic study of the child,* Vol. 6 (pp. 127–168). New York: International Universities Press.

Krystal, H. (1973). *Psychic reality.* Paper presented to the Michigan Psychoanalytic Institute, Farmington Hills, MI.

Krystal, H. (1981). The aging survivor of the Holocaust. *The Journal of Geriatric Psychiatry, 14*, 165–189.

Krystal, H. (1985). Trauma and the stimulus barrier. *Psychoanalytic Inquiry, 5*, 131–161.

Krystal, H. (1988). *Integration and self healing.* Hillsdale, NJ: Analytic Press.

Krystal, H. (1991). Integration and self healing in post traumatic states. *Journal of Geriatric Psychiatry and American Imago, 48*, 93–118.

Krystal, H. (1995). Trauma and aging: A thirty-year follow-up. In C. Caruth (Ed.), *Trauma: Exploration of memory* (pp. 76–99). Baltimore: Johns Hopkins University Press.

Krystal, H. (1997a). Late life effects of trauma: Adult catastrophic and infantile type. *Journal of Geriatric Psychiatry, 30*, 61–81.

Krystal, H. (1997b, January). *Reflections on the psychology of survival and readjustment.* Address to the Second Reunion of Jewish Graduates from German Universities after World War II, Boca Raton, FL.

Krystal, H. (1997c). The trauma of confronting one's vulnerability and death. In C. Ellman & J. Reppen (Eds.), *Omnipotent fantasies and the vulnerable self* (pp. 149–185). Northvale, NJ: Jason Aronson.

Krystal, H. (1998). What cannot be remembered or forgotten. In J. Kauffman (Ed.), *Loss of the assumptive world: A theory of traumatic loss* (pp. 213–220). New York: Brunner-Routledge.

Krystal, H. (1999, May). *Psychoanalytic approaches in posttraumatic, alexithymic, psychosomatic, and addictive patients.* Paper presented at the Michigan Psychoanalytic Society "Milestone Program," Farmington Hills, MI.

Krystal, H., & Krystal, A. D. (1994). Psychoanalysis and neuroscience in relationship to dreams and creativity. In M. P. Shaw & M. A. Runco (Eds.), *Creativity and affect* (pp. 185–212). Norwood, NJ: Ablex Press.

Kumin, I. (1997). *Preobject relatedness: Early attachment and the psychodynamic situation.* New York: Guilford Press.

Lanzmann, C. (1985). *Shoah: An oral history of the Holocaust.* New York: Pantheon.

Laub, D. (1995). Truth and testimony: The process and the struggle. In C. Caruth (Ed.), *Trauma: Exploration of memory* (pp. 61–75). Baltimore: Johns Hopkins University Press.

Lifton, R. J. (1976). *Life of the self.* New York: Simon & Schuster.

Lifton, R. J. (1986). *The Nazi doctors: Medical killing and the psychology of genocide.* New York: Basic Books.

Mark, B. (1988). *The scrolls of Auschwitz.* Tel Aviv, Israel: Oved.

Meerloo, J. A. M. (1959). Shock, catalepsy, and psychogenic death. *International Record of Medicine, 172,* 384–393.

Minkowski, E. (1946). L'anesthésie affective. *Annals of Medicopsychology, 104,* 8–13.

Niederland, W. G. (1961). The problem of the survivor. *Journal of Hillside Hospital, 10,* 233–247.

Ornstein, A. (1985). Survival and recovery. *Psychoanalytic Inquiry, 5,* 99–130.

Ornstein, P. H. (1997). Omnipotence in health and illness. In C. Ellman & J. Reppen (Eds.), *Omnipotent fantasies and the vulnerable self* (pp. 117–130). Northvale, NJ: Jason Aronson.

Sachs, N. (1967). *O the chimneys.* New York: Farrar, Straus & Giroux.

Schore, A. N. (1994). *Affect regulation and the origin of the self: Neurobiology of emotional development.* Hillsdale, NJ: Erlbaum.

Seligman, M. E. P. (1975). *Helplessness: On depression, development, and death.* San Francisco: Freeman.

Shaw, R. (1967). *The man in the glass booth.* London: Chatto and Winders.

Sifneos, P. (1967). Clinical observations on some patients suffering from a variety of psychosomatic diseases. *Acta Medica Psychosomatica: Proceedings of the 7th European Conference on Psychosomatic Research, Rome, 7,* 452–458.

Westerlundh, B., & Smith, G. (1983). Perceptgenesis and the psychodynamics of perception. *Psychoanalysis and Contemporary Thought, 6,* 597–640.

Wilkinson, A. (1994, January 24). A change of the vision of God. *The New Yorker, 69,* 51–68.

# 5

# ON GENOCIDAL PERSECUTION AND RESILIENCE

*Ira Brenner, MD*

Resilient: (1) Returning to an original position, springing back, recoiling, etc.; also looking back. (2) Elastic; resuming an original shape or position after compression, stretching, etc. (3) Of a person: Readily recovering from illness, shock, etc.; resistant to setbacks or adversity. From the Latin "resilire": to leap back or recoil (Brown, 1993).

Psychological resilience following overwhelming life experience has become the subject of great interest in recent years. In addition to its obvious importance in the military and the significance of revictimization in childhood survivors of sexual abuse, the events of September 11 have brought the issue home to all of us. Social catastrophes on our soil have shocked us into realizing that no one is immune from terrorism and its traumatic effects. Like at the October 2004 Convention of the International Society for Traumatic Stress Studies (ISTSS) held in Chicago, plenary sessions and symposia of the ISTSS include such titles as "Stories of Healing and Resilience: The Power of Culture and Community," "Turning Trauma and Recovery Into Art: Creative Languages of Injury and Resiliency," and "Fostering Intergenerational Resilience From War and Genocide." The latter symposium dealt with American Indians, parents with PTSD, and the aftermath of war. Some of the research in progress presented preliminary data supporting the fact that some people with a prior history of trauma do not have an increased likelihood of developing PTSD in response to a major event. Furthermore, in those sexual abuse survivors who do not experience revictimization, resilience is associated with the perception of being in control and feeling competent. In addition, studies of disaster relief workers at Ground Zero suggest the significant finding that only a minority develop PTSD. In comparing their coping styles with those who did not develop PTSD, it is hoped to shed further light on resilience. According to self-reporting questionnaires, certain patterns were observed such as having self-directed anger but not self-blame and having coping styles characterized by seeking support from others, being accepting, and having the capacity to see the positive side of things. Such findings are then hoped to be operationalized in order to teach resilience to the at-risk population. The new field of "trauma preparation" offers a cognitive/behavioral model consisting of five stages: anticipation, pretrauma, trauma, posttrauma, and recovery. While these types of models and strategies might seem a bit foreign, superficial, and perhaps even a bit naive to the psychoanalyst who has the opportunity to explore the psyche in microscopic detail, the need for large-scale interventions is a reality in today's world. Most relevant to this issue is the fact that this brave new world of trauma owes much to those psychoanalysts who had the courage to listen to Holocaust survivors when no one else wanted to or was able to.

One of these pioneers is Henry Krystal, MD, whose 1968 book, *Massive Psychic Trauma*, has been a most powerful but quiet presence in my bookcase for many years. However, I did not realize that it was also having a profound effect on one of my patients until I moved offices and rearranged my bookcases. Frantic until she relocated it on a different shelf, this woman then revealed how fascinated she was by the title, imagining that it was her biography. Each day as she lay on the couch, she would commune with the book and get an odd sense of reassurance as the title would mirror her state of mind and remind her that her problems were deep and long-standing. She imagined that the answers to the riddle of her childhood were written on the pages of this mysterious book, fantasizing that there were very thin slices of her skin lying in between its pages or perhaps were the pages themselves. If only she could open the book, she would then know for sure what had happened to her and connect to her body and claim it to be her own. Over time, she was able to harness her defiance and unwillingness to submit, a trait originally used in the service of resistance, to confront adversity and create the kind of life she could only imagine in her dreams. This refusal to submit, a key to her resilience, was catalyzed by our hard work in analysis and is a quality of mind that we can see even under the most unspeakable conditions of genocidal persecution.

Genocide is the ultimate narcissistic injury. It is intended to obliterate the individual and his or her kind of all traces of his or her past, present, and future immediate and extended family. The term for this "crime without a name" was coined in 1943 by the jurist Raphael Lemkin when he learned what was happening to the Jews of Europe (Marrus, 1987). It occurs when a human being is progressively deprived of rights, possessions, home, loved ones, dignity, and ultimately the right to live simply because he or she is a member of an identifiable group. The resulting assault on the ego is utterly overwhelming, and when flight to safety is not possible, regression in the service of survival may be necessary in order to avoid the depletion and total despair that may lead to suicide. On an individual level, Ferenczi (1929/1955), in his essay "The Unwelcome Child and His Death Instinct," described how maternal aggression intensifies the internalized aggression of the unwanted child, who is more prone to get sick and die. When this familial paradigm gets enacted on a large scale in a society, the helplessness and impotent rage may contribute to the demise, or near demise, of a whole people. Although other groups, such as gypsies, homosexuals, and Jehovah's Witnesses, were treated mercilessly as well, the German government's "Final Solution to the Jewish Problem" did not allow any exceptions for the Jews. By the end of World War II and the liberation of the concentration camps, it has been estimated that two thirds of the Jewish population of Europe and about one third of the worldwide Jewish population was murdered. Of the 18 million civilian deaths in Europe, one out of every three, or 6 million, were Jewish. Over 1.5 million children were included in this incomprehensible number.

Krystal's follow-up studies with over 1,000 Holocaust survivors over 40 years has offered him a unique perspective on the vicissitudes of massive psychic trauma. He has played a key role in establishing the legitimacy of psychological damages due to persecution, and our current understanding of the nature of post-traumatic stress disorder owes much to his research. He essentially focuses on three elements: (1) the stages of the traumatic process, (2) those factors in the psyche that prevent psychic trauma, and (3) the sequelae of trauma. I will briefly review them, link them to developmental theory, especially Mahler's and Winnicott's, and offer some of my own ideas based on my work with Judith Kestenberg. I will then present highlights of our current understanding of their neurobiology. In describing the stages of the traumatic process, Dr. Krystal describes the catatonoid reaction, which is beyond fear, one of submission and becoming a robot. If it does not progress to a malignant state leading to death, it actually may have some survival value. He also describes a different kind of death in the concentration camps, that of the Musulman state, one of total depletion and punctuated by intermittent, ineffectual rages. He tells us that in the chronic robot state there is a symbolic death and a permanent death imprint characterized by desensitization and identification with death and the dead. Here we can see some of the enormous challenges for survivors of such trauma to bounce back.

The second element that he describes is one of prevention. He reminds us of the stimulus barrier, and the example he gives of the functional blindness in some Cambodian refugees is especially interesting in that he tells us that it is different from a conversion reaction or repression and is much more akin to a repudiation, disavowal, and essentially a dissociative process. I too have seen a number of patients with dissociative identity disorder who had various dissociated selves who were, indeed, blind or deaf or had other functional sensory impairments that essentially served the same purpose of not seeing, hearing, or knowing. In the traumatic state, the information processing is impaired and the disturbances of perceptive, cognitive, sensory, motor, affective, conscious, and regulatory functions serve as a way of warding off overwhelming input that goes beyond ego defenses. The scope of attention is severely narrowed as in a hypnotic trance. This constriction due to external overwhelming factors is in contrast to the constriction of perception due to the upsurge of instinctual strivings where one's external world narrows as Hartmann has described. He says that "The animal's picture of the external world narrows and broadens as the demands of his instincts become stronger or weaker; its center shifts according to whether he is hungry, in heat, etc. to those elements which are directly related to the gratification of the instinct" (Hartmann, 1939/1958, p. 58). Here, the constriction of perception is for a totally different purpose.

The third element is the sequelae of massive psychic trauma. Krystal observed a persistence of cognitive disturbances in the 30-year follow-ups and uses, for some of his data, the survivor testimonies, many of which have a constricted, "facts only" quality to them. Here, there are isolated memory fragments, disturbances in registration and recall, and not the continuous chronology that we might expect. There is defensive reprocessing of memories, amalgams of dreams and fears, and generation of traumatic, screened memories to ward off the totally unthinkable. Also, in the catatanoid reaction, he feels that there is primary repression resulting in a black hole in the information processing system. We may also consider this as repudiation and, again, to be in the realm of dissociation, truly a major obstacle in doing analytic work with such severely traumatized individuals. He also points out that there can be four different kinds of splitting of one's self-representation. One can be a fixation on the past. Another is believing and not believing what has happened and how. A third involves a splitting of identity and, again, this is more in the realm of dissociative disorders, which, in his experience, is rare in Holocaust survivors.[1] The fourth is that there can be splitting within the self between the victim and the perpetrator. So, we may expect dissociation, disavowal, inability to mourn—which has much to do with intergenerational transmission, the legacy of trauma for the children of survivors, who often are the ones who may do the mourning a generation later for their parents' unresolvable losses—survivor guilt, the question of where was God when all this was happening, enormous problems with faith, and alexithymia. But it is important to consider that symptoms themselves, from an adaptive standpoint, are a creative effort of the human psyche to try to solve the problem of overwhelming trauma. That fine line between adaptive and maladaptive, repetition and mastery, and transcendence and denial is what resilience is all about.

Dr. Krystal's particular interest in the death camps, the signature of the Third Reich, led him to conclude that "the 'healthy' infantile omnipotence is the most important asset and the emotional mainspring of extraordinary reserves for dealing with life's stresses and potential trauma" (Krystal, 2003, p. 4). Krystal believes that "almost every survivor has preserved a secret spark of omnipotence which whispers to him that he is very special and so he managed to survive the incredibly overwhelming and humiliating near-death experiences . . . but these secrets of unspeakable horror translated into the language of infantile omnipotence and narcissism may be concealing this message: 'Do you want to know how it is that I survived? The secret is, my mother loved me!'" (Krystal, 1997, p. 159). He cites Kumin's (1997) work on synchronous pre-object relatedness as well as Shore's (1994) ideas about right hemispheric communication between mother and infant as the foundation of the requisite secure, healthy attachment. Here Dr. Krystal emphasizes the developmental aspects of omnipotence in contrast to its use defensively.

Winnicott's contributions figure prominently in this discussion. Influenced by Klein, who elaborated upon Freud's assumption of infantile omnipotence, Winnicott emphasized its developmental aspects of being the result of good-enough mothering and the infant's own creativity. The mutual influence of the child's activity in discovering the wonders of the mother's breast in concert with her attunement and availability allows for the creation of the breast as a part object in the transitional space between the two. However, since omnipotence is the product of collaboration between the dyad, things can go awry. Most notably, a "false self" personality organization may develop to compensate for the failure of the dyad to reinforce the infant's omnipotence. A pseudocompliant, social self, capable of reacting and eliciting some type of response from the other, perpetuates the illusion of omnipotence, but it is disconnected from the child's "true self." According to

Winnicott, the lifelong, intrapsychic fantasy of omnipotence manifests itself readily in the analytic situation where "there is no trauma that is outside the individual's omnipotence . . . in infancy, however, good and bad things [do] happen to the infant. . . . [T]he capacity for gathering external factors into the arena of the infant's omnipotence is in the process of formation" (Winnicott, 1960, p. 590). Accordingly, those who have been totally shattered by massive psychic trauma cannot resurrect an illusion of omnipotence without feeling that everything that has happened was their fault—such negative omnipotence lends itself to "if only . . ." fantasies (Akhtar, 1999) and profound survivor guilt.

Margaret Mahler's views about omnipotence are relevant here as well. She proposes two stages of omnipotence within Freud's phase of primary narcissism, a time that occurs in the immediate period of life after birth. The first stage, "normal autism," is characterized by no awareness of the maternal caretaker as she exists in what Ferenczi (1913) described as "unconditional hallucinatory omnipotence." Mahler's second stage, symbiosis, is then characterized by a vague awareness of an external, need-satisfying presence, which, paraphrasing Ferenczi, she described as a "conditional hallucinatory omnipotence." Many months later, during the 15th to 18th month of a practicing subphase, she observed that the toddler's elated mood, the feelings of omnipotence and conquest associated with locomotion and muscular activity, gave way to a deflation owing to a more realistic appraisal of his or her place in the world, that of being small, helpless, and dependent upon a mother who is a separate being. Although gender differences have been noted, for example, the girl's tendency to become more depressed than the boy, the young child may still hold on to the illusion of the parent's omnipotence for a longer period of time (Jacobson, 1964). To follow Mahler's reasoning a bit more, increased cognitive capacity associated with the newly acquired ability to stand upright not only is a milestone of the greatest evolutionary significance but also ushers in a period of enormous narcissistic vulnerability.

This "species-specific human dilemma . . . arises out of the fact that on one hand the toddler is obliged by rapid maturation of his ego to recognize his separateness, while, on the other hand, he is as yet unable to stand alone and will continue to need his parents for many years to come" (Mahler, Pina, & Bergman, 1975, p. 229). In what sounds like a formula for resilience, Mahler, Pina, and Bergman conclude that "the reestablishment and regeneration of self-esteem and confidence in the world [of the practicing subphase] will generally depend upon the pace and the timing of the replacement of omnipotence by sound secondary narcissism" (Mahler, Pina, & Bergman, 1975, p. 216). It is, then, during the rapprochement subphase when healthy self-esteem may develop and the foundation is laid down for the regulation of such mental processes.

In my own work on the subject with Judith Kestenberg (Kestenberg & Brenner, 1995), our study of child survivors of the Holocaust, we looked at the problem of resilience from a standpoint of narcissism in the service of survival. We wanted to add to Freud's notion that narcissistic libido is derived from the soma (Freud, 1920) and added that a narcissistic investment in every vital part of the body would guarantee survival and well-being. In addition, we considered that primary narcissism has its own developmental line as various organs and zones gain prominence and are more cathected than others. In addition, the movement patterns that are present in every living tissue could act as conveyors of libido and aggression. For example, two main patterns would be those of rhythmically alternating between growing and shrinking of the body shape. Growing to take in vital life- and comfort-giving substances, the organism expands as it grows. To expel noxious substances, it shrinks. These patterns of growing and shrinking are linked with the affects of comfort and discomfort with intake and discharge. They are part of the motor apparatus, and they underlie primary narcissism and diminish as we get older but never disappear as long as we still are living. We considered primary narcissism as a psychic reflection of growth and maintenance of life whose early manifestations are seen in the smile of contentment.

A second source of secondary narcissism would be from self-love and self-admiration when the child feels loved and approved and admired by important objects. As Freud has said, "If a man has been his mother's undisputed darling, he retains throughout his life a triumphant feeling and confidence of success which not seldom brings actual success along with it" (Freud, 1917, p. 156). Another change in shape is that in which parts of the body are extended to reach pleasant stimuli and are withdrawn from unpleasant stimuli as the stimulus loses its nourishing quality. These patterns underlie attraction and repulsion and form a basis for anaclitic relationships. This is the substrate of what Freud described as "secondary narcissism." We then distinguished between primary narcissism with its sources in the body and two kinds of secondary narcissism—one that arises from withdrawal from the object and from lack of love and the other when libido is drawn from the loving object. The primary sensory experiences associated with comfort are the biological basis for the investment of the body with primary narcissism. However, not only can the body or the whole self be invested with libido but also the mental apparatus or parts of it, like the id, ego, or superego. We then reasoned that the ego could be selectively invested with narcissism and, in further differentiation, that selected ego functions like memory or motor skills could be highly cathected, sometimes at the expense of others. So, we theorized that, from an economic viewpoint, a redistribution of narcissistic libido may be necessary in order to maintain physical survival.

Joseph Drexel (1980), a political prisoner who was tortured in Mauthausen for his anti-Nazi beliefs, wrote that he was forced to sing during his tortures. He used the songs as "an enlivening drug," which revitalized him. Oftentimes he felt a split within himself: his body was tied to the table and beaten, and one part of him felt the intolerable pain, the threat to his life as well as his desire to give up and die, while the other floated "without sensation and devoid of gravity but in a strange, spatial congruence with a martyred body" (p. 118). We speculated that his depersonalized overcoming of gravity and space was a revival of the primary narcissistic triumphs of early childhood associated with movement. Drexel was kept in solitary confinement in the dark. He was afraid of the darkness, which, to him, equaled a constriction and loss of space. However, he invested it with a narcissistic fantasy that the night simulated the wideness and infiniteness of space. In so doing, he could imagine that his thoughts could flow, and when they were carried by his waking dreams, he felt "held by the invisible spirits and suspended on the wings of memories" (p. 11). Here, being carried to safety seemed to be linked to nonverbal memories of a man, threatened by extinction, who conjures up feeling born again into a safe, holding environment. By retaining his dignity and self-esteem, and by regaining faith in his own ability to resist the pull toward death, he gained the will and the wherewithal to survive. Of course, it is well known that in other circumstances, dignity may have been retained but death could still not be averted, as young girls and boys went to the gas chambers singing their national anthems.

In those who did survive, short respites from deprivation or torture could allow them to regain their narcissistic equilibrium by enjoying bodily care. When Drexel was able to rinse himself with water, he felt a well-being that reminded him of having been newly bathed: "A strong will to live flowed through my blood vessels" (p. 105). It is also remarkable that a tortured person can become very aware of his or her inner organs. Drexel declared his love for his heart, which he addressed as if it were a beloved child:

> I held my breath and listened to its uneasy beats and a strange, almost affec-
> tionate love pulled me towards a small, courageous, bundle-like organ and
> its secret and wonderful, soft and unerring force. You small, wonderful
> being in my chest . . . I could trust you now . . . you would not disappoint
> me. (p. 102)

Is it possible that this investment of libido in an inner organ is a corollary to
withdrawal of libido from the external objects to the inside of the body, as if a
fetus rather than one's own caring mother were endowed with love? How precious our parts of the body can become after an expectation that some limbs
would be injured or lost is exemplified in Drexel's discovery of the lack of serious injury to his body, which "filled me with a wild satisfaction" (p. 102).
Another source of narcissistic nourishment came from the parting words of a
loving parent, which restored the child's wish to live. Identifying with the
mother, the child decided to care for herself as the mother or father did when
they were alive (Kestenberg & Brenner, 1995). The parent would seem to
love the child from beyond the grave, which bolstered the will to survive.

The confrontation with death, therefore, has a profound effect upon the
psyche (deWind, 1968). A redistribution of narcissistic libido may occur naturally in the normal course of aging, and with a gradual awareness of the
inevitability of one's death, the maintenance of self-esteem, self-worth, and the
right to live all have to be reconciled with the recognition of aging leading to
death. When one is forced to confront this normal developmental task pre-
maturely, it is out of phase and requires a tremendous reorganization of psychic forces. In a sense, it is the antithesis of a fixation. Therefore, in the face of
constant threats to survival, and the lingering deterioration in the body well
before old age, the employment of intensive narcissistic defenses may be fueled
by a distribution of narcissistic libido from nonessential cathexes of the self to
the body for certain essential bodily functions and to the ego ideal, all of which
may make the will to survive more effective. We tentatively agreed to call such
narcissism "tertiary," that is, a return to the overcathexis of the body to lifesaving ego functions and associated aspirations to live a long life. In such extraordinary, life-threatening circumstances, the ego and bodily functions that
maintain self-preservation would become invested or fueled by tertiary narcissism. Invoking the reservoir analogy of narcissistic libido (Freud, 1923), we
postulated that primary narcissism could coalesce with secondary narcissism
under such circumstances, which was forged into this tertiary narcissism. It

could then provide for additional resilience, which, in the case of child survivors, enabled them to endure until liberation.

The persistence of this putative redistribution of narcissism might explain some of the sequelae of massive psychic trauma. Specifically with regard to child survivors, the extent to which the Holocaust experience affected and colored their psychological growth would be influenced not only by the nature of the trauma, the stage of their development, and their premorbid mental health but also by a continuation of such a narcissistic configuration. On one occasion I witnessed in a group meeting of child survivors, the affirmation of life was dramatically enacted when the hostess for the evening lit a fire in her fireplace, forgetting to open the damper. Within seconds, the room, which was packed with unsuspecting child survivors, filled with dense smoke. Without panic, several people sprang into action opening the doors and windows, thereby "rescuing" everyone from what was becoming a gas chamber. The unspoken communication about protecting each other and their seeming readiness for danger was quite striking. The survival value of group formation was demonstrated quite early here, as it almost seemed that the group will to survive increased as each person recognized his or her value to the other. Thus, the group's narcissism increased in the face of danger, which was successfully averted. Many child survivors reported that they often sensed that it was a triumph just to wake up alive each day. Shortly after September 11, when air travel slowed to a trickle, a national meeting of child survivors had very few cancellations.

Despite the meaninglessness of time and the dangers that lie ahead, finding and having something to eat became a source of great pride and accomplishment. Appropriating a piece of clothing, such as a coat or a pair of shoes, was similarly a sign of great resourcefulness, along with finding shelter, escaping, running fast, eluding guards, and so forth. In addition, a number of child survivors attributed their survival to certainly highly valued traits or skills in themselves, which would reflect their primary narcissism. For example, having an Aryan appearance of blond hair and blue eyes was mentioned quite frequently. One woman recalled a harrowing train ride with her very Semitic-looking parents as false papers were being scrutinized. She felt that her looks confused the German officers, and they naturally assumed that she was not Jewish. She then felt a sense of omnipotence because she had saved herself and her parents. The pride that she had had in her pretty face prior to the war took on a life-and-death significance during persecution. Similarly, fluency in the German language was highly prized and had survival value. Another survivor credited his survival with a command of German so that he was able to translate and communicate with the Nazis. They, according to him, thought he was special, which made him feel protected. Feeling protected is related to feeling loved, and infant observation suggests that narcissism is heightened when the child is loved, approved of, and admired, which originates from the baby's tendency to incorporate the good that comes from the outside. The baby feels better when he or she is fed, cared for, and caressed. He or she then becomes more precious, owing to the good care that has been given. Thus, a loving object's behavior is another source of secondary narcissism that is antithetical to the first source of secondary narcissism, which arises from the lack of care or pain associated with the object.

Of course, pathological narcissism may occur, and while that may not enhance survival, it may be present in survivors nonetheless. Mrs. A, for example, who was in Auschwitz at age nine, became convinced that she was invisible and, therefore, unknown to her Nazi captors. In so doing, she felt invulnerable and safe from danger. During the selection in which her mother and younger sisters were sent to the gas chambers, she clung to her aunt, who shielded her. Mrs. A then began to feel that as long as she were hidden and not known about, she could not get hurt. Indeed, when Auschwitz was evacuated prior to the arrival of the Russians, she refused to leave her barracks, hiding under a bed and crouching in the corner. As a young woman after the war, she proceeded with her education, showing exceptional intelligence and a literary talent. Interestingly, she had her tattoo surgically removed while in college in the United States in order to try to erase her past and to assimilate. When confronted about her fantasy of being invisible and unknown to the Germans in Auschwitz, she became puzzled and bewildered. She could not remember having been tattooed, which clearly proved that she was not only known but had to be accounted for. In her mind, she survived as a sickly, malnourished, frightened young girl simply because *they* didn't know she was there. Prior to the war, she was raised in a very affluent, sophisticated family, the first grandchild on both sides of the family. She was indulged and became the center of attention, not only because of her birth order but also because of her intelligence and affability. She was healthy and proud and felt very special. The degradation of her parents left her with an indelible scar that filled her with profound anxiety, sadness, despair, and guilt. As the family's fortune declined, so did her hopes for survival. Mrs. A learned that she could no longer count on her parents anymore. However, she felt that she was nothing without them. One memorable event which reinflated her depleted sense of self-worth occurred on the train ride to Auschwitz. Starved, dehydrated, over-crowded, and exhausted beyond belief, her father traded a gold cigarette case for a drink of water for her. Aside from the obvious value of the water, the narcissistic nourishment seemed to be of tremendous value also. Here, again, she felt how important and how worthy she was in her father's eyes as he gave away such a valuable possession for water for a special daughter. In recalling this event, she paused from her despair and wanted to take great delight in this extraordinary moment.

The basic functions of nourishment are highly invested with narcissistic libido. Mrs. A's father bartered gold for water and intensified the pleasurable act of drinking. Starved and depleted, the miracle of water was further exalted by the father's demonstration of his love and devotion to her. Here, the secondary narcissism associated with the father's reflection of his love was interwoven with the primary narcissism of filling her belly with life-sustaining water. The fact that she survived does not prove that her narcissism was adaptive, however, in that adults protected her as much as possible.

The deployment of manic defenses against unresolvable mourning and loss warrant mention here also (Akhtar, 1992; Klein, 1935, 1940; Winnicott, 1935). Akhtar, synthesizing Klein's ideas, which were elaborated upon by Winnicott, observed that the manic defense is characterized by denying internal reality, a flight to external reality, the keeping of parental introjects in a state of suspension, and the using of opposites. While the awareness of this response to traumatic loss is not new and certainly not unique to the Holocaust, we found this potentially adaptive defense in adolescent survivors more frequently than in infant survivors, latency-age survivors, or adult survivors. As many experts have noted (Jacobson, 1957; Katan, 1961; Krystal, 1988; Wolfenstein, 1966; Zetzel, 1965), adolescence is the time of life for the maturation of affects, which facilitates the capacity for grieving at a higher level. While there is controversy over the extent to which younger children can truly mourn their lost objects, the adolescent is better prepared for a number of reasons. Specifically, there is the opportunity for a second individuation that bolsters object constancy (Blos, 1967), the acquisition of abstract thinking promotes a deeper comprehension of death, greater physical strength facilitates alloplastic adaptation in order to alter one's environment (Hartmann, 1939/1958), and sexual maturity enhances the capacity for new and enduring object relationships to supplant the loosened ties with one's parents.

In a rather unusual article in *Fortune* magazine (Loomis, 1998), five Holocaust survivors who became multimillionaire entrepreneurs and philanthropists were profiled. There were a number of common denominators in these men that support the hypothesis that their resilience was associated with a manic defense and an omnipotent fantasy:

1. All five went through at least part of their adolescence either in hiding, in slave labor or in concentration camps.
2. All five suffered object losses, including the sudden separation or traumatic loss of their fathers, either before or during the war.
3. All five were described as either very bright, precocious, mischievous, defiant, or energetic.
4. During their confinement, all five broke the "rules" and risked their lives trying to stay alive and to save other people's lives.
5. All five had unshakable confidence, optimism, and a conviction that they would and should somehow survive.
6. All five were either described by loved ones or described themselves as having traits consistent with omnipotence and a manic defense, for example, "this drive, this incredible drive"; "working six days a week . . . [and having] the attention span of a gnat"; "He was crazy. I didn't have a husband"; "I've been through the war and I'm not going to take any crap from anybody"; "I figured I could handle just about anything"; and "Business is war. I don't believe in compromise. I believe in winning" (Loomis, 1998, p. 80).

One of these men, Sigi Ziering, survived from the ages of 11 to 17 with his mother and brother. He did not show any emotion for over 20 years until May 1997, when he, along with 105 other founding members of the U.S. Holocaust Memorial Museum in Washington who donated at least $1 million each, were treated to a parade of flags representing the U.S. Army divisions that liberated the camps in 1945. In his speech, Ziering proclaimed, "Today, I cried because the worst memory of the ghetto and the camps was a feeling of total isolation and abandonment by the rest of the world. This feeling of utter despair and hopelessness weighed more heavily on us than the constant hunger, the beatings and the imminent death facing us every minute" (Oliver, 2000, p. 20). Ziering, whose indefatigability earned him a PhD in physics, a career working on nuclear reactors and space projects, and ultimately a position as the CEO of a very successful company that developed radioimmunoassay materials, never forgot about the element of luck. In describing the selection process at a camp he landed in prior to liberation, he mused, "With German precision the guards went at their jobs alphabetically [each week] and never got to Z" (Loomis, 1998, p. 82). Yet he did not rely on chance or divine intervention. He was tireless and very productive. Living out the stark motto on the iron gates of the death camps, "Arbeit Macht Frei," he bluntly stated his philosophy of life and secret of survival: "Unless you work, you're destined for the gas chambers" (Oliver, 2000, p. 20). He outwitted the Nazis at their own deadly game. And, true to his work, it was noted in his obituary three years after the interview at age 72, "He survived the Nazis but never stopped working until about a year ago when he was diagnosed with brain cancer" (Oliver, 2000, p. 20).

The Nazis tried to deprive their victims of their dignity, their spirit, and their pervasive will to live and learn. They deprived them of vital objects, such as air, warmth, food, and life-sustaining people like parents, spouses, and children. Under these circumstances, the libidinization of the self as a valuable, dignified person who is loved and cherished by his or her own people and the libidinization of sensory experiences and satisfactions of the past contributed to raising the self-esteem and the will to survive. These mechanisms not only prompted actions that would save the individual but also enhanced the desire of others to save the individual too. A survival that led to the continuation of the heritage and the perpetuation of one's genes through his or her children was also experienced as a triumph over evil and a further justification for living. In Dr. Krystal's words,

> In concentration camps and related experiences, no one survived without some help from others. The preservation of some capacity for social interaction was a great aid in maintaining one's sense of humanity. The ability to form temporary alliances for survival and, when possible, to help someone constituted a rare source of re-fueling a sense of being a good person and maintaining some self-respect. When people were able to stay together with a group from 'home,' they acquired a source of support to their humanity. (2003, p. 17)

One of the most remarkable aspects of aging children and adolescent survivors is the persistence of both their ego strengths and their vulnerabilities throughout the life cycle. This phenomenon is also seen in those Armenians who survived genocidal persecution in Turkey earlier in the last century. Although not studied as extensively, their accounts and their memories of atrocities reflect a similar indelible impact. Like resilient sapling trees that have had to grow at unusual angles in order to bypass obstructions to sunlight, those who at a young age endured genocidal persecution have followed their own twisting and turning paths in order to grow. From chronic psychosomatic disturbances in the very young to characterological disturbances in the older ones, many have bypassed certain developmental tasks but have nevertheless functioned well until illness, loss, or old age set in (Kestenberg & Brenner, 1995). In addition, their survival ordeals are indelibly imprinted in their psyches and may repeat themselves in symbolic or in actual scenarios until they die.

In conclusion, to put all these protective measures into a schematic context with a wider applicability, consider Anthony's model of the buffering system, drawn from his work with the so-called invulnerable child (Anthony & Cohler, 1987). In his diagram, he has six concentric circles representing a different layer. The innermost circle is neonatal cortical sleepiness. The next circle is the protective shield or stimulus barrier. The next layer of defense is maternal protection. The next circle is ego resilience, then family safeguards, and finally community bulwark. We can see that the malignant assault on victims in the death camps could destroy this buffering system and render human beings into zombielike robots. Such dissociative functioning could be seen to be derived from that innermost layer of neonatal cortical sleepiness. To survive such horror and to reenter the world of the living is truly a miracle of human resilience.

# References

Akhtar, S. (1992). *Broken structures.* Northvale, NJ: Jason Aronson.

Akhtar, S. (1999). *Inner torment.* Northvale, NJ: Jason Aronson.

Anthony, E. J., & Cohler, B. J. (1987). *The invulnerable child.* New York: Guilford Press.

Blos, P. (1967). The second individuation process of adolescence. *Psychoanalytic Study of the Child,* 22, 162–186.

Brown, L. (Ed.). (1993). *The new shorter Oxford English dictionary.* Oxford: Clarendon Press.

deWind, E. (1968). The confrontation with death. *International Journal of Psychoanalysis,* 49, 302–305.

Drexel, J. (1980). *Rueckkehr Unerwuenscht: Joseph Drexel Reise Mathausen der Widerstand Kreis Ernst Niekisch* (W. R. Berger, Ed.). DTV Dokumente. Muenchen: Deutsch Taschenbuch VerlagMemoir.

Ferenczi, S. (1913). Stages in the development of the sense of reality. In *Contribution to Psycho-Analysis* (pp. 181–203). Boston: Richard G. Badger.

Ferenczi, S. (1955). The unwelcome child and his death instinct. In M. Balint (Ed.), *Final contributions to the problems and methods of psychoanalysis* (pp. 102–107). New York: Basic Books. (Original work published 1929.)

Freud, S. (1917). A childhood recollection from Dichtong Und Wahrheit. *Standard Edition* 17:145–156.

Freud, S. (1920). Beyond the pleasure principle. *Standard Edition* 8:3–66.

Hartmann, H. (1939). *Ego psychology and the problem of adaptation* (D. Rapaport, Trans.). New York: International Universities Press [1958].

Jacobson, E. (1957). Normal and pathological moods. *Psychological Study of the Child, 12,* 73–113.

Jacobson, E. (1964). *The self and the object world.* New York: International Universities Press.

Katan, A. (1961). Some thoughts about the role of verbalization in early childhood. *Psychological Study of the Child, 16,* 184–188.

Kestenberg, J. S., & Brenner, I. (1995). Narcissism in the service of survival. In T. Cohen, M. H. Etezady, & B. Pacella (Eds.), *The vulnerable child, Vol. 2,* pp. 35–50. New York: International Universities Press.

Klein, M. (1935). A contribution to the psychogenesis of manic-depressive states. In *Love, guilt and reparations, 1921–1945* (pp. 262–289). New York: Free Press [1975].

Klein, M. (1940). Mourning and its relation to the manic-depressive states. In *Love, guilt and reparations, 1921–1945* (pp. 344–369). New York: Free Press [1975].

Krystal, H. (1968). *Massive psychic trauma.* New York: International Universities Press.

Krystal, H. (1988). *Integration and self healing.* Hillsdale, NJ: Analytic Press.

Krystal, H. (1997). The trauma of confronting one's vulnerability and death. In C. Ellman & J. Reppen (Eds.), *Omnipotent fantasies and the vulnerable self* (pp. 149–185). Northvale, NJ: Jason Aronson.

Krystal, H. (2003, May 3). *Resilience.* Presented at the Margaret Mahler Symposium, Philadelphia, PA.

Kumin, I. (1997). *Preobject relatedness: Early attachment and the psychodynamic situation.* New York: Guilford Press.

Loomis, C.J. (1998, April 13). Everything in history was against them. *Fortune,* 66–84.

Mahler, M. S., Pina, F., & Bergman, A. (1975). *The psychological birth of the human infant.* New York: Basic Books.

Marrus, M. R. (1987). *The Holocaust in History.* New York: Meridian.

Oliver, M. (2000). In memoriam—Sigi Ziering; survived Nazi camps. *American gathering of Jewish Holocaust survivors, 15,* 20.

Ornstein, P. W. (1997). Omnipotence in health and illness. In C. Ellman & J. Reppen (Eds.), *Omnipotent fantasies and the vulnerable self* (pp. 117–138). Northvale, NJ: Jason Aronson.

Shore, A. (1994). *Affect regulation and the origin of the self: The neurobiology of emotional development.* Hillsdale, NJ: Lawrence Erlbaum Associates.

Winnicott, D. W. (1935). The manic defense. In *Collected papers: Through pediatrics to psychoanalysis* (pp. 129–144). London: Tavistock.

Winnicott, D. W. (1960). The theory of the parent-infant relationship. *International Journal of Psychoanalysis, 41*, 585–595.

Wolfenstein, M. (1966). How is mourning possible? *Psychoanalytic study of the child, 21*, 92–126.

Zetzel, E. R. (1965). Depression and the incapacity to bear it. In M. Schur (Ed.), *Drives, affects, behavior* (pp. 243–274). New York: International Universities Press.

# Note

1. Let me just mention here that there is a population of hospitalized, aging Holocaust survivors in Israel that consists of patients who have been chronically hospitalized for decades, and it is quite likely that in this group some of the patients who have been diagnosed as schizophrenic may, in fact, be profoundly dissociated child survivors.

# 6

# AN AUTOBIOGRAPHICAL STUDY OF RESILIENCE

## Healing From the Holocaust

*Henri Parens, MD*

While in this study I shall focus on resilience following trauma experienced during the Holocaust, the resilience manifested in this context resulted from the same basic adaptive processes and character factors that contribute to resilience in coping with trauma in general.

On May 28, 2006, as has become our custom recently, Savic—one of us "Three Musketeers" of Rivesaltes, Vichy-France—called me. (Savic and I were incarcerated from the time we were 11 years old in this notorious French "camp de concentration," as Vichy called it.) Santa Barbara (where they live), he told me, had been hit for weeks with the most unkind and uncommon weather for that region. The rain, while encumbering to humans, had, however, been a source of renewal of life of remarkable vigor. Along with the lush oaks came also the lush weeds. Savic told me that razing the weeds down the day before seemed nigh ineffective as they were now again about 3 inches high. What resilience, I quipped. Can we adjudge everything that grows vigorously to be resilient?

In his last book, *The Drowned and the Saved*, Primo Levi (1986/1989) pondered the fact that some survived the extermination camps and some did not; he rightly put much weight on the play of chance. His own scars were deep; but his resilience was amply evident in his ability to not only survive Auschwitz but to write of his experience of it. In large part, his resilience in Auschwitz derived from a healthy mix of his own endurance and ingenuity, his professional expertise (a chemist much needed by a rubber-exhausted war machine), his unknown "friend" Lorenzo Perrone—who, Levi emphasized, beyond giving him an additional piece of bread or a bowl of soup or a vest, reminded him that humanity had not died. And he tells us there was a large gift of chance. Nonetheless the effects of his Auschwitz experience left their mark. His characterologic depression, biographically proposed by Carole Angier (2002) to be of pre-Holocaust origin, which continued[1] after the

Holocaust, may have led him to suicide. He spoke vividly of his contributing survivor guilt: "The comrade of all my peaceful moments, . . . the pain of remembering . . . attacks me like a dog the moment my conscience comes out of the gloom" (Levi, 1947/1996, p. 142).

There is general consensus that resilience is the product of interactions of one's biology, psychology, and chance. Increasingly, the interactive roles of our biology and psychology are recognized to reciprocally sustain and foster or undermine one another (Kendler, 1993; Kendler & Eaves, 1986; Rutter, 2000, 2006; Southwick, Vythilingam, & Charney, 2005). Chance, on the other hand, is unfathomably governed. Even brilliant math gurus can only give us probabilities that can never robustly predict the play of chance.

## On the Psychobiology of Resilience

Resilience lies in the nucleus of Darwin's "survival of the fittest." The earliest medical notion of "resilience" was construed as the product of "good" rather than "poor" protoplasm, a pejorative but not completely wrong medical concept. But we have come to recognize that psychology has much to say about this pejorative concept. From the times of Walter B. Cannon (1928), Hans Selye (1950), Franz Alexander (1961), and others, we have increasingly become able to ascertain that biochemical-physiological, neurobiological, and psychosocial factors mediate and determine the reaction of the individual to stress including his or her coping and recovery reactivity, that is, resilience. Leon J. Saul (1947/1960) often asked: "How is it that some children are born with a silver spoon in their mouth and can't make it in life?" (late 1960s, personal communication). Similarly, Margaret S. Mahler asserted on a number of occasions that "some children can extract libidinal supplies from a rock" (late 1960s, personal communication). While we recognized this critical adaptation capability, they, however, did not explore the question of "resilience."

For a brief period, some spoke of children's "invulnerability" (Anthony, 1974). The eventual recognition of "resilience" goes back especially to Lois B. Murphy (1962) and Norman Garmezy (1971), who some 50 years ago pleaded that we look at what is healthy in our patients, not just at their pathology. After years of study, Garmezy (1985) pointed to three domains of experience that make resilience possible:

1. personality dispositions of the child;
2. a supportive family milieu; and

3. an external support system that encourages and reinforces a child's coping efforts and strengthens them by inculcating positive values.

Fifteen years later, Luthar, Ciccheti, and Becker (2000) came to a very similar proposition. According to Hauser, Allen, and Golden (2006), Garmezy's and Luthar, Ciccheti, and Becker's propositions came "to be described in terms of processes rather than as traits or situations" (Hauser et al., 2006, p. 307). Thinking of resilience as process gives a significant dimension to our understanding of resilience in that it speaks to a capability that is influenced by time and experience; it is in essence a developmental process and can therefore be subject to regression and to growth.

In addition, viewing resilience as process, looking at the complex of factors engaged by or that give rise to resilience is equally of great interest, especially since factors can more readily be discerned than processes. Hauser et al. (2006) tell us for instance that Ann Masten (2001, p. 234) observed that "the short list of protective factors on which resilience studies have converged [include] 'connections to competent and caring adults; cognitive and self-regulation skills and positive views of self; and the motivation to be effective in the environment'" (2006, pp. 6–7; see Southwick et al., 2005, below). Taking a big leap, Hauser et al. have furthered the inquiry by asking, *How* does resilience arise? In a creatively thought-out study, they searched for evidence of resilience factors in a population of teenagers who, a decade before, had been placed in a therapeutic residential facility because of serious social adjustment problems. Their search for insight into resilience led them to "concentrate on three themes—relatedness, agency, and reflectiveness—which [they] found tightly woven in the narratives of [the] resilient teens" they studied (2006, p. 39).[2]

In an informative review, Southwick, Vythilingam, and Charney (2005) look at component factors operative in the psychobiology of resilience. They speak to the wide spectrum of neurochemicals, genetic factors, and anatomical brain areas operative in the individual's reaction, successful or not, to stress. Duly emphasizing the interplay of our biology (genetic and biochemical physiology) and experience in determining the individual's vulnerability and resilience to stress, Southwick et al. also review the equally wide range of psychosocial factors that seem to play a role in or are evidence of resilience. They touch on the magnificent experiencing of positive emotions and optimism, humor, cognitive flexibility, acceptance of reality rather than resignation or resistance to it, altruism, capacity to recover from negative events, social supports, and positive role models (Southwick et al., 2005, pp. 268–279). And they include "spirituality" as a protective factor. They wisely place "religion" under the heading of "spirituality" rather than the other way around.[3]

Southwick et al. raise en passant, but do not discuss, the challenging and enormously important notion of "stress inoculation," which they suggest might lead to "stress resilience," a potential strategy of great interest—and misgiving—to prevention. They note that

> preclinical and clinical work suggests that moderate childhood stressors that can be successfully managed or mastered are likely to cause stress inocula-tion and stress resilience to subsequent stressors. On the other hand [they observe rightly], severe stressors that cannot be managed or mastered are more likely to lead to stress sensitization [i.e., traumatization] and vulner-ability to future stressors. Thus, [they propose that] although children should not be exposed to stressors that are overwhelming, they are likely to benefit from moderate stressors that they can successfully master. (2005, pp. 280–281)

In this, they enunciate a principle we (Parens & Rose-Itkoff, 1997a; Parens, Scattergood, Duff, & Singletary, 1997) have emphasized that is critical to optimizing child rearing and that is applicable across a number of develop-mental challenges such as in setting limits, the application of discipline, and making demands for compliance and for performance, and it also applies to the notion that "the modest dose of anxiety that comes from not knowing" leads kids to want to learn, while excessive anxiety interferes with successful learning. It is assumed by mental health developmentalists that a challenge within the child's capability to master leads to increased adaptive ability; a challenge that overwhelms the child undermines the child's ability to cope and renders him or her vulnerable. The vernacular holds some wisdom, that "if [this challenge] doesn't kill me, it'll make me stronger."

Framing his approach to the question in attachment theory, Boris Cyrul-nik has written extensively on resilience (1999, 2003/2005, 2004). In fact, among his widely read—in Europe especially—books that address the phe-nomenon of resilience one is entitled *Un Merveilleux Malheur* (1999, "A mar-velous misfortune"), emphasizing that, even when the misfortune is large, the processes and psychosocial factors that constitute and give rise to resilience pro-pel some individuals to remarkably generative reactivity and creativity.[4] Anticipating Hauser et al. (2006), Cyrulnik illustrates numerous cases of a trauma-tized child's constructively turning to others and taking responsibility for his or her own fate (2003/2005). So, too, Judy Kestenberg and Ira Brenner (1996) reported in their study of child Holocaust survivors how, indeed, the horren-dous experience of their variable individual Holocaust experiences elicited in a number of adolescents acts of unexpected capability, even bravery as evi-denced in 15-year-old Yehuda Nir's (2002) participation in the Warsaw Ghetto uprising, in 17-year-old Mark Solant's (2006) various efforts to survive and help other kids, and possibly in my own case, which I shall detail shortly. So, too, in their stunning study, Hauser et al. (2006) report their findings on "resilient teens," who defied the prediction that their harshly severe disturbed adolescence would slate them for disturbed adulthood as burdens to their fam-ilies and to society. Indeed, as they ask, "how . . . do some individuals emerge stronger than they were from experiences that destroy others" (2006, p. 6)?

## A Case Study of Trauma and Resilience

Here, I cannot let privacy, embarrassment, or reservation impede my efforts to understand and explain—hoping to help us find ways to foster resilience in children and in our patients. Theorists' theories cannot but be born from their own experiences. While anonymity facilitates clinical work, I find that when theorists open their experiences to view, their theories are rendered more cogent by our understanding what led to their generation.

Max Schur (1972) postulated that the guilt three-year-old Freud experi-enced following the precocious death of his brother Julius might have led to Freud's lifelong preoccupation with death, a preoccupation that has led some to postulate that, following World War I, in which his oldest son participated, Freud (1920) proposed that an inborn death instinct is the source of human aggression. It is well known that Freud observed, "There is no question of get-ting rid entirely of human aggressive impulses; it is enough to try to divert them to such an extent that they need not find expression in war" (1932/1933, p. 212), an optimistic, sober note from our master-teacher. However, I have long argued (Parens, 1979/2007, 1991, 2001, 2005) that the death instinct has not been of good service to our understanding of human aggression; that it has yielded to easy rationalization and abdication of respon-sibility for our own very human hostile destructiveness.

We know and appreciate why Margaret Mahler (Stepansky, 1988) homed in so vigorously on the overriding influence—for good and bad—of the mother on the development of the child; and why she saw the father as a "knight in shining armor." So, too, Susan Coates (2004) tells us that when she herself "came to recognize how much Bowlby's personal and intellectual style was a response to the cumulative weight of the losses he suffered, [she] came to better appreciate the personal sources of his passionate—at times even provocative—allegiance to attachment theory" (p. 573).[5] And might we better understand why Heinz Kohut gave to narcissism so enlarged a berth that a mother or father would be relegated in the child's mind to being a "self-object," a concept that stands in opposition to the achievement of the highly desirable separation-individuation process that leads to an integrated sense of self and of love-objects? And for that matter why did Melanie Klein conceptualize primitive object relatedness in terms of "part-objects," hypercathecting the mother's breast when the infant's foremost locus of attachment is the mother's face (the space between the forehead and the eyes to be specific [Spitz, 1965])?

All these theory generators made enormous contributions to our understanding of human experience—even if, at times, at some cost to those who buy into their theories too exuberantly. In teaching I ask students to anchor themselves in theories but to heed Charcot's brilliant dictum, which I paraphrase as "Theory is great, but it doesn't prevent facts from being what they are."

In the course of "self-analytically" writing about my Holocaust experience (Parens, 2004), I learned why I gave so much energy and time to the healing children's psychic pain, to the study of aggression and the development of strategies for minimizing its hostile destructive trend, and to the prevention of traumatization of children by their own parents and society, and why in my advancing years I am focusing on the nature of prejudice and to the prevention of its malignant form—all, I believe, by-products of resilience in coping with my Holocaust experience.

## Motivations to Heal From Massive Trauma

Healing from the Holocaust has required active, vigorous, continuous, indeed lifelong efforts, conscious and unconscious. It has required efforts to cope with pain and loss of family, even uprooting from one's ongoing life and home; to mediate and sublimate one's omnipresent reactive rage; to accept the Kafkaesque reality and have a sustainable explanation for what happened, all in order to repair, to regenerate, and to prevent maladaptive effects and sequelae of this specific trauma. The will to live, to overcome, must prevail over passive surrender to brutally sadistic traumatization. Speaking of his death-camp inmates in Auschwitz, Buchenwald, and Dachau, Henry Krystal noted the consequences of the psychological shock, exhaustion, and passive surrender to the death-camp mortifying abuses leading, in some around him, to human degradation into the "walking dead," the "Musulman" (Krystal, 1968, 1978).

## A Temporal Examination of Psychological Determinants of Resilience

My own experience leads me to add a temporal dimension to our understanding of resilience. Whether acute or chronic, trauma acts upon the individual at a given point in time. What the state of the individual is, what his life conditions are at the time of occurrence, is critical with regard to how the trauma will impact on him or her. The trauma itself will impact the individual according to its parameters. And recovery from traumatization will in addition depend on the state of the individual after the trauma has ceased and the state of his objectal universe, both in the short term and in the long term (Parens, 1999a). Thus, what conditions prevail before, during, and after the trauma all codetermine its impact on the individual. And, similarly, before, during, and after can be usefully considered along the Garmezy-Luthar triadic processes that may or may not give rise to resilience. Here, I put this thinking into a psychoanalytic frame:

Pretrauma state/parameters:

1. Self: age; ego functioning (strengths and weaknesses); superego functioning; status of psychic conflict and character defenses; history of hostile destructive load/ patterns of reactivity (Note: The psychosocial factors enumerated by Southwick et al. [2005] can be subsumed under ego and superego functioning and characterologic defenses.)
2. Family relationships: types of attachment; quality of object relatedness (also noted by Kestenberg & Brenner, 1996)
3. Community support systems including school, street, and community neighborliness and societal mores

Transtrauma parameters:

1. Nature of trauma: what it is; what it means to the self; how intense its impact; how long did it take place
2. Self: same parameters as above
3. Family relationships: same parameters as above; also, object losses; object substitutions; behaviors of objects in support network; behaviors of trauma-inflicting objects
4. Community support systems during traumatic era—as emphasized by Ornstein (Ornstein, 1985; Ornstein & Goldman, 2004)

Posttrauma state/parameters:

1. Self: same parameters as above; also, consider status over time; creativity, operation of adaptation-enhancing defenses, generativity, short-term, episodic, long-term
2. Family relationships: continuation of pretrauma relationships; mourning of losses; reconstitution of family relationships
3. Community support systems cultivated (self-generated), recreated, and maintained—richly addressed by Cyrulnik (1999, 2003, 2004)

## Chance

During the pretrauma period (assuming there is one), trauma period, and posttrauma period (assuming that the traumatic conditions do come to a close), in each time frame, chance has its own unfathomable rules of governance. Many humans protect themselves—consciously and unconsciously—against the existential anxiety generated by our equally unfathomable fate by considering all things to be predetermined and prescribed. To those, there is no chance; it's all in the hands of God; except for those who see God as did Spinoza: God has no program; God does not ordain events. With this concept of "The Unknown," I said in *Renewal of Life* that "God cannot prevent holocausts" (Parens, 2004, p. 172).

That humans are challenged by chance is a matter of everyday life. That humans challenge chance is a matter of gambling, be it casino gambling or, on a much larger scale, chancing an unforeseeable outcome, as did Hitler in taking over the demilitarized Rhineland, then annexing Austria (Anschluss), then invading Czechoslovakia, and, after ridiculing Britain's hapless Chamberlain and America's President Roosevelt, attacking Poland, launching World War II and the Holocaust.

## My Story

As I have reconstructed it, my early years were good ones despite the fact that my parents divorced when I was about four years old. My mother left Lodz, where I was born, in order to get to Brussels, where some of my family had for some time established itself. She took me with her, but left my brother, older than I by about three years, with my father and my large family in Lodz; my father and mother had a number of siblings. Life in Brussels was warm, and while economically not easy, it was good; we had good family ties, good health. I was a good student, I think due to go into fifth, perhaps sixth grade when the Third Reich struck and tore my world apart.

## What Happened to My World

On May 10, 1940, the Germans attacked Belgium. I was 11. In chaos many among us left Brussels, heading wherever the train taking us to asylum in France would take us. At that time the French received us very nicely. We spent the summer of 1940 in a French village. I learned some natural lessons, like helping a farmer pick his strawberries for a few pennies; and as food got increasingly scarce, at some risk, stealing potatoes or apples from some blameless farmers' fields. (Have you ever seen a bull and a cow mate? That massive beast with an equally massive organ mounted on that poor cow! Phiew! It's OK, the cow survived.) Sometime in early October, we were rounded up and sent to a detention camp in Toulouse.

## The Camps

Everything was gray in Toulouse. We were there only a few days and were then taken to Recebedou, our first concentration camp. In Recebedou, families remained intact. Brick barracks, partitioned and with the aid of a blanket strung up as a curtain, families could have some privacy. While eating was regular, the food quickly became inadequate; the diet was minimalist, with barely a piece of meat now and then; starvation began to set in. No school; parents occasionally set up some classes. We also developed a scout troop that met occasionally. Besides hunger, uprooting, incarceration, and the cold, the most troubling problem for us kids was idleness; it's amazing how good school is for a kid. We were in Recebedou for about three or four months when we were selected to be moved to another camp, Rivesaltes.

Rivesaltes was a descent into the second ring of hell. Quoting from *Renewal of Life*,

> We arrived on a winter-wind-blowing day to a gray plain, some 20 kilometers from foothills of the Pyrenees Mountains, a plain spread with barracks that immediately struck me as cheaply-built, desolate, depressing. I remember our arrival there, now 60 years later: it was a bleak part of France, at a bleak time, on this bleak day. (Parens 2004, p. 42)[6]

> Rivesaltes barracks were one large open box: dormitory, eating place, dwelling place, all packed in one's own bed area, our bed serving all furniture purposes, chair, table, etc. The barracks were lined along their length with beds on each of the long sides. No stove. I guess that in addition to whatever we could put on ourselves, clothes and blankets when it got very cold, our own bodies provided whatever heat there was. We did gather wood in Rivesaltes to make small fires outdoors. The bed frames were made of 2 x 4 wood beams across which stretched single, straightforward wires, north to south and east to west. A coarse-cloth mattress sack filled with straw, one coarse-wool gray blanket. Sheets? Not included. Now, my emphasis on the coarseness of both the straw-filled mattress and the blanket just made itself clear to me about one hour before this writing. I feel compelled to explain.

Soon after I decided the time had come for me to write about my witnessing and living a piece of the Holocaust, during a stretch of time from the end of July to August 14, 2002 when I began writing, it seemed I had managed to make contact with some poison-ivy and soon started to develop a typical, very itchy rash. Those who react allergically to poison-ivy know what I'm talking about. The problem is that having been the victim of this miserable allergic reaction before, I had become well acquainted with the various structural features and color-bound manifestations through which poison-ivy evolves during its season. But my diagnosis brought with it a dilemma: there is and there was no poison ivy on our property. As the course of my nasty and very itchy skin ailment dragged on, my Dermatologist and my Internist agreed to eliminate from my average-expectable aging-optimizing medications those medicines that might possibly cause some skin rash. My reactive skin rash had by now turned from an acute condition . . . to a somewhat chronic one. . . . My astute Dermatologist was puzzled by what I was harboring. It came to him by both a process of elimination and years of clinical know-how about . . . skin disorders, to pursue in good doctorly fashion a line of thought that caused him some unease. Gently, hesitatingly probing of his psychiatrist-patient, if he was having some emotional problems, he asked, "Henri, excuse my wondering but, is something especially troubling you these days? This really looks like 'Nummular Eczema' (a specific form of the widely known skin disorder that tortures children and adults) which has strong emotional determinants (especially stress and rage) acting on a skin diathesis (specific inborn vulnerability due to some organ or system sensitivity)." I smiled, I think, and barely shaking my head in thought I told him, "Bernie, I think you just hit it on the head." And I went on to explain that I noted with some constancy, that during those times when I was writing . . . my Holocaust story, I was almost continually itching, at times squirming, and then I would feel compelled to apply the topical agent . . . he had prescribed for me and/or take an antihistamine. Both stress and rage come with this writing, quiet but not so quiet rage, as in this writing, as Rachel (my wife) has wisely said, "It's a self-analysis; it may even help you more [than an analysis]." (pp. 42–43)

## In Rivesaltes, Life Went On

What they fed us was just as bleak as the time in history, the plain, the barracks; the whole package. Food was brought to us in man-carried drums. In the mornings we got one piece of darkish bread, at times with one spoon of watery brown syrup, probably an attempt to make the bread more palatable. It really wasn't necessary to try to make it palatable; starvation convinced us it was. . . . Midday we were treated to watery soup with some kind of vegetation in it; I am not a gardener but I doubt many of us knew what vegetable it was. In the evening, we again got a piece of bread and some cut-up turnips or rutabagas. It is well known that hunger will make us, even most kids, overcome our distaste and even disgust with certain foods. Just as I self-protectively then did not allow myself to feel intolerant of my sack-cloth and wool bedding, so too, I swallowed turnip and rutabaga without puking. (pp. 46–47)

Even in the face of these miseries, life went on in Rivesaltes; it would in all but the most dire of circumstances. Children, biologically promised the right to a long life ahead, feel the need to go on. This does at times require denial of existing circumstances and conditions, just as patients with cancer or prisoners on death row often deny they are at death's threshold and plan for the future. Several kids about my age, 2 other boys and 2 girls, at times organized ourselves into activity. It seemed to fall into place naturally. In 1940–41, in Rivesaltes, we did not have any schooling, that is, the expectable schooling kids get in Western Europe. Experience was our schooling now. . . . Idleness gets boring. Other than our individual meanderings not far from our barrack and the uniquely programmed activity of wood gathering for our small outdoor fires that succeeded at briefly warming our thinning selves, we kids spontaneously fell into two memorable activities. For the boys, playing The Three Musketeers, and on several occasions, the boys and girls spent a couple evening hours dancing. Yes, dancing in Rivesaltes. Only kids could be that, what? Nuts? Unaware that we were increasingly at risk, targeted for further abuse, and denigration, we played, we danced. Sometimes kids are smarter than grown-ups. We had our priorities right: Live while you can; there are no absolute signs that tomorrow will be worse! I know—often we can't let ourselves know. The fact is, we did that; we played Les Trois Mousquetaires and we danced. Whose idea it was, what made us think we could dance, I can't recall. I guess it was a community-of-5 effort. I provided the music. During my earliest . . . years . . . I found that . . . it feels oddly good to sing. . . . Not so surprising; my mother . . . would sing; I liked it when she sang. . . . In Rivesaltes my singing was subdued; . . . at this time, in this place, [it] was a paradoxical thing to be doing. We were kids 11–12 years old. Until you are at death's door, life goes on. (pp. 48–50)

## Escape From Rivesaltes

My mother knew something very bad about our fate. I was not looking ahead; she was. As if out of the blue, she said she wanted me to escape from Rivesaltes! She conveyed its seriousness and risk. She was telling me and she was asking me if I would escape without her. . . . Without her, that was the big part. I saw her wish on her face. "Yoh, Ma, ch'vet tun vus du zugst" ("Yes, Ma, I'll do what you say") [I probably] said to her in Yiddish.

      Our life together had made me fairly self-reliant, within limits of my age. She knew me. I trusted her; and she could count on me to do what she wanted me to do. That was our history, my mother and me. (p. 53)

I think I slept well-enough, the night into May 1, 1941, Labor Day in Europe. We were up fairly early. We waited till after we were regaled with our morning piece of bread. I do not remember our good-byes. I probably could not bear it, rejected its imprinting in my memory. Knowing my mother, we no doubt hugged and held one another somewhat longer than usual. I was to be inconspicuous from beginning to end. I felt odd and uncomfortable, with double layers of underclothes, socks, shirts and pants. I was already very skinny by then, so I probably did not look over-bloated. I left, armed with the potato sack I had used to collect wood for our still needed source of heat.

I walked to the specified outer area of the camp, in the direction that would head me toward the highway to Perpignan, as close as possible to the camp-adjacent railroad tracks. I played the part well, I think, of taking seriously the task of bending down to pick up dead bits of wood among the briar. Casually I looked around to see where the guards were located. I was in luck; I didn't see any guards at all—maybe they were all in the latrine at once; it was May 1. I bent down, and still seeing no one, I dropped to the ground. With that, I could feel my whole body racing . . . my heart pounding. I know how I react when I get a sudden scare. . . . I must have felt my escape set in motion just by this act. I had not felt any fear before that moment.

Determined now, I started to crawl toward the mound-elevated train track. I soon found that what I knew before of the briar was so, the live bushes have big spines that hurt when, . . . I hit them head on. I used the potato sack to shield my hands and forearms as I crawled, more carefully, but as quickly as I could. Within some 20 feet from the train-track-mound I stopped, raised my head slowly as little as I needed to again see if there were any sentinels, and saw none. The mound rose about 5 feet high. Bracing myself for it, I quickly bounded up and started to run. I cleared the mound, the tracks and landed on the other side of it. Shielded now from direct view from camp-side, I had not stopped; semi-crouched I continued to run, more scared now than before. . . . I was running scared shitless through a still barren vineyard, the ground was sandy, I tripped on something, crashed harmlessly into the ground, immediately got myself back up and continue to run as if I hadn't stopped. Beyond the vineyard I continued my course through shrubs and trees. Once in those, feeling less visible, I slowed my pace some; I didn't stop. Unexpectedly, I had reached the highway. Good fortune had it that the highway was sided by deep ditches that ran along each side, all the way from where I met the highway to Perpignan. This, I guess my mother didn't know, that there was a protective ditch I could use for as long as it went. Also fortunate, there was no water in the long ditch, nearly a trench, along the road.

The macadam paved road, a two-lane, unmarked affair, ran to Perpignan, some 10 kilometers into the city. I marched as best and as fast as I could in the ditch. May 1; no farmers in the fields; no idea if anyone saw me during those kilometers into Perpignan. . . . I got there at about 2 or 3 in the afternoon. Once into the small city, I had no difficulty finding the railroad station. I made a point of not looking into anyone's face, as we do when we hope no one will see us. I can't tell how much I looked unusual. Skinny kids I guess were not a novelty then, anywhere. I worried most about my cloth shoes, that they might give me away as a penniless, homeless waif and who knows where he might've come from. Perpignan was not a war devastated zone, . . . it's not as though I could have been taken for some poor orphaned kid whose parents got killed when their house was blown to bits by some bomb. To be as invisible as possible was one of my prime tasks. But I had to buy a train ticket.

I got to the train station, had no difficulty seeing the ticket counter; as casually as I could I asked for a ticket for the next train to Marseille and its cost. The next train was at about 11 p.m. that evening. I had the money needed, handed it over. . . . To my relief, the clerk just handed me the ticket and some change.

Once I got my ticket, I realized to my distress that I had hours to wait. It was about mid-afternoon and the train left late that night. I could not stay in the station. I needed a secluded place where I could hide until nightfall at least. . . . Not difficult to figure out: find a toilet with cubicles with doors and I had it made. Not a savory place, but it would keep me hidden. I was not bored in that stall. I was out of Rivesaltes even if only for a few hours, with the promise of more. (pp. 57–58)

In time, I got to the train station. The train came, I got on.

## The Train From Perpignan to Marseille

Standing room only! I don't know how long we had traveled so far, one hour, two, more? . . . I felt an odd feeling of near-peace, maybe it was sleepiness; I had been on my feet, had run like hell and walked a good number of kilometers and had not slept since many hours now. . . . Nor had I eaten since my piece of bread in the morning. . . . No problem; I was not thinking of sleep or of food. . . . I was rather in a state of alertness somewhat dulled by the train's moving rhythm. There was more space between my standing-room-only-neighbor on my right than on my left. In fact the one on my left moved closer, he quietly said to me, "Je sais d'où tu viens" ("I know where you're coming from").

I was scared to death. I had been running like hell, I was scared shitless much of the time up to now; this time I was petrified. I had not gone that far on my journey. To be sure, this was the end of me. I was never this close to filling my pants with the contents of my nearly empty gut. He must have sensed it because he said, "N'aies pas peur." ("Don't be frightened.") His tone gave me the courage to hesitantly look at him. "T'as faim?" ("Are you hungry?") Dramatically relieved by his look and tone, I nodded my head. He must have looked me over well . . . : I know where you're coming from and are you hungry? He provided me with my first meal in 9 months. He did not have to do this; he could have just turned away. I best remember his sympathetic reach toward me, and what he did. Other than that, there was nothing remarkable about him, an average enough businessman or who knows what. I felt protected with him in the station. [He was my first "Lorenzo."[7]] He helped me understand at least what some of the many travelers might be doing on this train. He was going to Grenoble to ski! While we were in concentration camps, some were skiing! . . . Not all evil people, either. Life just went on, even while so many of us were imprisoned and starving in camps! . . . When I re-embarked on our train to Marseille, seats were now available; many had transferred to go elsewhere. I was wakened by the train conductor—we were in Marseille. (pp. 59–61)

## Safety: The OSE Homes

I easily found the address my mother had given me: Le Bureau d'Oeuvre de Secours aux Enfants (OSE). As soon as I walked in I felt safe. They knew where I came from before I told them. I do not consider these rescuers "Lorenzos" because by their work they were dedicated to help others.

I was immediately taken to the OSE Home in Boulouris: La Feuille. This was asylum. There were perhaps 30 kids there; the starvation level was the same; but the OSE workers made us feel safe. Within several months we moved to St. Raphael: La Villa Mariana. From there the older kids at long last could go to school. Being among the oldest, I was responsible to get us there and back. I was Villa Mariana for one year when I was informed that my mother had put my name on a list for children to go to America—without their families. The OSE brought our parents to Marseille to say good-bye to us. They were then returned by agreement, by the OSE, to Rivesaltes. I remember little of our good-byes.

During our brief sojourn in Marseille, I was overjoyed to find that Savic, my Rivesaltes co-Musketeer, had also been selected to make the trip, he, directly from Rivesaltes. From Marseille we sailed to Casablanca, where we stayed for three weeks waiting for our ship, the World War II–neutral Portuguese Serpa Pinto—this was June 1942—to take us across the Atlantic to New York's Ellis Island. Once in America, Savic and I requested that we be placed in the same city.

## The Start of My New Life

Pittsburgh, America—

> [We were] were placed with the Wagner family. . . . At 13 I was not aware then as I have been now for a long time, how enormously generous, how deeply decent, Faye and Harry Wagner were; and how lovely and accepting their 3 young daughters were, Phyllis, then 8, Sandy, 5, and Evie, 2, . . . in accepting two 13-year-old strangers into their home. We were Jewish refugees and quite a number of families in America opened their homes to us. (p. 91)

Faye was a remarkable woman. My dilemma with her was that I could not call her "Mrs. Wagner"; that was too removed from how I felt about her. I could not call her "Mom"; that was out of the question, I had my mother. How I came to it I don't know, but I came to call her "Lady." I said it with warmth, and I felt she knew it. She was, truly, a Lady. I came to really love her, to love all of them. Who wouldn't? Faye and Harry made it possible for Savic and me to pick up living our life, which had been so brutally trampled by Nazism, by malignant prejudice.

> No, we did not pick up living our life. . . . Before the war I was in a world with my mother, my uncles, aunts, cousins, friends, my school, Bruxelles,

speaking French and Yiddish. My father and my brother were in Lodz, apart but accessible, in my world. . . . [It was a good world.] This life, as of May 1942, . . . was the start of my new life; my old life had been violated, fragmented; and it is taking the rest of this life in America to bring some closure to what happened to my life of origin. . . . As it did even in Rivesaltes, life went on; and from the fragments, with the help of many on the way, it evolved into this very different, new and eventually very good life. (pp. 91–93)

## Entry Into Our "New World"

Our New World was, is, an asylum; not for everyone to be sure—which I have undertaken to do all I can to change—but it was for us. Richly endowed by my world in Brussels, on the heels of what the OSE, the American Quakers, The Jewish Social Service Agency and individuals embedded in these services—Mme Mazur, Mora, Aranka of the OSE in France—had done, the sympathy of my "Lorenzo" on the train to Marseille, now came the enormous generosity of the Wagner family that gave me not only asylum but also loving care and made it possible for me to reorder my life and start my adulthood reconstituted, ready to take on what lay ahead with a mix of anxiety, confidence, optimism, and hard work. During these formative adolescent years the family of Donald Steinfirst opened their home to me, Donald seeing to it that I got a scholarship to get a degree in music at what was then Carnegie Tech; dear Emma Steiner, the choir director at Alderdice High School, who launched me into music; the list of those who have helped goes on and on. And it is crowned by the woman I married, our three sons, now our grandchildren. Because of them, I have become who I am, a very gratified man.

For me as well as for others (Sonnert & Holton, 2006), healing from the Holocaust has left painful scars, but it also has led to much good. First, a few words about the scars, then about the good. Both give evidence of resilience since scars too are evidence of healing.

## Scars and Resilience

For André Malraux, la condition humaine . . . is that man who has only one life, is willing to lose it for an idea. . . . I am borrowing Malraux's phrase to carry another meaning. I am speaking of the fact, not just that we suffer, but as my own past and decades of work have taught me, that we humans create much of that suffering ourselves. That man makes members of his own Society suffer is documented by the continuing emergence of testimonies that detail the dreadful Holocaust atrocities survivors suffered and massacres they witnessed. [Since then, 2,000,000 were massacred in the Killing Fields of Cambodia, masses were murdered in Bosnia's ethnic cleansing, 800,000 Hutus were murdered in several weeks in Rwanda, and now we witness the mounting murders in Darfur, by April 2007 estimated to be over 200,000.] We are all well exercised in causing others suffering. (p. 107)

Looking back, three dates stand out for me. On May 1, 1941, at 12, I escaped from Rivesaltes. In May 1942, I left Marseille for America on the OSE Convoy #3.

On August 14, 1942, my mother was sent to Auschwitz. About two years after the Allies' victory in Europe in 1945, I learned that my mother had been sent to Auschwitz on August 14, 1942, four months after I had arrived in America. I have repeated "August 14, 1942" in an effort to inscribe it in my brain. My brain long resisted its inscription. A friend, visiting the Wannsee Conference Center in Berlin in 2005, saw a large photo display of Jews closely watched as they board a cattle train in Drancy, for Auschwitz. It was convoy #19. My mother was on this convoy.

According to Serge Klarsfeld, this is the day convoy #19, carrying [1,015] persons left Drancy, destination Auschwitz. [Only one among them survived.] . . . Transports from France to Auschwitz started on March 27, 1942. At the outset of their odious collaboration, the Vichy-French plan executors worked with such alacrity and efficiency that they sent their first train convoy of Jews before the Germans were ready to receive them, causing an embarrassment for the poor German Nazis! But by August, the time convoy #19 was shipped out, the dispatching to the Death Camps in Poland of Jews who had sought refuge in France seems to have proceeded smoothly. And since the "Final Solution" once set in motion [7 months earlier] called for expeditiousness, no doubt the transfer of [these victims] from Rivesaltes via Drancy to Auschwitz probably took no more than three days. Once there, extermination was efficiently expedited.

On August 14, my mother was sent to Auschwitz. What a terrible return to her homeland. Had I not escaped, I would have returned to my birth land with her. I have thought often, "And with her to our grave." (pp. 116–117)

In the years that followed, pertinent to my Holocaust experience among my travels—most for lecturing purposes—in addition to returning to Brussels a number of times, I went to Israel, to several cities in Germany including Munich and Berlin, retraced my journey from Brussels through France, revisited Rivesaltes, and visited Drancy.

My journey in Israel was singularly meaningful to me. Entering Tel Aviv airport I was exhilarated seeing shop signs written in large Hebrew letters, amazed by the car-rental guy writing up our contract in Hebrew! Of course, this was Israel; but until then, nowhere in the world did I imagine such free everywhere public display of "Jewishness." Even in my advancing years I was awed by the open display of being Jewish. Jews are well enough accepted in America, but I don't see such highly open displays—except for those among us who do walk about in Hasidic attire. With this and my painfully draining visit to Yad Vashem, the Holocaust memorial in Jerusalem, I felt deeply the scars malignant prejudice has inflicted in my psyche.

My travels in Germany have been full of trepidation. In Munich, where I now have lectured on five different occasions, I have been surprised by the anxiety I feel even when walking the streets with very dear German friends. So too when, jogging early in the morning in Cologne, I heard a rather rowdy group of probably nice college-age kids bringing their night to a fun-filled conclusion; I became anxious and was glad that I was on the other side of the wide street. Interestingly, knowing that Berlin is the avant-garde city of Germany, that Hitler hated Berlin, that it was the home of Bertolt Brecht and Kurt Weill, and I was in the good hands of a psychologist-analyst guide, I was much more comfortable. In addition, seeing the Memorial to the Burning of Books with its subterranean white empty bookshelves, and seeing the long line of German kids waiting to go into the stark, fortress-prison-like Jewish Museum, all make me like Berlin.

## Retracing My Stay in Hell: Return to Rivesaltes

In 1997, Rachel and I attended International Psychoanalytic meetings in Barcelona. We went because from there in less than an hour we could be in southern France. Karl, who was finishing a medical fellowship in South Africa, as well as Sabina and their two boys, also joined us. Together, we traveled by van to southern France, then on to Brussels.

We stopped at the Gendarmerie in the village Rivesaltes for directions to
their local concentration camp; yes, it was still there. . . . We got into the
van and now slowly, we followed the gendarme's directions. The camp was
less than a mile from the village. I felt that familiar gut sink, . . . that grave
pensive sorrow I know, when I first saw the remnants of that hell. And I felt
a sweep of gratitude; the French had not destroyed the evidence; they had
not swept it under the carpet as they did of Gurs, another camp, not far
from Rivesaltes. Where Gurs was, now lays a lovely village. No; Rivesaltes,
the remnants were there.

I felt sick. I recognized the remnants of what I had known. . . . Sabina
caught a shot of Rachel seeming to explain something to 6-year-old Elliot,
probably in response to one of his many questions; they were standing in
front of one of the barrack-shells. Barbed-wire, rolled, crumpled together
lay here and there, probably marking where the periphery stood; in one
place a small stretch of it stood, leaning somewhat collapsed. In the photo
of that stretch, Sabina caught a picture of me with 1-year-old Arthur on my
back and, twenty feet ahead, Karl carrying Elliot. I think that Elliot must
have wanted to be held by his father, perhaps sensing that this was a
moment of wanting to be very close to him. A face-on shot of them shows
Karl looking grim, serious and sad all in one; Elliot looks puzzled.

In the pain, I took some pleasure in seeing the fragmented walls, no
roofs, debris scattered on the remaining floors, of the boxes that once held
us captive. . . . The shame of Vichy-France spread over it all. (pp. 147–148)

## Of Burdens That Follow From What Befell
the Jews of Europe

### Problems for my Family

One of the largest torments I continue to experience following from what
happened to me is the pain and the burden this past has caused my wife
and our three sons. No survivor has escaped this; we can't prevent it; wives
and kids cannot not be burdened by it. Now my grandchildren have begun
to ask me, with a note of seriousness and caution, "Zaida, were you in the
war?" (p. 166)

The sins of the father will be visited on the child. . . . I understand how it
happens. . . . But what sins did I commit in all this? The pains of the father

will be visited on the child. That's what applies to us; and it makes me weep. A father cannot have better sons than I have. And, I am hung in a paradox: I want my sons and my wife to put it all to rest; but I want us all to remember it, and I want to remind others of it, hoping they will not let it happen again, nor wish to perpetrate it again. (p. 170)

### My Problem With God and With Liturgy

"Why did God let this happen to us?" God too was a victim of the Holocaust. Elie Wiesel said it better than anyone. Compelled to watch another hanging in Auschwitz, this time of a young teenager too light to be effectively strangled by his own weight pulling on the hangman's noose. Writhing to breathe as he hung, it took one half hour—and he stopped. Forced to watch, someone behind Wiesel asked, in vain, a second time, "So where is God?" Wiesel felt within himself a voice that answered, "Where he is? . . . Here he is—he is hanging here, on this gallows" (Wiesel, 1958, *La Nuit*). (Parens, 2004, p. 172)

I am now [78]; I still don't know about God. I am not anti-God. . . . I see God more as what I understand to be Spinoza's idea of God. . . . God is in everything, everywhere. God cannot prevent Holocausts. (Parens, 2004, p. 172)

## Why Has It Taken So Long to Write What Happened to Us

We are all aware that after five or more decades of silence, a number of survivors of the Holocaust have now written memoirs. There were a few powerful ones published soon after the Holocaust that have left their mark on society, such as Rudy Vrba's *Escape From Auschwitz*, Primo Levi's *If This Is a Man*, Elie Wiesel's *Night*, and best known of all, *The Diary of Anne Frank*. Why did it take so long for survivors to write of their experiences? My own experience informs me that it was just too painful to do. I have hidden behind the curtain of being a psychoanalyst who must maintain anonymity, and I realized that as a doctor I could not burden my patients with my traumatic past. Yes, but it is also clear to me, and my nummular eczema and a four-year stint with an intense photosensitivity triggered by our first effort to go to Israel, are sure evidence of my somatic response to the torture of remembering. I know now how large my resistance has been to writing my witness report of what happened to me and my world. And this is confirmed by the emotional turmoil I experienced in the writing of my self-analytic memoirs as well as by the striking relief I have experienced since they were published (2004).

## Guilt, Shame—Mine—That of Survivors

> Guilt. Mind-boggling. You suffered; but someone you love deeply suffered more and [somehow] it's your fault. We brilliant animals function that simply! Survivor guilt. . . . Did survivor guilt propel Levi to end his life? (p. 184)

> I too have contemplated . . . guilt at having survived. . . . Generally, I don't feel guilty that I survived. But now and then a most distressing feeling gets hold of me invariably attached to a thought that is difficult to dismiss. I have wondered if my escape from Rivesaltes labeled my mother as an "undesirable, recalcitrant guest of the Rivesaltes Concentration Camp" and contributed to her being selected for further descent into hell, first of course to the dead-bodies-gas chambers, with their feces and urine remains, and then sanctification by burning in hell. Did my escape contribute to that?
>    Why did Primo Levi from three floors up throw himself to his death? Contemplating his being chosen to work in the Laboratory, out of the winter cold, no beatings, no threats, no insults, Chemist Levi reflects guilt-burdened . . . that the others were not shielded as he, he tells us that "the comrade of all my peaceful moments, . . . —the pain of remembering . . . attacks me like a dog the moment my conscience comes out of the gloom." [I ask you,] Where does one draw the line? When does one say, "No, I will not be privileged; I will stay and suffer with the others?" When does one do that? Should I have refused to escape from Rivesaltes, should I not have left my mother alone? Should I have refused to leave France for America? Should I have gone with her to Auschwitz? (pp. 185–186)

Though I have written my memoirs, I have not yet been able to do some things I should do. I have not been able to find out once and for all what happened to my father, my brother, and the large family I left in Poland. Nor have I been able to visit Auschwitz, where I know my mother was murdered. (Between the time of the writing of this chapter and its publication, Rachel, two of our sons, and one grandson will finally have visited Auschwitz and Lodz.)

## Evidence of Resilience

While I have talked about psychic scars, aftereffects of my Holocaust experience, embedded in that text is also evidence of resilience, especially in the reconstruction of my family—not by recovering those lost, but with the help of Rachel by creating our new family. There are now three vibrant generations of the Parens family. And with the help of many, for now many years, I have become the professional I am.

## How Have I Come Professionally to Where I Am?

As I wrote in 2004, "La condition humaine, that we suffer, and that we humans create much of that suffering ourselves, has pre-occupied me from the time of my youth. I have especially searched in my field for ways to explain why we make others suffer and to find ways to get us to stop causing avoidable suffering to others" (p. 199). No doubt it determined my becoming a child psychiatrist-psychoanalyst. The main setting of my work has been the clinical situation. But both my clinical work and teaching—half-time faculty appointment in academic, psychiatric training facilities, as well as in a psychoanalytic training program—compelled me into research. It was only in the writing of my memoirs that I came to recognize how my research in child development was unconsciously driven by my Holocaust experience.

In 1968 I was invited to the Medical College of Pennsylvania to develop psychoanalytically informed research in child development. In 1969 we developed a project, with a strong protocol, to study correlations of qualitative aspects of the mother-child relationship with the development of three specific ego functions in the child. Following a summer program much appreciated by the community, when we called for volunteers, nearly 50 mothers responded. Given that we could not work with so large a number of subjects, we selected those seven who at the time were pregnant. The project was started in September 1970. We met in a group setting, twice weekly—except for the month of August—the mothers, their infants, and their children who were not yet in school, that is, less than four years old, and the research staff. Within the first year the group was enlarged to 10 mothers. To direct observation, in time, we added responding to the mothers' questions about their children's behaviors, eventually optimizing the mothers' parenting and therewith their children's development, as was documented by a 19-year follow-up study (Parens, 1993). We worked together for seven years. During this time, the project evolved into a highly productive undertaking.

Within six months of launching the original project—correlating mother-child relationship with infant's developing adaptive functions—I was drawn into two unpredicted directions:

1. The study of the development of aggression in childhood was compelled by my fascination with unanticipated aggressive behaviors in the infants—unaware then that I was unconsciously driven to understand how hostility, hate, and human destructiveness develop.
2. The recognition that informing parents of strategies to optimize their children's development constituted a method for optimizing parenting followed from the fact that this is just what was happening. That the parents became eager students of parenting education made us aware that we had developed a replicable method for parenting education intended to optimize children's emotional growth. I want to note parenthetically here that my principal project collaborator, Elizabeth Scattergood, on the occasion of the 32-year follow-up reunion of our project and seeing the appreciation of the project mothers for what they verbalized they feel we did for them years before, made the interpretation to me that my interest in helping these mothers probably had something to do with my mother. She is probably right: I want to help mothers, possibly feeling that I did not help my mother enough, that I did not prevent her murder.

Both interests led to much study, publication, and the development of programs both educational and interventional, and eventually led us to strategies for the prevention of emotional disorders in children including the development of high-level hostility, hate, and violence (Parens, 1979/2007, 1987, 1993; Parens & Rose-Itkoff, 1997a, 1997b; Parens, Scattergood, et al., 1997; Parens, Scattergood, Singletary, & Duff, 1987). The interweaving of these two areas of study was initiated upon our discovering the cardinal hypothesis that experiences of excessive psychic pain lead to the generation of hostility and hate in humans (Parens, 1979/2007). This gave rise to the consequent hypothesis: If children can be reared by parenting strategies that minimize avoidable experiences of excessive emotional pain, these children will become less hostile than those reared under conditions of parental abuse, especially physical, and far too underrecognized, emotional abuse (Parens & Rose-Itkoff, 1997a, 1997b; Parens, Scattergood, et al., 1997). In the evolution of my thinking I hypothesized then that by far, home—more than school or the community—is where children who hate and destroy are produced. In time, I would modify this view slightly.

Knowing of my past and my study of aggression and prevention efforts, colleagues asked me to address the multicultural challenge to "live together with our differences" (personal communication, S. Akhtar, 1997; R. Gogineni, 1997). I had long thought of prejudice; this launched me into its study: What gives rise to prejudice? Are we all prejudiced, as so many have said? My bias to frame my explorations in terms of development is pretty well a signature of my psychoanalytic work. It served my inquiry well. Attachment, prewired to occur in early life, when looked at in detail yields factors obligatory to that development that make us all have prejudices. That is, specificity of attachment, or to whom we attach, is fostered by separation anxiety and protected by stranger anxiety; and, once in progress, attachment also brings with it identification with one's caregivers. The influence of these two obligatory developmental factors led me to postulate that prejudice is universal. But this prejudice does not bring with it the wish to destroy others. We just prefer to be or are more comfortable "with our own." This, therefore, is benign prejudice. My work on aggression informed me that it is the hostilification of this benign prejudice that produces malignant prejudice. From 1997 on my studies on prejudice multiplied, and they continue to this day. From 1999 on, my studies of prejudice became personalized, leading eventually to my writing my Holocaust memoirs (Parens, 2004).

In time, side by side with developing strategies toward the prevention of "experience-derived emotional disorders in children and of high-level hostile destructiveness" in children (Parens 1993, 1996, 2001; Parens & Rose-Itkoff, 1997a, 1997b; Parens, Rose-Itkoff, et al., 2005; Parens, Scattergood, et al., 1987, 1997), my studies on prejudice opened the door toward the prevention of malignant prejudice (Parens, 1999a, 1999b, 2007a, 2007b, 2007c).

I insist that we can, and we must, act to reduce malignant prejudice. "Some say Humans murder, it's in their nature. My clinical and research work do not support these indictments. We are not born murderers. But we can become that way" (Parens, 2004, p. 268). And equally so, we can become people who refuse to murder. Idealism? I feel a kinship with Primo Levi. We have traveled different roads to be sure, but I end up with the same question he posed: "What can each of us do so that in this world pregnant with threats at least this threat . . . [of a return] of the concentration camp world . . . will be nullified" (Levi, 1989, p. 21)? We have to strive to nullify it.

I have come out of my Holocaust misery with the strong conviction that
we cannot eliminate our differences. We, everywhere, must put our ener-
gies into exposing 'malignant distortions' [about other people, those of
other ethnicity than ourselves]. . . .

We must not let it happen to us again.

We must not make it happen to others.

We must not be victims, and

We must not be perpetrators.

We must learn

To live together

With our differences. (Parens, 2004, p. 270)

## References

Alexander, F. (1961). *The scope of psychoanalysis*. New York: Basic Books.

Angier, C. (2002). *The double bond*. New York: Farrar, Straus & Giroux.

Anthony. E. J. (1974). The syndrome of the psychologically invulnerable child. In
E. J. Anthony & C. Koupernik (Eds.), *The child in his family: Vol. 3. Children
at psychiatric risk* (pp. 529–544). New York: Wiley.

Bowlby, J. A. (1958). The nature of the child's tie to his mother. *International Journal of Psychoanalysis, 41*, 350–373.

Cannon, W. B. (1928). *Bodily changes in pain, hunger, fear, and rage*. New York:
Appleton-Century.

Coates, S. W. (2004). John Bowlby and Margaret S. Mahler: Their lives and theories.
*Journal of the American Psychoanalytic Association, 52*, 571–601.

Cyrulnik, B. (1999). *Un merveilleux malheur*. Paris: Odile Jacob.

Cyrulnik, B. (2003). *Le murmure des fantômes*. Paris: Odile Jacob. English transla-
tion: *The whispering of ghosts* (S. Fairfield, Trans.). New York: Other Press, 2005.

Cyrulnik, B. (2004). *Parler d'amour au bord du gouffre*. Paris: Odile Jacob.

Fonagy, P. (1999). Psychoanalytic theory from the viewpoint of attachment theory
and research. In J. Cassidy & P. R. Shaver (Eds.), *Handbook of attachment: Theory, research and clinical applications* (pp. 595–624). New York: Guilford Press.

Freud, A. (1960). Discussion of Dr. John Bowlby's paper. *Psychoanalytic Study of the
Child, 15*, 53–62.

Freud, S. (1920). Beyond the pleasure principle. *Standard Edition* 18:1–64.

Freud, S. (1927). The future of an illusion. *Standard Edition* 21:3–66.

Freud, S. (1933 [1932]). Why war? *Standard Edition* 22:195–218.

Garmezy, N. (1971). Vulnerability research and the issue of primary prevention.
*American Journal of Orthopsychiatry, 41*, 101–116.

Garmezy, N. (1985). Stress-resistant children: The search for protective factors. In J. E. Stevenson (Ed.), *Recent research in developmental psychopathology* (pp. 213–233). Oxford: Pergamon Press.

Hauser, S., Allen, J., & Golden, E. (2006). *Out of the woods: Tales of resilient teens.* Cambridge, MA: Harvard University Press.

Kendler, K. S. (1993). Twin studies of psychiatric illness. *Archives of General Psychiatry, 50,* 905–915.

Kendler, K. S., & Eaves, L. J. (1986). Models for the joint effect of genotype and environment on liability to psychiatric illness. *American Journal of Psychiatry, 143,* 279–289.

Kestenberg, J. S., & Brenner, I. (1996). *The last witness: The child survivor of the Holocaust.* Washington, DC: American Psychiatric Press.

Krystal, H. (Ed.). (1968). *Massive psychic trauma.* New York: International Universities Press.

Krystal, H. (1978). Trauma and affects. *Psychoanalytic Study of the Child, 33,* 81–116.

Levi, P. (1989). *The drowned and the saved* (R. Rosenthal, Trans.). New York: Vintage. (Original work published 1986 as *Sommersi e i salvati.*)

Levi, P. (1996). *Survival in Auschwitz* (S. Woolf, Trans.). New York: Simon & Schuster. (Original work published 1947 as *Se questo e un uomo.*)

Luthar, S. S., Ciccheti, D., & Becker, B. (2000). The construct of resilience: A critical evaluation and guidelines for future work. *Child Development, 71,* 543–562.

Masten, A. S. (2001). Ordinary magic: Resilience processes in development. *American Psychologist, 56,* 227–238.

Murphy, L. (1962). *The widening world of childhood: Paths toward mastery.* New York: Basic Books.

Nir, Y. (2002). *The lost childhood.* New York: Scholastic Press.

Ornstein, A. (1985). Survival and recovery. *Psychoanalytic Inquiry, 5,* 99–130.

Ornstein, A., & Goldman, S. (2004). *My mother's eyes: Holocaust memories of a young girl.* Cincinnati, OH: Emmis Books.

Parens, H. (1979). *The development of aggression in early childhood.* Northvale, NJ: Jason Aronson. (Second edition, 2007)

Parens, H. (1987). Cruelty begins at home. *Child Abuse and Neglect, 11,* 331–338.

Parens, H. (1991). A view of the development of hostility in early life. *Journal of the American Psychoanalytic Association, 39*(Suppl.: *On Affects,* T. Shapiro & R. Emde, Eds.), 75–108.

Parens, H. (1993). Toward preventing experience-derived emotional disorders: Education for parenting. In H. Parens & S. Kramer (Eds.), *Prevention in mental health* (pp. 121–148). Northvale, NJ: Jason Aronson.

Parens, H. (Speaker). (1996). Prevention of violence via parenting education. Panel: Violence in School (E. Sholevar, Chair). In "Furman Initiative" at Meetings of the American Academy of Child and Adolescent Psychiatry. (AACAP Audio-cassette Library, CP 6908 [2 cassettes]).

Parens, H. (1999a). Toward the prevention of prejudice. In M. R. Fort Brescia & M. Lemlij (Eds.), *En el umbral del milenio, Vol. 2* (pp. 131–141). Prom, Peru: SIDEA.

Parens, H. (1999b, May 15). *Some influences of the Holocaust on development: One man's experience.* Address to the Annual Meeting of the American College of Psychoanalysts, Washington, DC.

Parens, H. (2001). Toward the prevention of violence and malignant prejudice. In *The psychoanalysis of change and change in psychoanalysis: Symposium in honor of Dr. Lotte Koehler* (pp. 1–20). Munich: Muenchen Forum fuer Neuere Entwicklungen in der Psychoanalyse. (Also translated and distributed in German.)

Parens, H. (2004). *Renewal of life: Healing from the Holocaust.* Rockville, MD: Schreiber.

Parens, H. (2005). The 2nd Vamik Volkan Lecture: Renewal of Life—Healing from the Holocaust. *Mind and Human Interaction, 14*(1), 2–17.

Parens, H. (2007a). Toward understanding prejudice: Benign and malignant. In H. Parens, A. Mahfouz, S. Twemlow, & D. Scharff (Eds.), *The future of prejudice: Psychoanalysis and the prevention of prejudice* (pp. 21–36). New York: Rowman & Littlefield.

Parens, H. (2007b). Roots of prejudice: Findings from observational research. In H. Parens, A. Mahfouz, S. Twemlow, & D. Scharff (Eds.), *The future of prejudice: Psychoanalysis and the prevention of prejudice* (pp. 81–95). New York: Rowman & Littlefield.

Parens, H. (2007c). Malignant prejudice: Guidelines toward its prevention. In H. Parens, A. Mahfouz, S. Twemlow, & D. Scharff (Eds.), *The future of prejudice: Psychoanalysis and the prevention of prejudice* (pp. 269–289). New York: Rowman & Littlefield.

Parens, H., & Rose-Itkoff, C. (1997a). *Parenting for emotional growth: The workshops series. (1) On the development of self & human relationships; (2) On aggression; (3) Conscience formation; (4) Sexual development in children.* Philadelphia: Parenting for Emotional Growth. © TXu 842–316 & 317.

Parens, H., & Rose-Itkoff, C. (1997b). *Trauma: Workshops: On helping children and parents cope with it.* Philadelphia: Parenting for Emotional Growth. © TXu 842–316.

Parens, H., Rose-Itkoff, C., Pearlman, M., Reid, K., Turrini, P., Fallon, T., et al. (2005). Into our 4th decade of prevention via parenting education: Where we have been—where we are going. *International Journal of Applied Psychoanalytic Studies, 3,* 17–38.

Parens, H., Scattergood, E., Duff, S., & Singletary, W. (1997). *Parenting for emotional growth: A curriculum for students in grades K thru 12: Vol. 1, The textbook;*

*Vol. 2, The lesson plans.* Philadelphia: Parenting for Emotional Growth. © TXu 680–613.

Parens, H., Scattergood, E., Singletary, W., & Duff, A. (1987). *Aggression in our children: Coping with it constructively.* New York: Jason Aronson. (Translated into German and Russian [1997].)

Rutter, M. (2000). Resilience reconsidered: Conceptual considerations, empirical findings and policy implications. In J. P. Shonkoff & S. J. Meisels (Eds.), *Handbook of early childhood intervention* (2nd ed.) (pp. 651–682). Cambridge: Cambridge University Press.

Rutter, M. (2006). *Genes and behavior.* Malden, MA: Blackwell.

Saul, L. J. (1960). *Emotional maturity.* Philadelphia: Lippincott. (Originally published 1947.)

Schur, M. (1960). Discussion of Dr. John Bowlby's paper. *Psychoanalytic Study of the Child, 15,* 63–84.

Schur, M. (1972). *Freud: Living and dying.* New York: International Universities Press.

Selye, H. (1950). *The physiology and pathology of exposure to stress.* Montreal: Acta.

Solant, M. (2006, August 25–28). Personal communication on "Jewish Rescue and Resistance During WWII" panel at the 18th International Conference of Holocaust Child Survivors, Second Generation and Families, Dearborn, MI.

Sonnert, G., & Holton, G. (2006). *What happened to the children who fled Nazi persecution.* New York: Palgrave Macmillan.

Southwick, S. M., Vythilingam, M., & Charney, D. S. (2005). The psychobiology of depression and resilience to stress: Implications for prevention and treatment. *Annual Review of Clinical Psychology, 1,* 255–291.

Spitz, R. (1960). Discussion of Dr. John Bowlby's paper. *Psychoanalytic Study of the Child, 15,* 85–94.

Spitz, R. (1965). *The first year of life.* New York: International Universities Press.

Stepansky, P. E. (Ed.). (1988). *The memoirs of Margaret S. Mahler*

# Notes

1. Remarkable and yet to be explained, according to Janet Maslin, who reviewed Carole Angier's biography of Primo Levi (*New York Times,* Thursday, June 13, 2002), Angier believes "that Primo Levi was depressed before and after Auschwitz, but not in it." Remarkable and yet to be explained is that during their stay in extermination as well as nonextermination concentration camps in Poland, Germany, and France, inmates tended to not develop common colds (despite exposure to severe weather conditions), nor common ailments; rather, many died of typhoid and of starvation. This type of finding suggests the complex relation between stress conditions and illness/resilience.

2. Hauser et al. tell us that "*reflectiveness* is curiosity about one's thoughts, feelings, and motivations, and the willingness to try to make sense of them and handle

them responsibly. *Agency* is the conviction that what one does matters, that one can intervene effectively in one's own life. *Relatedness*—engagement and interaction with others—may be highly valued even when there are no helpful others around, and this may predispose youngsters to be able to use supportive connections when they are available" (2006, p. 39).

3. Freud's (1927) pathologizing appraisal of the role of religion in humans' coping with their existential anxiety has not served us well, and it has burdened some among us familiar with his views who experience a sense of spirituality without giving it a religious denominational appellation.

4. A recent study, *What Happened to the Children Who Fled Nazi Persecution*, by Gerhard Sonnert and Gerald Holton (2006), is brought to mind by Cyrulnik's thesis—though not by the title of his book.

5. Indeed, in his passion Bowlby was highly provocative in his depreciating critique of Anna Freud's theorizing about attachment (Bowlby, 1958), which, I believe, eventually contributed to what has long been the unfortunate rift between ego psychology and attachment theory. It may be that only by being independent from ego psychology, or rather from the "psychoanalytic establishment," has attachment theory been able to achieve its remarkable and highly valuable yield. Just as Fonagy (1999) rightly believes that A. Freud's, R. Spitz's, and M. Schur's critiques of Bowlby's theorizing (all in *The Psychoanalytic Study of the Child, Vol. 15,* 1960) were crass, so did I find Bowlby's critique of Anna Freud's theorizing crass. Coates adds to our understanding of the rift by commenting on Bowlby's disappointing supervision experience with an unduly unyielding Melanie Klein. In the play of authoritarianism and narcissistic injury, Hegel's presence was in the air: "thesis—antithesis—. . . ."

6. Quotations in the remaining text are taken from the author's Holocaust memoirs, *Renewal of Life: Healing From the Holocaust* (Parens, 2004) with permission from copyright owner.

7. See the beginning of this chapter where I speak of Lorenzo Perrone, Primo Levi's unknown "friend," who reminded him that humanity had not died. Perrone's acts were so powerfully symbolic I refer to such persons as "Lorenzos."

# 7

# RESILIENCE, SUBLIMATION, AND HEALING

## Reactions to a Personal Narrative

*Barbara Shapiro, MD*

I thank Dr. Parens for sharing his experiences with us. His story gives a personal face to the ways in which some children and adults are remarkably resilient in the face of significant trauma. The psychoanalytic literature on resilience is relatively sparse, and Dr. Parens's narrative, along with the other chapters in this book, adds to our understanding of this vital set of strengths.

Dr. Parens stresses that in our work with patients the frame must include a focus on strengths, natural health, and resiliencies—in the evaluation, in the dynamic formulation, and in the treatment. I absolutely agree, and must add that Dr. Parens does not just say this; it is inherent in how he approaches patients. I know this because he was one of my supervisors when I was a psychoanalytic candidate.

Unfortunately many papers in our psychoanalytic literature and certain aspects of candidate training rest on a medical model of diagnosis and psychopathology. As a small but telling example, the forms for candidate case reports, certification, and training analyst application ask for "diagnosis." Such medicalized thinking privileges conflict, developmental and constitutional vulnerabilities, and the psychopathological effects of trauma, while ignoring inherent health, strengths, resiliencies, and developmental context. Yet we depend on the actual and potential strengths of our patients for their ability to work with us and to heal. Part of the psychoanalytic process is for the analyst and analysand to understand and appreciate strengths and resiliences and not just vulnerabilities and pain.

Here I will first discuss the personal narrative, or story. Then I will turn to the nature of resilience. Finally I will focus on Dr. Parens's story to discern what factors and qualities might have contributed to his resilience as a child and as an adult. From now on I will refer to Dr. Parens as Henri, because he is Henri to me, and because I will discuss the resilience of the child, and the child was Henri and not yet Dr. Parens.

## Some Thoughts About the Personal Narrative

We can examine resilience using two basic research paradigms. One research method consists of cross sectional or longitudinal outcome studies of groups of children or adults who have experienced trauma (Luthar & Zelazo, 2003; Masten & Powell, 2003). The other research approach is to analyze personal narratives or individual case studies, either singly or as a group (Hauser, Golden, & Allen, 2006). This is ethnographic research. Both research paradigms have accepted methodologies and provide different but complementary ways of examining aspects of the human condition, including resilience. Henri's chapter contributes to research on resilience as an ethnographic single-case study.

His story also exemplifies other aspects of the personal narrative. The personal narrative is, of course, at the core of psychoanalysis. This is how we work with people, and how we come to understand people and human nature. Personal narrative can be understood as both reflecting and transforming experience. It reflects the person's experience and makes possible a new experience (Hauser et al., 2006; Leffert, 2007). In addition, the personal narrative enables past experiences to be shared with others, may offer comfort although it is birthed with pain, provides material for research, and becomes part of history.

One starts with raw experience, which especially with trauma is often chaotic, incoherent, and nonverbal. Over time, the feelings and content are put into words, and then into a story, which gets told, reshaped, and retold. The content comes to include circumstances, experiences, relationships, external information, and the social and cultural milieu. Gradually these stories are worked through, organized, and integrated into a form that more or less explains the flow of events over time. These narratives continue to be reworked throughout our lifetimes.

In psychoanalytic therapy or analysis, the narrative is shared with another. It becomes part of what Ogden calls the analytic third (Ogden, 1994). The experience and the story are transformed, both by the co-constructed narrative itself and by the process of co-constructing the narrative.

We as analysts tend to think of a dyadic narrative. However, Henri has now shared his story with a much larger community. It has become a group narrative. I postulate that sharing a narrative with a group transforms aspects of experience, as does a dyadic narrative, for us and for Henri. The transformative aspects may be different than in a dyadic narrative, as the form, motivations, and context are different. The co-construction of the narrative involves all of us—the storyteller, the discussants, the listeners, and the readers. You, the reader, experience the story through your lens, and Henri sees and imagines his colleagues hearing and reading his story. In addition, there is spoken and written feedback and discussion, which in turn contributes to the evolution of the narrative.

In the personal narrative, one can slowly sort out the complicated issues of what happened over time; how things evolved; what is one's own responsibility and the accountability of others; what could have been controlled or prevented and what could not; what made others do what they did; why bad things happen to innocent people; the role of the bystander and the helper; the role of outright evil; the role of chance, fate, or predestination; the place for faith and spirituality; and the confusions and parallel worlds—such as being helped by someone who was going skiing in the midst of genocide. We humans are meaning seekers.

Telling a story can be both tremendously comforting and enormously painful. Telling and retelling stories is central to healing and recovery from trauma. However, we must remember that some stories perpetuate trauma. They become rigid, fixed, or hateful and/or consist of fantastical elaborations that take on a life of their own and are not anchored in everyday reality. This kind of story then transmits and replays the trauma—for the person, transgenerationally to children, and to the community and society. So when I talk here of the personal story as healing and transformative, I am talking about a certain kind of story—a story that is open, developing, growing, establishing links and meanings, with increasing freedom of thought, feeling, reflection, and understanding.

Henri brings up the problems of transgenerational transmission of trauma. He says, "Kids cannot not be burdened by it." He very poignantly points out that it is not just the sins of the father that are passed on for seven generations, but also the pains of the father. Even in strong and resilient families, trauma and suffering are transmitted in small but persistent and reoccurring ways—for example, subtle verbal and nonverbal discontinuities of affect and content, silences, tones of voice, and body language when certain things are discussed—or not discussed (Hesse & Main, 2000). Children recognize suffering and despair even when they cannot name it as such, and it becomes part of their own personal narrative and sense of self.

## Some Thoughts About the Nature of Resilience

Henri points out that resilience is lifelong, a process, not a singular entity. It is different for different people at different times. The plasticity of the brain gives us the capacity to recover, albeit with scars. Resilience may coexist with vulnerability. For example, at certain developmental nodes such as adolescence, childbirth, death of a loved one, life-threatening illness, perhaps the beginning of an analysis, we are more vulnerable, and yet at the same time new growth is more likely to appear. The vulnerability breaks things up a bit. The resilience enables transformation and growth. We see many severely traumatized people who come to us plagued with problems, who with help are better able to work, love, and play, although scars persist. That person's resilience makes him or her able to use the therapeutic opportunity for reflection and growth, and the growth then makes the person more resilient.

In some studies resilience is equated to the absence of psychopathology. However, resilience is not the absence of scars, vulnerabilities, and suffering but rather is the result of a positive set of strengths. Sometimes resilience is equated with survival; however, such an equation seems to idealize the fact that someone has lived through tremendous adversity. Resilience does not guarantee physical survival, and physical survival does not guarantee emotional survival. Henri points out the importance of luck, chance, and circumstance. Some people survive physically but their souls are murdered (Shengold, 1989).

There are different gradations and types of resilience, but resilience basically involves the capacity to flexibly and creatively use opportunities for survival, growth, and development, as they arise. However, moral questions arise as we examine resilience. Many creative and intelligent individuals survive tremendous trauma and then traumatize, injure, or demean others while they themselves prosper materially. Certain aspects of resilience have contributed to their survival and prosperity, but the resilience has not extended to the qualities of compassion and moral empathy.

## Henri's Resilience: Some Observations and Extrapolations

Based on his story, I consider Henri to be remarkably resilient. His resilience was made of many factors, such as intelligence, creativity, social skills, likability, and physical strength. There were many sources on multiple levels: his own constitution, his mother and family, his community, the goodwill of some strangers, and luck. I will enumerate some of the sources of resilience for Henri. These sources of resilience are not unique to Henri, but form the basis of potential resilience for all of us.

1. He loved and loves his mother, and clearly his mother loved him. As he says, his early years were by and large good ones. This early attachment, nurturance, and love formed the basis for future reciprocity of love and nurturance, and a coherent sense of self with other.

2. His mother did not just love him. Her love was what we think of as true or ideal parental love. Parents should want their children to survive, even if they themselves do not. But, as we well know, even well-intentioned parents may not be able to transcend their own narcissism—to think of the life and survival of the child, independent of themselves. Here, in the parent-child dyad, is the capacity for reflective function and mentalization (Coates, 1998; Fonagy & Target, 1998), altruism, empathy, and compassion.

3. He had an extended family. It was not one without problems, but no one needs families without problems, if they even exist. They just need to be good enough. The extended family is the first community. Henri-and-his-mother were not alone in the world.

4. I would venture to say that Henri was a gifted child and certainly an adult with a superior intellect. Many studies of resilience cite intellectual capacity and problem-solving ability as correlating with resilience (Masten & Powell, 2003). My own clinical experience with people who have been severely traumatized is that flexible intellectual capacity—the ability to see and understand patterns and meanings—contributes immensely to resilience and adaptation.

5. Henri was and is creative. Clearly he was creative in solving problems during his escape. He was able to play, and describes his use of fantasy. As an adult, his work on aggression, running parent-child groups, and on prevention has been remarkably creative. Creativity may have a great deal to do with resilience, as it involves flexibility and the ability to sublimate and transform (see Yates, Egeland, & Sroufe, 2003).

Fantasy play is the beginning of creativity. Play, in and of itself, helps children heal from trauma. Child therapists see the remarkable transformation, right in their own offices. When we see severely traumatized children for therapy or analysis, they are often remarkably inhibited in their play. The play is inflexible, repetitive, and controlling. Over time the play becomes more creative, and fantasy is given free rein. Play heals children in real life, and not just in psychotherapy. We see in Henri's story an initial inhibition of play, and then the resumption. Clearly the capacity for play existed before the trauma and was not destroyed.

6. Henri was musically gifted—another aspect of his creativity. For artistically talented and creative people, engaging in their art is a powerful means of expressing and working through trauma. Additionally, although I don't know what Henri's musical ear added, I would speculate that playing or singing music requires the ability to hear oneself—to have simultaneously an observing and an experiencing ego, which relates to the capacity for reflection. Often the capacity for reflection is destroyed by trauma, and the initial therapeutic work involves developing the capacity for mentalization and reflection (Coates, 1998; Fonagy & Target, 1998). Reflection is necessary for the formation of an evolving personal narrative. Additionally, music is organized and evolving over time. It is a nonverbal equivalent of a narrative. Clearly not all resilient people are musical, but for Henri this ability may have played a role.

7. Henri's mother developed a realistic escape plan and arranged for his transport to America. This was a woman who herself was resilient, a creative problem solver, who had the hope and optimism to plan ahead for her son, beyond her own being. She trusted her son's competence, assumed there were solutions and hope, trusted that a future was possible, and conveyed that to him. She also saw the reality—that if her son stayed he most likely would die. She did not deny or disavow the reality, or assume that the best route to survival was acceptance. She gave him the competence, confidence, sense of active agency, hope, and reality testing necessary to escape and survive. Henri would have internalized many of his mother's qualities and worldviews, enabling his continued resilience over time.

8. Mother and son were both able to handle overwhelming feelings without becoming paralyzed, passive, insane, or violent. In the escape the son did not succumb to terror. I am talking here of the ability to regulate affect—having an adaptive set of defenses (Yates et al., 2003). Of course then the terror and rage have to be dealt with later, but it is not helpful to experience the full emotional impact of a traumatic situation at the time of crisis.

9. Henri must have had physical resilience and good coordination and reflexes. Physical strength is not generally considered as part of resilience,

but in surviving certain kinds of trauma, like the Holocaust, physical strengths are necessary (but not sufficient).

10. Henri had social skills. For example, he played with other kids, and knew that to escape attention he needed not to look anyone in the face. These skills are separate from the capacity to love and likability. They consist of the ability to read other people. If one is going to survive in a hostile environment, the capacity to quickly understand the motivations and emotions of others, and what is expected socially, is immensely helpful.

11. Many other people helped, protected, loved, and nurtured Henri. There must have been something about him that got others to do this—perhaps an essential likability. Also Henri had the capacity to take in, to be helped. I imagine Henri identified with aspects of all those people. This would help mitigate the soul-murdering aspects of trauma. He would want to help, nurture, and protect others. His initial resilience was bolstered by these relationships and the resultant identifications and internalizations over the course of his development.

12. He had the ability to feel gratitude. Gratitude is different for a child and an adult. It has its own developmental line. Gratitude, when appropriate and deserved, is an important and potentially healing part of the personal narrative for adults—maybe not at the beginning or middle stages of analysis, but at some point. For some people, of course, no one helped, and gratitude exists only as potential capacity. Malignant shame and envy from trauma can destroy the capacity for gratitude, and are part of the soul-murdering aspects of trauma.

13. Henri describes a helping community in many different places. This community provided the physical and emotional resources necessary for his survival and development. Feeling oneself to be a part of a community, however that is defined, is necessary for most of us. For those whose families are murdered or destroyed, the presence of a helping community is life saving. Although it cannot replace family, it can serve many of the functions of family, and provides a sense of not being alone in the world.

14. The trauma was inflicted by others, and not by primary objects of attachment within the family. He was not faced with the unsolvable dilemma of being abused and terrified by someone who was also his "primary haven(s) of safety" (Hesse & Main, 2000). Henri's base of a loving mother, an extended family, and a nurturing community were not destroyed from within. A helpful split based in reality preserves the good mother and all her derivatives.

# Conclusions

Overall, Henri's sources of resilience parallel the literature on resilience (Luthar & Zelazo, 2003; Masten & Powell, 2003). He had a loving and resourceful family and community. He was intelligent, was an excellent problem solver, had good social skills, was likable, and had the capacity for play, reflection, and compassion. He and his mother were able to regulate affect in an adaptive manner (Yates et al., 2003), and had an active sense of agency. The trauma was not inflicted by a member of his community.

These factors viewed separately would seem to be basic common sense. However, the actual process of resilience rests on how these factors dynamically intertwine and reinforce one another within each unique individual, family, and community. To put it simply, the whole is greater than the sum of the parts.

As Henri points out, resilience is an ongoing developmental process, lasting throughout the lifetime. As an adult, Henri became a physician, a psychiatrist, a child psychiatrist, a psychoanalyst—a "healer of children, from their emotional pain." He contributed significantly to the understanding of aggression, violence, prejudice, and genocide. He worked with parents toward preventing emotional problems in their children. Prevention has been a central and consistent endeavor for Henri. These activities arose from the specifics of his trauma, without directly repeating it. Rather, the trauma was reworked while simultaneously providing healing. This is sublimation—a resilient use of defense. It is what Henri calls "the sublime defenses." True resilience involves the ability to use past adversity to find meaning for oneself and be of some sort of benefit to others. Work and relationships that are meaningful and beneficial to others then cycle back and add to strength and healing.

In one sense, resilience is a blessing and a privilege. But just like the quality of sensitivity, it is double edged, as it almost inevitably leads to guilt. Henri survived and his mother did not. Both were resilient, but the survivor is left with the quandary that Henri describes: wanting to rescue and wanting to atone—for the indecency of happiness.

Henri says that it is "taking [him] the rest of [his] life in America to bring some closure." This bespeaks an underlying truth; significant trauma is never totally healed, no matter how resilient the individual. The pain, suffering, and scars may be eased enough that the person can love, work, and play. However, the process of healing, like resilience, is lifelong. Throughout life, trauma rises up and affects the individual in different ways at different times, particularly during developmental nodes. I think Henri's telling and writing about his story are key aspects of this process. Henri now shares his story with many others, including his colleagues, who themselves participate in this work of therapy and healing that has been so meaningful to him and to others. He has put it together into a coherent and probably ever evolving narrative, from which others can learn and he can continue to heal.

# References

Coates, S. W. (1998). Having a mind of one's own and holding the other in mind: Commentary on paper by Peter Fonagy and Mary Target. *Psychoanalytic Dialogues, 8*, 115–148.

Fonagy, P., & Target, M. (1998). Mentalization and the changing aims of child psychoanalysis. *Psychoanalytic Dialogues, 8*, 87–114.

Hauser, S., Golden, E., & Allen, J. (2006). Narrative in the study of resilience. *Psychoanalytic Study of the Child, 61*, 205–227.

Hesse, E., & Main, M. (2000). Disorganized infant, child, and adult attachment. *Journal of the American Psychoanalytic Association, 48*, 1097–1127.

Leffert, M. (2007). A contemporary integration of modern and postmodern trends in psychoanalysis. *Journal of the American Psychoanalytic Association, 55*, 177–197.

Luthar, S., & Zelazo, L. (2003). Research on resilience: An integrative review. In S. Luthar (Ed.), *Resilience and vulnerability* (pp. 510–549). New York: Cambridge University Press.

Masten, A., & Powell, J. (2003). A resilience framework for research, policy, and practice. In S. Luthar (Ed.), *Resilience and vulnerability* (pp. 1–25). New York: Cambridge University Press.

Ogden, T. H. (1994). The analytic third: Working with intersubjective clinical facts. *International Journal of Psychoanalysis, 75*, 3–19.

Shengold, L. (1989). *Soul murder: The effect of childhood abuse and deprivation.* New Haven, CT: Yale University Press.

Yates, T., Egeland, B., & Sroufe, A. (2003). Rethinking resilience. In S. Luthar (Ed.), *Resilience and vulnerability* (pp. 243–266). New York: Cambridge University Press.

# 8

# PSYCHOLOGICAL AND BIOLOGICAL FACTORS ASSOCIATED WITH RESILIENCE TO STRESS AND TRAUMA

*Steven M. Southwick, MD,*

*Fatih Ozbay, MD,*

*and Linda C. Mayes, MD*

Resilience: In psychology, the term resilience refers to the capacity to positively cope with stress and adversity. The American Psychological Association defines resilience as "the process of adapting well in the face of adversity, trauma, tragedy, threats or even significant sources of stress—such as family and relationship problems, serious health problems or workplace and financial stressors. It means bouncing back from difficult experiences" (American Psychological Association, n.d.). Ann Masten in her research with children has found that those who are resilient "have a good outcome in spite of serious threats to adaptation and development" and that resilience is the rule rather than the exception (Masten & Coatsworth, 1998). That is, most children are surprisingly resilient and possess what Masten has called "ordinary magic" (Masten, 2001).

Most researchers consider resilience to be multidimensional in nature. Thus, people who are faced with adversity can exhibit competence in some psychosocial domains, but not in others. For example, Kaufman, Plotsky, Nemeroff, and Charney (2000) found that two thirds of maltreated children were resilient in the academic domain but only 21% were socially competent. Similarly, traumatized adults may demonstrate resilience in areas such as work but falter in other areas, such as family relationships. Domains that have been identified as essential for optimal functioning include educational resilience, emotional resilience, behavioral resilience, and relationship resilience. Typically, at-risk or traumatized individuals display an unevenness of functioning across domains. As noted by Masten (2001), it is unrealistic to expect that anyone, no matter how resilient, will consistently perform at a uniformly high or low level across all areas of his or her life. Thus, some researchers define resilience as excellence in one salient domain with at least average adjustment in other adjustment domains. However, other researchers require that a resilient individual excel in multiple psychosocial domains.

Resilience is also dynamic rather than static. Resilience trajectories may be uneven and vary across domains, with some people demonstrating resilience at one age but not another, or in one circumstance but not another. While some children may flourish and adapt well to stress in early childhood, they may be far less resilient in adolescence when faced with a new set of challenges.

In this chapter, we briefly review a number of psychodynamic, neurobiological, genetic, developmental, and learning processes that have been associated with resilience to stress. We also focus on the association between resilience and role models, mentors, and social support. As such, our review is limited and does not adequately reflect the enormous complexities involved in the construct of resilience and positive adaptations to stress.

## Psychodynamic Mechanisms

For as much as psychoanalysis as a field has focused on the outcome of trauma and stress, psychodynamic writers and theoreticians have been less explicit regarding resilience. However, more contemporary perspectives that integrate theories of attachment into psychoanalytic models of object relations have far more to say about the role of internalized objects or internal working models as buffering stress and adversity as well as the ups and downs of everyday life (Fonagy, 2001; Fonagy, Gergely, Jurist, & Target, 2002). Attachment perspectives are essentially models of stress or emotion regulation (Cassidy & Shaver, 1999)—how children and adults use important other persons in their lives to downregulate negative emotions and upregulate positive or rewarding states of being. In this way, contemporary psychodynamic approaches are easily integrated into neurobiological models of the balance between stress regulation and reward systems that are so key to, for example, models of drug use and addiction (Brady & Sinha, 2005).

The key features of the psychodynamic model of attachment relevant to resilience are how early caregiving enhances or does not enhance secure attachment in infants and young children, how these early experiences of being cared for shape templates of what one might expect generally from relationships with others, and how relationships with others provide or do not provide safety and security. These early templates may be thought of as internal working models in the language of attachment theory or internalized object representations in the language of more traditional psychoanalytic theory. Secure attachment or secure models of attachment emerge from early relationships that are appropriately contingent on a child's needs and buffer the child from overwhelming stress but also give the child sufficient challenge and opportunities to solve problems or regulate his or her own feelings so that he or she begins to develop a sense of autonomy, separateness, and individuality. Too-perfect contingency or too much protection is just as distorting of internalization processes as too little or neglectful care with frequent exposure to stress and chaos, though the templates of internalization will be different in each of these cases. From these internalized models or internalized object representations, children have a perspective on the world of others as trustworthy, responsive, caring, helpful; as frightening, abandoning, unsafe; or as unpredictable, uncaring, and not reliable under extreme need or stress.

From the perspective of psychodynamic attachment theory, these templates come into play especially in times of stress. In other words, we call on important others in our minds when we are distressed and frightened, and if our internalized others are secure, we are also able to use real persons in the external world for comfort and companionship during stress. So in one way, resilience from a psychodynamic point of view is based largely on the security or complexity of one's internalized object world. This notion ties into ideas of "good enough parenting" and "stress inoculation"—as each of these is relevant to how parents provide sufficient protection and emotional buffering that changes with the developmental needs of the child. Another psychoanalytic concept relevant to this is the "stimulus barrier," or how the child's capacity to tolerate negative experiences from both internal and external sources changes over time. The source of that change is not only maturation but how parents buffer the environment just enough so that the child is not overwhelmed but at the same time has the experience of mastery that in turn contributes to a sense of individuality and emerging self.

There are other psychodynamic concepts that are also relevant to resilience, each of which may in many ways be linked to internalization or attachment processes. These include capacities such as flexibility, imagination, curiosity, and the ability to be alone. Each of these might be considered aspects of ego functioning—and thus relevant to psychoanalytic models of ego psychology in which mature or resilient coping is related to a range of ego strengths—or the ability to maintain an intact sense of self in the face of nearly overwhelming internal or external affects. From the point of view of object relations, these key ego strengths are shaped in the course of early caregiving. Secure children are more curious, more flexible, and more imaginative and have a greater access to their internal fantasy world compared to insecure children—and there are strong empirical data now to support this association (Sroufe, 2005; Sroufe, Egeland, Carlson, & Collins, 2005). At the same time, endowment also contributes to the emerging of these ego strengths—and there is a back-and-forth relationship between a child's capacity to respond adaptively and a parent's ability to understand his or her child and respond appropriately.

Defenses are also relevant to psychoanalytic models of resilience inasmuch as the range and choice of defenses leave an individual more or less open to both relationships and the world around him or her. It may well be that the resilient individual relies on a range of defenses that protect him or her at the most overwhelming moments but do not completely shut out or shut down memory and processing so that after the crisis, the resilient person may return to the stress and more effectively process and metabolize the experience.

## Neurobiological Mechanisms

Physiological and behavioral responses to threatening events are associated with processes in specific neural circuits. Traumatic stress alters the chemistry of the brain and may lead to structural changes as well. The emotional and cognitive consequences of these changes may include anxiety, memory impairment, and increased sensitivity to alcohol and drugs. In general, stress-related changes in the brain limbic system (hippocampus, amygdala, and hypothalamus) and in the prefrontal cortex are implicated in stress reactions (Charney, 2004). The hippocampus is a brain structure that is responsible for registering memories, whereas the amygdala plays an important role in regulating fear and aggression by sending signals that activate autonomic and hormonal responses to stress. These signals are associated with behavioral responses to stress, including "freezing" in response to danger (LeDoux, 1996). The hippocampus and the amygdala work in tandem to store fearful memories. The prefrontal cortex acts as a key region for attenuating both autonomic and neuroendocrine responses to stress. Prefrontal cortex supports "executive functions" such as decision making and the shifting of attention to newly relevant stimuli that predict reward or punishment (Damasio, 1997). Repeated exposure to unavoidable stress may lead to "learned helplessness," which is a learned sense of futility. Lesions of the rat medial prefrontal cortex cause serotonin hyperactivity and enhance learned helplessness (Amat et al., 2005), implicating a role for the prefrontal cortex in mediating sense of control, which may be a critical feature of resilience to stress.

## Autonomic Nervous System Responses to Stress

The autonomic nervous system (ANS) is responsible for regulating involuntary functions such as heart rate, blood pressure, and digestion. When activated by stress, the sympathetic nervous system (SNS) increases heart rate and blood pressure. Some people are prone to demonstrating an unusually strong SNS response to stress. Dienstbier (1991) has suggested that performance is best during optimal SNS activation: relatively low baseline levels of epinephrine with robust increases in epinephrine and norepinephrine (NE) in response to challenges, followed by relatively rapid return to baseline levels. Neuropeptide Y (NPY), an amino acid that is coreleased with norepinephrine when the SNS is strongly activated, is thought to play an important role in maintaining SNS activity within an optimal activation range (reviewed by Southwick et al., 1999). Morgan et al. (2000, 2002) demonstrated that high levels of NPY are associated with better performance in highly resilient special operations soldiers (Special Forces) undergoing extremely stressful training procedures. In comparison, combat veterans diagnosed with PTSD have reduced levels of NPY (Rasmusson et al., 2000). Galanin is another peptide that is involved in neuroendocrine control, cardiovascular regulation, and anxiety and may also be associated with resilience to stress. Like NPY, galanin is coreleased with NE when SNS activity is high. In rats, central administration of galanin reduces the neuronal activity at the locus coeruleus, and when injected into the amygdala, it blocks the anxiogenic effects of stress (Bing, Moller, Engel, Soderpalm, & Heilig, 1993; Moeller, Sommer, Thorsell, & Heilig, 1999). The balance between NE, NPY, and galanin may determine the overall net effects of SNS hyperactivity, supporting the notion that the regulation of noradrenergic activity within an optimal window may be a neurobiological characteristic of resilience to stress (Yehuda, Brand, Golier, & Yang, 2006).

## Hypothalamic-Pituitary-Adrenal (HPA) Axis Responses to Stress

The hypothalamus secretes corticotropin-releasing factor (CRF) in response to acute and chronic stress. The stimulation of CRH-1 (corticotropin-releasing hormone–1) receptors may cause anxiety-like responses. In contrast, the activation of CRH-2 receptors has anxiolytic effects (Bale et al., 2000, 2002). The optimal regulation of these two different types of CRH receptors appears to moderate behavioral and neurobiological responses to stress and may facilitate psychobiological resilience to stress-induced disorders such as PTSD and depression. CRH stimulates the anterior pituitary gland to synthesize and release adrenocorticotropin hormone (ACTH), which in turn leads to release of adrenal cortisol and dehydroepiandrosterone (DHEA). Cortisol mobilizes and replenishes energy stores, contains the immune response, and affects behavior through actions on multiple neurotransmitter systems and brain regions (Yehuda, 2002). However, if stress remains chronic, prolonged elevations of cortisol may cause hippocampal damage as evidenced by reductions in dendritic branching, a loss of dendritic spines, and a reduction in the growth of new granule cell neurons in the dentate gyrus (Sapolsky, 2003). Damage to the hippocampus may weaken its ability to reduce HPA activation, resulting in even greater glucocorticoid levels, and a vicious cycle may ensue. In contrast to cortisol, DHEA exerts anti-glucocorticoid and anti-glutamatergic activity in the brain and may confer neuroprotection (reviewed in Charney, 2004). The administration of DHEA has antidepressant effects in patients diagnosed with major depression (Wolkowitz et al., 1999). Numerous studies indicate that DHEA may play an important role in stress resilience. For example, Morgan et al. found a negative relationship between DHEA/cortisol ratio and dissociation and a positive correlation between DHEA/cortisol ratio and performance among elite Special Forces soldiers during intensive survival training (Morgan et al., 2004). Lower DHEA levels have been shown to be associated with more severe PTSD symptoms in women with PTSD (Rasmusson et al., 2004). Similarly, allopregnanolone, another neuroactive steroid, exerts negative feedback inhibition to the HPA-axis. Rasmusson et al. (2006) have demonstrated lower cerebrospinal fluid levels of allopregnanolone in those diagnosed with PTSD compared to controls. In conclusion, DHEA and allopregnanolone may confer resilience to stress by helping to terminate HPA-activation (Yehuda et al., 2006).

## Genetic Mechanisms

Heritability refers to the proportion of variation in a trait that is directly explained by genetic factors. Numerous heritable factors, such as those linked to variability in personality traits, trauma exposure history, and psychophysiological reactivity, affect an individual's response to stress and trauma. Several twin studies focusing on Vietnam War veterans have shown that genetic factors play a significant role in PTSD. True et al. (1993) found that heritability accounts for 32% of the variance in liability for PTSD. Stein, Jang, Taylor, Vernon, and Livesley (2002) replicated this finding in a smaller civilian sample by demonstrating that the overall heritability estimate of PTSD was 38%. These findings support the notion that some individuals are less prone to develop trauma-related psychopathology due to their genetic makeup.

Although relatively little is known about the molecular genetic basis of stress resilience, a number of genes associated with the SNS and HPA-axis recently have been implicated in positive coping responses to stress. For example, alpha-2 adrenoreceptor gene polymorphisms (i.e., variations in the gene) appear to play a role in baseline catecholamine levels, intensity of stress-induced SNS activation, and the rate of catecholamine return to baseline after stress. Among healthy subjects, Neumeister et al. (2002) found exaggerated total body noradrenergic spillover at baseline, exaggerated yohimbine-induced increases in anxiety and total body noradrenergic spillover, and a slower-than-normal return of total body noradrenergic spillover to baseline after yohimbine infusion among homozygous carriers for the alpha-2cDel322-325-AR polymorphism. These individuals may be more vulnerable to stress and possibly more likely to develop psychopathology, such as PTSD or depression, in response to trauma.

Gene environment interactions are of critical importance in understanding responses to stress and trauma. Recently the link between genetic factors and environmental factors has been clearly demonstrated in a study by Caspi et al. (2003), who found that the risk for developing depression in response to trauma is increased by having one or two copies of the short allele of the serotonin transporter promoter gene polymorphism. In the absence of exposure to traumatic stress, rates of depression did not differ between subjects with and without the short allele. Additionally, increased amygdala neuronal activity in response to fear-inducing stimuli has been reported in healthy subjects with the serotonin transporter polymorphism that is associated with reduced 5-HT expression and increased fear and anxiety (Hariri et al., 2002). On the other hand, in the Caspi et al. (2003) study, subjects with the long allele of the serotonin transporter promoter gene polymorphism had a lower risk for developing depression in association with highly stressful life events. Similarly, the long allele has been associated with decreased vulnerability to social stressors in women (Grabe et al., 2005). The long allele of the serotonin transporter promoter gene polymorphism is the first genetic variation that has been identified as a potential resilience factor.

While environmental factors, such as stress and trauma, can interact with genetic variations to increase risk for negative coping responses and possible stress-related psychopathology, environmental factors can also protect the individual from the negative consequences of stress, even in individuals with genetic risk factors. In a study of severely maltreated children, Kaufman et al. (2006) found that positive social support appeared to protect against depression in maltreated children, even in vulnerable children with the short allele of the serotonin transporter promoter gene. The results suggested that the negative sequelae associated with early life stress are not inevitable and that risk for negative outcomes can be modified by genetic and environmental factors.

## Developmental Mechanisms

Studies on development have consistently shown that early stressful experiences can have long-term effects on neurobiological, emotional, and behavioral responses to future stressors (Kaufman et al., 2000). Developing animals that are forced to confront overwhelming and uncontrollable stressors that they cannot master tend to display an exaggerated or sensitized sympathetic nervous system and/or hypothalamic-pituitary-adrenal response to stress as adults. In contrast, developing animals exposed to mild to moderate stressors that are under their control and that they can master tend to become stress inoculated with a reduced overall response to future stressors (reviewed in Kaufman et al., 2000).

When a neurobiological system becomes sensitized, its biochemical (and related physiological and behavioral) activity increases over time in response to a given level of stress (reviewed in Southwick et al., 1999). For example, separating rat pups or infant monkeys from their mother for substantial periods of time can result in long-term increases in CRH and NE drive (central components of the stress response), reduced central benzodiazepine binding (important for reducing and containing the stress response), altered neuronal development (reduced fiber densities) in some areas of the brain, increases in anxiety-like behaviors, impaired cognitive performance, and decreases in social interaction (reviewed in Kaufman et al., 2000). These animals develop stress-sensitized neurobiological systems that hyper-respond to future stressors with exaggerated behavioral, physiological, and biochemical responsiveness to subsequent stressors (reviewed in Kaufman et al., 2000).

In some cases the capacity to respond more readily to future stressors may be adaptive for survival because the organism is better prepared for future dangers. However, stress sensitization may also be maladaptive, leaving the organism in a hyperreactive state where it becomes hypervigilant, continues to act biologically and cognitively as if a danger still exists even when no real danger is currently present, and overresponds to relatively minor stressors (Southwick et al., 1999). It has been hypothesized that exaggerated emotional reactivity during childhood increases vulnerability to the later development of stress-related disorders such as depression and PTSD (Kaufman et al., 2000).

In contrast, preclinical research suggests that early exposure to mild to moderate stress that can be controlled may actually enhance the capacity to cope with stress in the future (reviewed by Dienstbier, 1989). Controlled exposure to stress as a means to enhance future resilience is known as *stress inoculation*. In studies of squirrel monkeys, Parker, Buckmaster, Schatzberg, and Lyons (2004) found that stress inoculation via brief intermittent maternal separation during postnatal weeks 17–27 led to diminished anxiety responses on subsequent exposure to a novel environment. Stress-inoculated monkeys were also found to have lower basal plasma ACTH and cortisol levels and lower stress-induced cortisol levels. At 18 months of age, these same monkeys were administered a response inhibition test and were found to have superior prefrontal cortex function as compared to non-stress-inoculated monkeys (Parker, Buckmaster, Justus, Schatzberg, & Lyons, 2005). These results suggest that early, mild, and controlled stress may alter key neurobiological systems and thus serve to reduce reactivity to future stressors.

Rodents reared in a nurturing environment have also been found to demonstrate enhanced tolerance to stress in adulthood. Rat pups that receive 15 minutes of handling per day during the first three weeks of life are less reactive to stress and less fearful in novel environments as adults compared to rat pups that are not handled (Ladd, Thrivikraman, Huot, & Plotsky, 2005). They also have reduced ACTH and corticosterone responses to stress and demonstrate a more rapid return of corticosterone levels to baseline after exposure to stress. It appears that early environments may influence and shape the development of stress-related neurobiological systems with early deprivation and uncontrollable stress promoting future exaggerated neurobiological stress reactivity (stress sensitization) and early nurturing or mild to moderate stress having a positive effect on future stress reactivity (stress inoculation). Of note, animal "adoption" studies have shown that even after stress-induced neurobiological and behavioral alterations have occurred, it may be possible to modify these alterations by subsequent supportive maternal caregiving and/or pharmacological interventions (Caldji et al., 1998; Kuhn & Schanberg, 1998).

Far less is known about the effects of early environment on later neurobiological stress reactivity in humans. In one study, pediatric inpatients with previous positive separation experiences (i.e., staying with grandparents for short periods of time) experienced less stress during their hospital stay (Stacey, 1970). Childhood exposure to mild stress has also been associated with reduced heart rate and blood pressure responses to distressing laboratory tests in adolescents (Boyce & Chesterman, 1990). Further, Norris and colleagues have reported better psychiatric outcomes among adult natural disaster and torture survivors who had experienced similarly traumatic events earlier in their lives (Basoglu et al., 1997; Knight, Gatz, Heller, & Bengtson, 2000; Norris & Murrell, 1988).

The notion that manageable and controlled doses of stress can have "steeling" or stress-inoculating effects has been incorporated into a number of clinical therapeutic approaches for the treatment and/or prevention of trauma. Using a stress-inoculation-based intervention, Wells, Howard, Nowlin, and Vargas (1986) demonstrated that preoperative stress inoculation was associated with less postoperative pain and anxiety. Similarly, stress-inoculation training has been shown to be an effective treatment for chronically stressed community residents (Long, 1985). The neurobiological basis for stress-inoculation effects in human subjects is not yet well understood.

## Learning Through Imitation

Mature role models and mentors are critical for the development of resilience. At every stage of life, humans learn through observation and imitation of others. This is particularly true during childhood and adolescence, when the nervous system is changing rapidly and when styles of thinking and acting are becoming consolidated and habitual. In his *Social Learning Theory*, Albert Bandura (1977) described how attitudes, values, skills, and patterns of thought and behavior are transmitted from one person to the next through imitation and modeling. According to Bandura, with support from a host of behavioral research, observational learning involves more than simple mimicry. Instead, through observation and imitation, the learner acquires conceptions and rules of behavior that later serve as guides for action. By forming rules, the learner can develop values, thoughts, and behaviors that resemble those of his or her role model but that can be adapted to the particular circumstances of the learner.

In general, learning by imitating role models and mentors requires repetition. When cells in the brain are actively used, they transmit their messages more efficiently and form new connections with other cells. In response to repetitive activation, synaptic transmission is increased, new branches and connections are formed, and the cortical areas that are stimulated have been shown to increase in size and shape. For example, when adult squirrel monkeys repetitively use one, but not both, of their hands to perform tasks that require dexterity and fine motor skills, the area of the brain responsible for movement of the active hand increases in size (Nudo, Milliken, Jenkins, & Merzenich, 1996). Similarly, violinists have been found to have greater cortical brain space devoted to fingers of the left hand compared to fingers of the right hand, presumably because fingers of the left hand are constantly engaged in precise movements across the strings of the violin while fingers of the right hand hold the bow, which requires far fewer precise movements. The differences in cortical space devoted to movement of left versus right fingers is greatest among violin players who began to play before the age of 12, when the brain is especially plastic (Elbert, Pantev, Weinbruch, Rockstroh, & Taub, 1995).

Recently, it has been suggested that learning through imitation may, in part, be related to mirror neurons (Gallese & Goldman, 1998; Rizzolatti et al., 1996). Mirror neurons are located in areas of the brain that process perception, emotions, language, and movement. When one person observes the behavior of another, mirror neurons fire in the same brain regions that are activated by the behaviors of the person being observed. In other words, during the process of observation, mirror neurons in the observer fire in the same brain regions as neurons that have been activated in the observed (Gallese & Goldman, 1998). It is possible that mirror neurons play a role in empathy, helping the observer understand the meaning behind observed behaviors.

In addition to the critical mentoring role played by parents, nonparental role models can also contribute to hardiness and resilience in children. Like parents, nonparental role models may play formative roles in development by providing dependable support, fostering self-esteem, demonstrating moral values, inspiring hard work, teaching skills, and passing on useful knowledge. Natural mentors, such as nonparental kin, neighbors, teachers, and coaches who are part of the mentored youth's natural social network, tend to be especially effective (Hirsch, Mickus, & Boerger, 2002). For example, adolescents with natural mentors have been found to have more positive attitudes toward school, a stronger belief in the importance of succeeding in school, better grades, less delinquency, lower rates of depression, and less marijuana use compared to those without natural mentors (Rhodes, Ebert, & Fischer, 1992; Rhodes, Grossman, & Roffman, 2002).

Although nonparental adult mentors who are not part of a mentee's natural social network, such as volunteers, tend to be less effective role models than parents and natural mentors, they nevertheless can facilitate the development of resilience. However, frequent contact over a long period of time appears to be important for success. In fact, a study of Big Brothers Big Sisters found that success was dependent on duration of mentoring and that mentees who met with their mentors for at least one year were less likely to skip a day of school and less likely to begin drinking alcohol or using illegal drugs than youth not enrolled in a mentor program. Some evidence suggests that volunteer mentoring that is infrequent and/or of brief duration may actually have a negative impact (Tierney, Grossman, & Resch, 1995).

## Social Support

The National Cancer Institute defines social support as "a network of family, friends, neighbors, and community members that is available in times of need to give psychological, physical, and financial help" (National Cancer Institute, n.d.). Social support is a complex construct that includes at least two important dimensions: first, a structural dimension characterized by network size and frequency of social interactions; and, second, a functional dimension that includes both emotional (such as receiving love and empathy) and instrumental (practical help such as gifts of money or assistance with child care) components (Charney, 2004). While both dimensions are important, most research has found the functional dimension (quality of relationships) to be a stronger predictor of good health than the structural dimension (quantity of relationships) (Southwick, Vythilingam, & Charney, 2005).

In general, poor social support appears to increase vulnerability to stress while positive social support of high quality seems to enhance resilience to stress. The effects of social support are far-reaching, extending to both physical and mental health. In fact, the effect of social support on life expectancy appears to be as strong as the effects of obesity, cigarette smoking, hypertension, or level of physical activity (Sapolsky, 2004). For example, increased morbidity and mortality in a host of medical illnesses has been associated with low levels of social support and social isolation. In the well-known Alameda County Studies, men and women without ties to others were 1.9 to 3 times more likely to die from ischemic heart disease, cerebral vascular disease, cancer, or a host of other diseases within a nine-year period compared to individuals with many more social contacts (Berkman, 1995).

Poor social support has also been associated with depression, anxiety, and post-traumatic stress disorder. In a study of 2,490 Vietnam veterans, Boscarino (1995), after controlling for level of combat exposure, found that veterans with low social support had approximately 180% greater risk for PTSD than veterans with high social support.

On the other hand, strong social support appears to have protective and buffering effects on mental and physical illness. Strong social support has been associated with decreased functional impairment in patients with depression (Travis, Lyness, Shields, King, & Cox, 2004), increased likelihood of recovery from depression (Sayal et al., 2002), and reduced risk of developing combat-related post-traumatic stress disorder. Compared to Vietnam veterans with low levels of social support, those with high support have been shown to be 180% less likely to develop PTSD (Boscarino, 1995). Similarly, among survivors of a cruise ship disaster (Joseph, Yule, Williams, & Hodgkinson, 1993; Resick, 2001), supper club fire (Green, Grace, & Gleser, 1985; Resick, 2001), and childhood sexual abuse (Conte & Schuerman, 1987), those with stronger social support have been reported as having better psychological outcomes. The relationship between strong social support and superior mental and physical health has been observed in diverse populations, including college students, new mothers, widows, unemployed workers, and parents of children with serious medical illnesses (Resick, 2001).

There are numerous possible explanations for the association between high social support, resilience, and positive mental and physical health. For example, it has been suggested that strong social networks and emotional support may foster effective coping strategies (Holahan, Holahan, Moos, & Moos, 1995), decrease involvement in high-risk behaviors (e.g., smoking, excess alcohol and fatty food intake) (Rozanski, Blumenthal, & Kaplan, 1999), reduce feelings of loneliness (Bisschop, Kriegsman, Beekman, & Deeg, 2004), increase sense of self-efficacy (Hays, Steffens, Flint, Bosworth, & George, 2001; Travis et al., 2004), and reduce exaggerated appraisals of threat (Fontana, Kerns, Rosenberg, & Colonese, 1989; Holahan et al., 1995). It is also possible that high social support may foster resilience and buffer against illness and illness progression through neurobiological actions.

Neural mechanisms underlying the processing of social information and regulation of social behavior (including social recognition, nurturing behavior, and the development of specific social preferences) are complex, involving multiple brain regions, numerous biological pathways, neurotransmitter systems, and neuropeptides. Two neuropeptides that have received considerable attention as they relate to social behavior are oxytocin and vasopressin. Oxytocin is known to play a role in maternal care (Insel & Young, 2001), regulation of social attachment, promotion of positive social interactions, and adult bonding (Heinrichs, Baumgartner, Kirschbaum, & Ehlert, 2003).

Oxytocin also appears to modulate the physiological and behavioral effects of stress. Oxytocin, which is released in response to fear and stress, has been shown to attenuate secretion of ACTH, corticosterone, and catecholamines in lactating rats (Heinrichs et al., 2003) and to reduce anxiety and stress-related behaviors in rodents (Carter & Altemus, 1997; Heinrichs et al., 2003). Similarly, reduced plasma ACTH, cortisol, and glucose responses to physical and psychosocial stress has been reported in postpartum lactating women compared to nonlactating women (Altemus, Deuster, Galliven, Carter, & Gold, 1995; Heinrichs et al., 2003). Additionally, healthy men who received oxytocin before being exposed to the Trier Social Stress Test experienced an increase in calmness during the test procedure while subjects who did not receive oxytocin experienced a decrease in calmness and an increase in anxiety (Heinrichs et al., 2003). It is possible that fear and stress-induced increases in oxytocin enhance social affiliation and that social support reduces arousal and negative appraisals of threat, and dampens stress hormone responses.

It should be noted that the optimal source of social support may depend on the developmental stage of the person who is receiving the support. For example, parental support seems to be more valuable in early adolescence than it is in late adolescence (Stice, Ragan, & Randall, 2004). Moreover, the type of social support seems to be important in conferring resilience to stress. In a sample of childhood sexual abuse survivors, a combination of self-esteem support (the individual perceives that he or she is valued by others) and appraisal support (the individual perceives that he or she is capable of getting advice when coping with difficulties) was most useful in preventing the development of PTSD (Hyman, Gold, & Cott, 2003).

## Conclusion

In this chapter we have briefly discussed some of the factors that are associated with resilience to stress. We particularly focused on the role of parents, mentors, attachment, development, and social support. Early secure models of attachment that depend on meeting the basic needs of the child and protecting the child from overwhelming stress but at the same time encourage the child to be independent, to solve problems, to deal with failure, and to regulate emotions appear to be critical for the development of resilience to stress in childhood, adolescence, and adulthood.

For the developing child, good enough parents and mentors enhance resilience by serving as "external regulators" whose ego capacities and strengths, including the ability to self-soothe, regulate emotions, control impulses, and delay gratification, may be "borrowed" until the child can gradually internalize them. By imitating and internalizing capacities and qualities of resilient parents and mentors, children and adolescents learn about courage, active coping, flexibility, and how to handle challenging situations. They also learn to imitate attitudes, beliefs, and behaviors known to be associated with resilience, including realistic optimism, the ability to face fear, self-discipline, perseverance, moral and ethical integrity, and the importance of taking responsibility for one's attitudes and actions. When development proceeds favorably, with time the individual acquires the ability to maintain an intact sense of self in the face of severe stress.

The good enough parent or mentor cares about and knows the child or mentee well enough to appreciate and understand the upper and lower limits of optimal stress exposure for that particular child or mentee. They understand that too little stress leads to weakening and atrophy, while too much stress (i.e., stress that is unmanageable or that cannot be mastered) can lead to emotional and physical breakdown. Stress that is optimal for growth, strengthening, and resilience tends to be stress that is out of the child or mentee's comfort zone but not overwhelming or unmanageable. Many parents and mentors have difficulty watching their child or mentee struggle with stress that is out of their comfort zone. To quiet their own discomfort, parents and mentors often "rescue" the child or mentee from stress that is uncomfortable but manageable. By doing so, they limit the child or mentee's opportunity to grow stronger and more resilient.

The capacity to handle life's challenges and hopefully to grow from stress is at the heart of resilience. Genetic and neurobiological factors interact with developmental and environmental factors to determine how an individual will handle stress. The formal and rigorous study of resilience is relatively new. We believe that this complex construct will be best understood using multidisciplinary approaches to research. Psychoanalysts, cognitive behaviorists, neurobiologists, sociologists, historians, and others have much to contribute to this important and rapidly expanding area of research.

# References

Altemus, M., Deuster, P. A., Galliven, E., Carter, C. S., & Gold, P. W. (1995). Suppression of hypothalamic-pituitary-adrenal axis responses to stress in lactating women. *Journal of Clinical Endocrinology and Metabolism, 80*(10), 2954–2959.

Amat, J., Baratta, M. V., Paul, E., Bland, S. T., Watkins, L. R., & Maier, S. F. (2005). Medial prefrontal cortex determines how stressor controllability affects behavior and dorsal raphe nucleus. *Nature Neuroscience, 8*(3), 365–371.

American Psychological Association. (n.d.). *The road to resilience.* Retrieved from http://www.apahelpcenter.org.

Bale, T. L., Contarino, A., Smith, G. W., Chan, R., Gold, L. H., Sawchenko, P. E., et al. (2000). Mice deficient for corticotropin-releasing hormone receptor-2 display anxiety-like behaviour and are hypersensitive to stress. *Nature Genetics, 24*(4), 410–414.

Bale, T. L., Picetti, R., Contarino, A., Koob, G. F., Vale, W. W., & Lee, K. (2002). Mice deficient for both corticotropin-releasing factor receptor 1 (CRFR1) and CRFR2 have an impaired stress response and display sexually dichotomous anxiety like behavior. *Journal of Neuroscience, 22*(1), 193–199.

Bandura, A. (1977). *Social learning theory.* Englewood Cliffs, NJ: Prentice-Hall.

Basoglu, M., Mineka, S., Paker, M., Aker, T., Livanou, M., & Gok, S. (1997). Psychological preparedness for trauma as a protective factor in survivors of torture. *Psychological Medicine, 27*(6), 1421–1433.

Berkman, L. F. (1995). The role of social relations in health promotion. *Psychosomatic Medicine, 57,* 245–254.

Bing, O., Moller, C., Engel, J. A., Soderpalm, B., & Heilig, M. (1993). Anxiolytic-like action of centrally administered galanin. *Neuroscience Letters, 164*(1–2), 17–20.

Bisschop, M. I., Kriegsman, D. M. W., Beekman, A. T. F., & Deeg, D. J. H. (2004). Chronic diseases and depression: The modifying role of psychosocial resources. *Social Science & Medicine, 4*(59), 721–733.

Boscarino, J. A. (1995). Post-traumatic stress and associated disorders among Vietnam veterans: The significance of combat exposure and social support. *Journal of Traumatic Stress, 8,* 317–336.

Boyce, W. T., & Chesterman, E. (1990). Life events, social support, and cardiovascular reactivity in adolescence. *Journal of Developmental and Behavioral Pediatrics, 11*(3), 105–111.

Brady, K. T., & Sinha, R. (2005). Co-occurring mental and substance use disorders: The neurobiological effects of chronic stress. *American Journal of Psychiatry, 162,* 1483–1493.

Caldji, C., Tannenbaum, B., Sharma, S., Francis, D., Plotsky, P. M., & Meaney, M. J. (1998). Maternal care during infancy regulates the development of neural systems mediating the expression of fearfulness in the rat. *Proceedings of the National Academy of Sciences of the United States of America, 95*, 5335–5340.

Carter, C. S., & Altemus, M. (1997). Integrative functions of lactational hormones in social behavior and stress management. *Proceedings of the National Academy of Sciences of the United States of America, 807*, 164–174.

Caspi, A., Sugden, K., Moffitt, T. E., Taylor, A., Craig, I. W., Harrington, H., et al. (2003). Influence of life stress on depression: Moderation by a polymorphism in the 5-HTT gene. *Science, 301*, 386–389.

Cassidy, J., & Shaver, P. (1999). *Handbook of attachment: Theory, research, and clinical applications.* New York: Guilford Press.

Charney, D. S. (2004). Psychobiological mechanism of resilience and vulnerability: Implications for successful adaptation to extreme stress. *American Journal of Psychiatry, 161*(2), 195–216.

Conte, J. R., & Schuerman, J. R. (1987). Factors associated with an increased impact of child sexual abuse. *Child Abuse and Neglect, 11*(2), 201–211.

Damasio, A. R. (1997). Towards a neuropathology of emotion and mood. *Nature, 386*(6627), 769–770.

Dienstbier, R. A. (1989). Arousal and physiological toughness: Implications for mental and physical health. *Psychological Review, 96*(1), 84–100.

Dienstbier, R. A. (1991). Behavioral correlates of sympathoadrenal reactivity: The toughness model. *Medicine and Science in Sports and Exercise, 23*(7), 846–852.

Elbert, T., Pantev, C., Weinbruch, C., Rockstroh, B., & Taub, E. (1995). Increased use of the left hand in string players associated with increased representation of the fingers. *Science, 270*, 305–307.

Fonagy, P. (2001). *Attachment theory and psychoanalysis.* New York: Other Press.

Fonagy, P., Gergely, G., Jurist, E. L., & Target, M. (2002). *Affect regulation mentalization and the development of self.* New York: Other Press.

Fontana, A. F., Kerns, R. D., Rosenberg, R. L., & Colonese, K. L. (1989). Support, stress, and recovery from coronary heart disease: A longitudinal causal model. *Health Psychology, 8*, 175–193.

Gallese, V., & Goldman, A. (1998). Mirror neurons and the simulation theory of mindreading. *Trends in Cognitive Sciences, 2*, 493–501.

Grabe, H. J., Lange, M., Wolff, B., Volzke, H., Lucht, M., Freyberger, H. J., et al. (2005). Mental and physical distress is modulated by a polymorphism in the 5-HT transporter gene interacting with social stressors and chronic disease burden. *Molecular Psychiatry, 10*(2), 220–224.

Green, B. L., Grace, M. C., & Gleser, G. C. (1985). Identifying survivors at risk: Long-term impairment following the Beverly Hills Supper Club fire. *Journal of Consultation and Clinical Psychology, 53*(5), 672–678.

Hariri, A. R., Mattay, V. S., Tessitore, A., Kolachana, B., Fera, F., Goldman, D., et al. (2002). Serotonin transporter genetic variation and the response of the human amygdala. *Science, 297,* 400–403.

Hays, J. C., Steffens, D. C., Flint, E. P., Bosworth, H. B., & George, L. K. (2001). Does social support buffer functional decline in elderly patients with unipolar depression? *American Journal of Psychiatry, 158,* 1850–1855.

Heinrichs, M., Baumgartner, T., Kirschbaum, C., & Ehlert, U. (2003). Social support and oxytocin interact to suppress cortisol and subjective responses to psychosocial stress. *Biological Psychiatry, 54,* 1389–1398.

Hirsch, B. J., Mickus, M., & Boerger, R. (2002). Ties to influential adults among black and white adolescents: Culture, social class, and family networks. *American Journal of Community Psychology, 30,* 289–303.

Holahan, C. J., Holahan, C. K., Moos, R. H., & Moos, P. L. (1995). Social support, coping and depressive symptoms in a late-middle-aged sample of patients reporting cardiac illness. *Health Psychology, 14,* 152–163.

Hyman, S. M., Gold, S. N., & Cott, M. A. (2003). Forms of social support that moderate PTSD in childhood sexual abuse survivors. *Journal of Family Violence, 18,* 295–300.

Insel, T. R., & Young, L. J. (2001). The neurobiology of attachment. *Nature, 2,* 129–136.

Joseph, S., Yule, W., Williams, R., & Hodgkinson, P. (1993). Increased substance use in survivors of the Herald of Free Enterprise disaster. *British Journal of Medical Psychology, 66,* 185–191.

Kaufman, J., Plotsky, P. M., Nemeroff, C. B., & Charney, D. S. (2000). Effects of early adverse experiences on brain structure and function: Clinical implications. *Biological Psychiatry, 48*(8), 778–790.

Kaufman, J., Yang, B. Z., Douglas-Palumberi, H., Grasso, D., Lipschitz, D., Houshyar, S., et al. (2006). Brain-derived neurotrophic factor-5-HTTLPR gene interactions and environmental modifiers of depression in children. *Biological Psychiatry, 59*(8), 673–680.

Knight, B. G., Gatz, M., Heller, K., & Bengtson, V. L. (2000). Age and emotional response to the Northridge earthquake: A longitudinal analysis. *Psychology and Aging, 15*(4), 627–634.

Kuhn, C. M., & Schanberg, S. M. (1998). Responses to maternal separation: Mechanisms and mediators. *International Journal of Developmental Neuroscience, 16*(3–4), 261–270.

Ladd, C. O., Thrivikraman, K. V., Huot, R. L., & Plotsky, P. M. (2005). Differential neuroendocrine responses to chronic variable stress in adult Long Evans rats exposed to handling-maternal separation as neonates. *Psychoneuroendocrinology, 30*(6), 520–533.

LeDoux, J. E. (1996). *The emotional brain: The mysterious underpinnings of emotional life*. New York: Simon & Schuster.

Long, B. C. (1985). Stress-management interventions: A 15-month follow-up of aerobic conditioning and stress inoculation training. *Cognitive Therapy and Research, 9*(4), 471–478.

Masten, A., & Coatsworth, J. D. (1998). The development of competence in favorable and unfavorable environments: Lessons from research on successful children. *American Psychologist, 53*, 205–220.

Masten, A. S. (2001). Ordinary magic: Resilience processes in development. *American Psychologist, 56*(3), 227–238.

Moeller, C., Sommer, W., Thorsell, A., & Heilig, M. (1999). Anxiogenic-like action of galanin after intra-amygdala administration in the rat. *Neuropsychopharmacology, 21*(4), 507–512.

Morgan, C. A., III, Rasmusson, A. M., Wang, S., Hoyt, G., Hauger, R. L., & Hazlett, G. (2002). Neuropeptide-Y, cortisol, and subjective distress in humans exposed to acute stress: Replication and extension of previous report. *Biological Psychiatry, 52*(2), 136–142.

Morgan, C. A., III, Southwick, S., Hazlett, G., Rasmusson, A., Hoyt, G., Zimolo, Z., et al. (2004). Relationships among plasma dehydroepiandrosterone sulfate and cortisol levels, symptoms of dissociation, and objective performance in humans exposed to acute stress. *Archives of General Psychiatry, 61*(8), 819–825.

Morgan, C. A., III, Wang, S., Southwick, S. M., Rasmusson, A., Hazlett, G., Hauger, R. L., et al. (2000). Plasma neuropeptide-Y concentrations in humans exposed to military survival training. *Biological Psychiatry, 47*(10), 902–909.

National Cancer Institute, U.S. National Institutes of Health. (n.d.). *Dictionary of cancer terms*. Retrieved from http://www.cancer.gov.

Neumeister, A., Konstantinidis, A., Stastny, J., Schwarz, M. J., Vitouch, O., Willeit, M., et al. (2002). Association between serotonin transporter gene promoter polymorphism (*5HTTLPR*) and behavioral responses to tryptophan depletion in healthy women with and without family history of depression. *Archives of General Psychiatry, 59*, 613–620.

Norris, F. H., & Murrell, S. A. (1988). Prior experience as a moderator of disaster impact on anxiety symptoms in older adults. *American Journal of Community Psychology, 16*(5), 665–683.

Nudo, R. J., Milliken, G. W., Jenkins, W. M., & Merzenich, M. M. (1996). Use-dependent alterations of movement representations in primary motor cortex of adult squirrel monkeys. *Journal of Neuroscience, 16*, 785–807.

Parker, K. J., Buckmaster, C. L., Justus, K. R., Schatzberg, A. F., & Lyons, D. M. (2005). Mild early life stress enhances prefrontal-dependent response inhibition in monkeys. *Biological Psychiatry, 57*(8), 848–855.

Parker, K. J., Buckmaster, C. L., Schatzberg, A. F., & Lyons, D. M. (2004). Prospective investigation of stress inoculation in young monkeys. *Archives of General Psychiatry, 61*(9), 933–941.

Rasmusson, A. M., Hauger, R. L., Morgan, C. A., Bremner, J. D., Charney, D. S., & Southwick, S. M. (2000). Low baseline and yohimbine-stimulated plasma neuropeptide Y (NPY) levels in combat-related PTSD. *Biological Psychiatry, 47*(6), 526–539.

Rasmusson, A. M., Pinna, G., Paliwal, P., Weisman, D., Gottschalk, C., Charney, D., et al. (2006). Decreased cerebrospinal fluid allopregnanolone levels in women with posttraumatic stress disorder. *Biological Psychiatry, 60*(7), 704–713.

Rasmusson, A. M., Vasek, J., Lipschitz, D. S., Vojvoda, D., Mustone, M. E., Shi, Q., et al. (2004). An increased capacity for adrenal DHEA release is associated with decreased avoidance and negative mood symptoms in women with PTSD. *Neuropsychopharmacology, 29*(8), 1546–1557.

Resick, P. A. (2001). *Stress and trauma.* London: Psychology Press.

Rhodes, J. E., Ebert, L., & Fischer, K. (1992). Natural mentors: An overlooked resource in the social networks of youth, African American mothers. *American Journal of Community Psychology, 20*, 445–462.

Rhodes, J. E., Grossman, J. B., & Roffman, J. (2002). The rhetoric and reality of youth mentoring. *New Directions for Youth Development, 91*, 9–20.

Rizzolatti, G., Fadiga, L., Matelli, M., Bettinardi, V., Paulesu, E., Perani, D., et al. (1996). Localization of grasp representation in humans by PET: Observation versus execution. *Experimental Brain Research, 111*, 246–252.

Rozanski, A., Blumenthal, J. A., & Kaplan, J. (1999). Impact of psychological factors on the pathogenesis of cardiovascular disease and implications for therapy. *Circulation, 99*, 2192–2217.

Sapolsky, R. M. (2003). Stress and plasticity in the limbic system. *Neurochemical Research, 28*(11), 1735–1742.

Sapolsky, R. M. (2004). *Why zebras don't get ulcers* (3rd ed.). New York: Times Books.

Sayal, K., Checkley, S., Rees, M., Jacobs, C., Harris, T., Papadopoulos, A., et al. (2002). Effects of social support during weekend leave on cortisol and depression ratings: A pilot study. *Journal of Affective Disorders, 71*, 153–157.

Southwick, S. M., Bremner, J. D., Rasmusson, A., Morgan, C. A., III, Arnsten, A., & Charney, D. S. (1999). Role of norepinephrine in the pathophysiology and treatment of posttraumatic stress disorder. *Biological Psychiatry, 46*(9), 1192–1204.

Southwick, S. M., Vythilingam, M., & Charney, D. S. (2005). The psychobiology of depression and resilience to stress: Implications for prevention and treatment. *Annual Review of Clinical Psychology, 1*, 255–291.

Sroufe, L. A. (2005). Attachment and development: A prospective, longitudinal study from birth to adulthood. *Attachment & Human Development, 7*(4), 349–367.

Sroufe, L. A., Egeland, B., Carlson, E. A., & Collins, W. A. (2005). *The development of the person: The Minnesota study of risk and adaptation from birth to adulthood.* New York: Guilford Press.

Stacey, M. (1970). *Hospitals, children and their families: The report of a pilot study.* London: Routledge & K. Paul.

Stein, M. B., Jang, K. L., Taylor, S., Vernon, P. A., & Livesley, W. J. (2002). Genetic and environmental influences on trauma exposure and posttraumatic stress disorder symptoms: A twin study. *American Journal of Psychiatry, 159*(10), 1675–1681.

Stice, E., Ragan, J., & Randall, P. (2004). Prospective relations between social support and depression: Differential direction of effects for parent and peer support? *Journal of Abnormal Psychology, 113,* 155–159.

Tierney, J. P., Grossman, J., & Resch, N. L. (1995). *Making a difference: An impact study.* Philadelphia: Public/Private Ventures.

Travis, L. A., Lyness, J. M., Shields, C. G., King, D. A., & Cox, C. (2004). Social support, depression, and functional disability in older adult primary-care patients. *American Journal of Geriatric Psychiatry, 12,* 265–271.

True, W. R., Rice, J., Eisen, S. A., Heath, A. C., Goldberg, J., Lyons, M. J., et al. (1993). A twin study of genetic and environmental contributions to liability for posttraumatic stress symptoms. *Archives of General Psychiatry, 50*(4), 257–264.

Wells, J. K., Howard, G. S., Nowlin, W. F., & Vargas, M. J. (1986). Presurgical anxiety and postsurgical pain and adjustment: Effects of a stress inoculation procedure. *Journal of Consulting and Clinical Psychology, 54*(6), 831–835.

Wolkowitz, O. M., Reus, V. I., Keebler, A., Nelson, N., Friedland, M., Brizendine, L., et al. (1999). Double-blind treatment of major depression with dehydroepiandrosterone. *American Journal of Psychiatry, 156*(4), 646–649.

Yehuda, R. (2002). Current status of cortisol findings in post-traumatic stress disorder. *Psychiatric Clinics of North America, 25*(2), 341–368.

Yehuda, R., Brand, S. R., Golier, J. A., & Yang, R. K. (2006). Clinical correlates of DHEA associated with post-traumatic stress disorder. *Acta Psychiatrica Scandinavica, 114*(3), 187–193

# 9

# FROM TRAUMA TO RESILIENCE

*Susan C. Adelman, PhD*

S teven Southwick's research presents us with two challenging questions: How does the neurobiology of trauma inform clinical work with traumatized individuals and how can we facilitate the development of resilience?

## Neurobiology of Trauma and
## Some Clinical Implications

There is an emerging relationship between the neurological understanding of brain function and some of the observations of psychological function that psychoanalytic clinicians have described from their extended observations. Perhaps this can be thought of as two hands reaching toward each other. While how individuals function will never be fully explained by neurology, it seems likely that we will eventually be able to demonstrate core emotions that have inborn systems in the brain (Panksepp, 1998). Research into the brain may eventually explain a great deal about what Freud called, according to his translators, instinctual drives, the biological underpinnings of human motivation.

Dr. Southwick has described how the fear system operates in the brain. This complex system is involved in many of the clinical conditions that we see, ranging from post-traumatic stress disorder to phobias and other anxiety disorders. Neuroscientists are also working to discover other emotional systems that are inborn in our brains. Although which these might be has not been finally established, many researchers include seeking systems connected with curiosity and appetitive states (hunger and sex), a rage system, a fear system involved in "fight or flight," and a panic-separation system connected with attachment, separation distress, social bonding, and mothering (Panksepp, 1998; Solms & Turnbull, 2002). Increasing knowledge of these biological systems and how they function and interact may ultimately inform a more profound understanding of how the human species has survived and also refine the understanding of the emotional dimensions of life. It was Freud's (1895) dream in the Project for a Scientific Psychology that this would happen, and we are beginning to see the dream realized (Schore, 1997).

In thinking of the emotional systems of the brain, it helps to keep an evolutionary perspective. With regard to fear in particular, it is important to remember that the human brain evolved over millions of years. The ability to survive danger was selected for and is built in at a biological level. The fear system is capable of immediate, intense, completely focused one-time, permanent learning of all aspects of a danger situation. Higher cortically based functions are not active in this learning. Rather, as Southwick, Ozbay, and Mayes explain (chapter 8), more primitive parts of the brain mediate rapid encoding of everything perceived, even the most incidental detail. Survival requires instant reaction to danger. Anyone lucky enough to survive the first encounter needs to instantly recognize signs associated with it to avoid future encounters.

As with other biologically necessary systems, the fear system operates whether we are aware of it or not. Further, conscious representation of the emotion may be quite incidental, from an evolutionary point of view, to the fact that the necessary behavior is undertaken. An easy example is that reproductive behavior occurs in all animals but the awareness of sexual feelings, that is, the consciousness of emotion and thoughts about sexuality, is certainly not present in most. This is one of LeDoux's (1996) critical points, and with it, his acknowledgment that Freud was correct in understanding that most of our emotional life is, indeed, not conscious.

John Bowlby, influenced by the biological research of his time, also believed that evolutionary and ethological perspectives were critical to an accurate understanding of how humans develop, function, and, therefore, survive. In particular, he asserted that an attachment system must be inborn and interactive with the infant seeking interaction, the mother's maternal behavior "reciprocal," and the development of attachment related to the mother's sensitivity to the baby's cues. He also described how when the infant is frightened, what calms the infant is the "sight, sound or touch of the mother" (Bowlby, 1969/1982, p. 179). That is, the attachment system mitigates trauma. Anna Freud and Dorothy Burlingham reported that young children who had been partly buried in bombings during World War II showed no signs of "traumatic shock" if they were with their mothers (Freud, 1973, pp. 160–161). Werner (1989) documents how resilient children can be as long as they have a caregiver who is emotionally and physically available. Van der Kolk and McFarlane, prominent trauma researchers, say that "in fact, the most powerful influence in overcoming the impact of psychological trauma seems to be the availability of a caregiver who can be blindly trusted when one's own resources are inadequate" (1996, p. 32). An area in which future brain research may contribute to part of our understanding of how psychoanalytic therapy helps traumatized patients is how the therapist may function as a trustworthy attachment figure and how the attachment system interacts with the fear system.

With the studies of Dr. Southwick and others (Damasio, 1999; LeDoux, 1996) comes the confirmation from neuroscience that some of what is observed clinically by analytic therapists is unconscious not because of repression but because of other memory systems in the brain. This seems to apply especially to some experiences connected with intense anxiety. Anniversary reactions to traumata and sudden intrusions of anxiety that are hard to explain have both long been a focus in work with patients as clinicians try to understand the sources of the feelings and to help the patient move from intense, wordless emotion to feeling with declarative memory and, later, with symbolic thought. How this works at the level of the brain is now much clearer. Neuroanatomical researchers like Dr. Southwick describe the brain as having not one but multiple memory systems for the same event. To quote Joseph LeDoux, "Conscious, declarative or explicit memory is mediated by the hippocampus and related cortical areas, whereas various unconscious or implicit forms of memory are mediated by different systems. One implicit memory system is an emotional (fear) memory system involving the amygdala and related areas. In traumatic situations, implicit and explicit systems function . . . in parallel" (LeDoux, 1996, p. 202) but record different information. The hippocampus perceives the perceptual, but it is the amygdala system that is responsible for the muscle tension, blood pressure changes, and hormonal, brain, and bodily changes (LeDoux, 1996, p. 202). But, LeDoux continues, "the explicit memory system is notoriously forgetful and inaccurate" while the memories in the amygdala seem relatively permanent (LeDoux, 1996, p. 203). Thus, there are two independent memory systems for trauma operating in the brain.

For clinicians, the knowledge that the amygdala controls the somatic reactions for fear and that it never forgets means that we should trust the body, the physical responses of the patient, as containing critical information whether or not the patient can report what he or she is feeling or why. Freud knew this and described it eloquently: "He that has eyes to see and ears to hear may convince himself that no mortal can keep a secret. If his lips are silent, he chatters with his fingertips; betrayal oozes out of him at every pore" (Freud, 1905). Freud also stated, "The ego is first and foremost a bodily ego" (Freud, 1923). Kramer and Akhtar (1992) and their colleagues have written movingly of nonverbal communications and their clinical importance.

Researchers have also found that in individuals with post-traumatic stress disorder, when the trauma is activated, there is a decrease in activation of the part of the brain most centrally involved in the transformation of subjective experience into speech (Broca's area) (Van der Kolk, 1996, p. 287). The clinician's task is a complex one of approaching the trauma but not reactivating it as part of the work of helping traumatized patients begin to find words for their experiences.

In addition, profound enough traumata may actually cause hippocampal dysfunction so that at the moment of trauma no memory develops that could later be consciously accessible. In severe trauma, that is, the full facts of what actually happened may not ever be available (Turnbull & Solms, 2003, p. 72). In these situations, the clinician and patient need to work together to observe the contexts of fear arousal and their associations as a way into regaining some knowledge of the trauma. With these pieces, rather than with a full memory that cannot be recovered because it does not exist, the patient has the option of reconstructing a story that is meaningful to him or her. This may be the best available strategy for moving the somatic reactions to the more flexible, symbolically encoded higher cortical regions.

The two processing systems in the brain for memory of trauma, the amygdala, and the hippocampus and related cortical areas, also point to the complexity of understanding trauma. There is, on the one hand, a permanent fear response that can be reduced in intensity but cannot be erased completely. The understanding, or meaning assigned to what happened, is created by the cortical functions of the brain and has a great impact on how the whole experience is integrated. Van der Kolk and McFarlane (1996) illustrate this beautifully with a case of a woman who was raped but did not develop PTSD until she found out, months later, that her rapist had not only raped but also killed another woman. Now she understood herself as having almost lost her life, and she developed full-blown post-traumatic stress disorder (Van der Kolk & McFarlane, 1996, p. 6). Thus, in treating the traumatized, we cannot overestimate either the reality of what happened to them or how they understood what happened. Both factors influence the defensive strategies they develop that may either facilitate or impede integration of the trauma.

A very brief history of psychoanalytic concepts of trauma may be help-ful. Freud struggled with the concept of trauma throughout his life and work. In one of his earliest works, "Studies on Hysteria," he and Breuer stated that "hysterics suffer mainly from reminiscences . . . the traumatic experience is constantly forcing itself upon the patient and this is proof of the strength of that experience: the patient is . . . fixated on his trauma" (Breuer & Freud, 1893, p. 7). His early idea was that the reports of sexual abuse by patients were true and led to alterations in consciousness, even a "splitting of con-sciousness." Later, with the development of the understanding of the sexual life of children and the Oedipus complex, Freud moved away from his earlier position toward understanding that it was his patients' sexual and aggressive drives and the defenses against them that produced their symptoms. Now the emphasis was on the internal construction of experience, the unique contri-bution of psychoanalysis.

But Freud did not ever abandon the reality of trauma. His thinking evolved over his lifetime. Freud described one of the ego's roles as maintain-ing homeostasis by regulating internal and external stimuli. In defining trauma, he said,

> We describe as 'traumatic' any excitations from outside which are powerful enough to break through the protective shield. It seems to me that the con-cept of trauma necessarily implies a connection of this kind with a breach in an otherwise efficacious barrier against stimuli. Such an event as an exter-nal trauma is bound to provoke a disturbance on a large scale in the func-tioning of the organism's energy and set in motion every possible defensive measure . . . the pleasure principle is for the moment put out of action. There is no longer any possibility of preventing the mental apparatus from being flooded with large amounts of stimulus, and another problem arises instead—the problem of mastering the amounts of stimulus which have broken in and [of] binding them, in the psychical sense, so that they can then be disposed of. (Freud, 1920, pp. 29–30)

Freud also studied war neurosis (now post-traumatic stress disorder) and rep-etition compulsion and struggled with how to explain the intensity and per-sistence of human destructiveness.

Thus, psychoanalytic theory has delineated two theories of trauma. One is the "unbearable situation" model and a second, the "unacceptable impulse" model (Krystal, 1978). The two theories of trauma are both important, each capturing part of the reality of what happens in trauma and what must be worked with in the psychodynamic treatment of trauma. Ira Brenner (2004) has written a powerful book discussing the interplay between real external trauma and its impact on inner meanings, structures, and experiences and detailing the extremely complex therapeutic work with victims of massive trauma. But it has often been difficult for clinicians to maintain simultaneously awareness of both the "unbearable situation" and the "unacceptable impulse" and to know when to work from one or from the other.

## Implications for Psychoanalytic Clinicians

There are a number of modifications in treatment worth considering when working with traumatized people. Dr. Southwick suggests that it may be valuable to consider offering medication sooner rather than later, especially as it may help the stress-damaged hippocampus to recover, which, in turn, may facilitate psychotherapy.

The traumatized patient's dilemma in coming to psychoanalytic treatment is uncertainty as to whether revisiting his or her traumatic experiences, the intense feelings connected with them, and the complexity of feelings about his or her important relationships will be liberating or retraumatizing. Analytic treatment may be even more frightening when the patient is a survivor of childhood abuse at the hands of his or her parents. Where injury has occurred in the most intimate of relationships, the conscious wish of the patient is for healing and progress from constricting fears to a life filled with richer choices. But the emotional expectation is that he or she will be reinjured. Indeed, the patient, having internalized object relations based on his or her family experiences and understandings of them, will often repeat the relationships and experiences that were injurious to the patient in his or her life and in the therapeutic relationship (Freud, 1939, pp. 75–76).

Well-meaning therapists can also cause injury. Ira Brenner reports a profoundly traumatized patient whose previous therapists had repeatedly asked her to detail her abuse experiences, and this, she felt, accelerated her deterioration. By contrast, Brenner "assured her that my interest in her day-to-day safety took precedence over hearing the details of her horrible experiences. . . . I tried to focus on her here-and-now functioning, essentially offering to be an auxiliary ego and memory bank" (Brenner, 2004, p. 22). Eventually, when she felt ready, his patient initiated the deepening of the treatment.

Destructive reactivation of the trauma can also be caused by too-early defense interpretation that happens before there is a strong working relationship within which to process it. Defenses are erected by the ego, and interpretation aims to modify the defenses. But traumatized individuals have had the experience of the ego being overwhelmed, so exactly when interpretation is useful and tolerable must be carefully considered. Additionally, interpreting the trauma patient's wishes, if done too early in the treatment, may easily be experienced as supporting the patient in taking too much responsibility for what happened to him or her. It may be valuable, even for an extended time, to accept the patient's need for his or her defenses, to appreciate, get to know, and value them, and perhaps even begin to play and observe them together, all in the service of creating safety and a secure therapeutic working alliance. Validating the trauma may be important, so that the patient feels heard and less alone and can begin to develop a cognitive frame within which to think about what, in many cases, is not yet verbalized. To put this in terms of the brain, it is valuable to actively get the cortex involved in trying to make sense of the confusing experiences the person is having.

It is of the greatest importance in the psychodynamic treatment of the traumatized to respect their tremendous anxiety because trauma always involves profound helplessness. This requires working actively to create as much of a feeling of safety in the consultation room as possible. It may involve flexibly accepting great variations in the treatment frame in terms of how patients come to treatment and stay in treatment, thus allowing them a great deal of control. This is, of course, precisely what they were deprived of by the trauma.

Clinical data can provide an illustration. Courtney came to see me after spending a year in the therapeutic playroom with her two-year-old daughter and the daughter's psychiatrist. Her daughter had been sexually assaulted while in daycare and was now in a very good play therapy. Courtney herself had a history of violent and sexual abuse by her own father. She had always remembered the violent abuse but had suddenly and overwhelmingly remembered the sexual abuse as an adult after seeing her father abusing a young child. She was flooded with memories, became disorganized, and had to be hospitalized. She subsequently withdrew from her studies, spent years in supportive psychotherapy, and eventually was able to marry, have children, and work effectively in a firm.

Now she was in my consultation room, wanting more—she wasn't sure what—and she was terrified. Coming once a week, she sat in her chair, feet firmly planted on the ground, weight forward, ready to flee, which she did on several occasions. What she was comfortable talking about was how much she wished she could be in treatment with her daughter's psychiatrist. We explored her feelings about him and what she longed for from him. She tried to convince me that I could never fill his shoes and that she was not clear that our work could proceed. As she tried and sometimes succeeded in evoking in me feelings of inadequacy and rejection, we continued to meet. She also spoke a great deal about her current realities and we got to know one another better. She spent considerable effort caring for others, often finding them ungrateful. After almost a year Courtney began to visibly relax and became more self-reflective. She wondered if she was taking care of others so as not to have to deal with wanting to be taken care of herself and grudgingly began to say that she thought we could work together. We laughed together, appreciating how we could both understand how it was very reasonable of her to be reluctant to start the hard work she had come for.

Why did I decide not to interpret the defensive position Courtney was in during the first year of her treatment? Why did I not explore with her the multiple levels of her attachment to her daughter's psychiatrist and both their wishful and defensive uses? I was very aware of many of the functions of this attachment. She envied her daughter getting the effective treatment in childhood that she had lacked. She wanted to be the child who was loved. She was easily able to idealize the unobtainable man and scorn the available woman, long for oedipal victory. She was testing my ability to tolerate her devaluation, her hostility without retaliation. And, perhaps most important, she was using her attachment to the psychiatrist as a defense against her fear of engaging in the terrifying work we had before us. I chose to say nothing about any of these because I felt she was on the edge of not being able to stay in the room at all. I needed to accept and withstand whatever she needed to play out until she felt safe enough with me to proceed.

Safety and flexibility continued to be important throughout treatment. Courtney was now in analysis, on the couch four times a week. In one session, as she began to discuss her father's abuse, she said she wanted to lie on the floor. I asked her to explore what came to mind about this and what it felt like for her. She was not able to explain but said it felt important to do this. With a patient who had not been traumatized, I probably would have asked them to stay on the couch and see what emerged. With Courtney, there was intensity to her request and, as in the opening phase of treatment, I felt I needed to be guided by her sense of how to proceed. She got off the couch and went into "child's pose," a folded yoga position, on the floor to ease the pain of her cramping muscles as she now more fully explored her violent physical abuse. Similarly, when she became nauseated speaking of the sexual abuse, I brought her a plastic bucket. The message I wanted to convey was that I accepted whatever happened to her body as she moved forward in her work and that we, working together, could contain whatever came. Part of the memory of physical abuse is really in the memory of the body; and there are physical symptoms that come with remembering. Kramer (1990, p. 151) speaks of the "somatic memories" of incest victims.

After a period back on the couch, Courtney returned to sitting on the floor to "play," identifying with her daughter in the playroom. Thinking of Winnicott (1971), I also understood her doing this as connected with her need for "playing" to occur between us and, by this, to create a safe, transitional space in which to let her explorations flourish (Winnicott, 1971, p. 38). Courtney subsequently remembered that her mother had only allowed her to play in the closet as a child. Now she was able to verbalize how the couch had begun to feel like the closet and, in her larger floor space, begin to work on her feelings about her mother. This patient was eventually able to deal with her terror of being out of the closet in her own life and was able to joyfully embark on a career that had a level of expression of her creative talents that had been closed to her before her treatment.

The sequence of enacting, remembering, and then reflecting is part of many therapies with adults who were abused as children. It allows them autonomy within an intimate relationship that they were denied in childhood. It also allows the therapist to be the good, nonabandoning object because being abandoned by protective objects is always part of the traumatic experience (Huizenga, 1990, p. 120; Laub & Auerhahn, 1993, p. 287). It enlarges the sense of what space there is for safe playing between people (Winnicott, 1971), one of the most damaged areas in the abused. It is also critical to the development of reflective function, which is so central to affect regulation and resilience (Fonagy, Gergely, Jurist, & Target, 2002). With our knowledge of the permanence of the brain's recall of trauma, we can be more confident that these modifications in treatment will not obscure the underlying fears and conflicts although they may alter how and when they emerge. This was the case with Courtney. In the course of our work, I became the abuser she hated; the cold, indifferent, rejecting mother; the longed for, sexually desired, unobtainable mother; and the ally as Courtney gleefully destroyed her abusing father and then missed her supportive, caring father.

Joseph Sandler (1960) spoke of the feeling of safety, of security, as not merely the absence of anxiety but as a positive state, a feeling of well-being that he thought connected with the earliest experiences of nurture and comfort. "It is a feeling which bears the same relation to anxiety as the positive body state of satiation and contentment bears to instinctual tension . . . the quality of feeling which we can oppose to the affect of anxiety, representing in a sense its polar opposite" (p. 353). Sandler felt that creating and maintaining a sense of safety was an ongoing activity. He understood many repetitive behaviors, particularly in children and more disturbed patients, as creating a predictable, controllable, safe world. In this, he also described how fear and the need for its opposite, safety, can be one of the motivations for people's behavior and life choices.

## Trauma and Resilience

Dr. Southwick has reported on the numerous factors that go into the development of resilience, among them genetics, parenting, stress experiences, and social support. These factors interact with one another in complex ways.

Examples of the interactions between genes, their expression, and parenting come from studies on rhesus monkeys. In one, infant monkeys with a genetic predisposition to abnormal neuroendocrine development had this vulnerability expressed only if they were maternally deprived. When the genetically vulnerable monkeys were raised by nurturing mothers, however, this genetic vulnerability was not expressed at all. From a behavioral and neuroendocrine standpoint, these vulnerable but well-cared-for monkeys were identical to the monkeys who did not have the vulnerability. In another study, female monkeys bred to be highly reactive were raised by foster mothers who were unusually nurturant. These infants grew up to be precocious, secure, powerful in the group, and, contrary to their reactive temperament, extremely nurturant mothers themselves (Suomi et al., reported in Fonagy et al., 2002, pp. 116–117).

Interactions between parenting, stress, and neurological development are also now extensively documented. Schore, referencing multiple studies, says, "DNA production in the cortex increases dramatically over the first year (of life) and interactive experiences directly impact genetic systems that program brain growth . . . the changing social environment . . . powerfully affects the structure of the brain" (Schore, 2003, p. 23). Further, Schore reports that the brain of the infant grows tremendously in the first two years. This is especially true of the right hemisphere, the part particularly concerned with affect and affect regulation. This research merges with the extensive attachment research and literature, which describe the complexity of mother-infant interactions. Thus at the level of genetic expression, the development of the brain, and the emotional systems, resilience is tremendously influenced by experiences of mothering. Both the brain and attachment research mesh powerfully with child analytic clinical observations including those of Anna Freud, Spitz, Margaret Mahler, and many others.

Resilience has also been studied in relation to childhood trauma. A recent study explored resilience in adults who were part of Sylvia Brody's prospective study of infants and their mothers that has continued for over 30 years. As adults, 13% reported serious abuse in their childhoods that had not been previously known. Although a number of the abused had made relatively successful adaptations, marrying, working and being parents, there was joylessness to most of their lives. "My life is a longing" (Massie & Szajnberg, 2006, p. 479) said one. The authors point to both resilience and lasting damage in self-esteem, trust, and emotional stability—that "seemingly adequate coping . . . always came at the price of emotional vulnerability and compromised potential" (Massie & Szajnberg, 2006, p. 471). It is worth remembering that most of the trauma patients seen in outpatient offices are resilient in the sense that they have not had the major life consequences that trauma victims often have: suicide, criminality, addiction, and prostitution, just to name a few.

A clinical example may be illustrative. Jennifer was a patient who would have been considered resilient. She came to me with an acute loss and through psychoanalytic psychotherapy was able to tap her deeper resilience: the capacity for reworking her understanding of herself, her object world, and, with it, her life choices. She also illustrates the role of safety in the life and in the treatment of the traumatized.

Jennifer's husband had just abandoned her, suddenly and unexpectedly leaving her for another woman. He had been her rock, her base. She had always been fearful and he had held her hand through her frightening experiences. How had she not known he was capable of this? She hadn't known he was having an affair. And then, after he left, she found a carton filled with cigarette butts. She hadn't known he was a smoker. Shocked, grieving, and furious, Jennifer had seen her world turned upside down in an instant. We worked for most of a year on her intense emotions and new realities. At the end of the year, she said she felt better but still had a phobia about being in moving vehicles that was limiting her career development; could I help her?

I told her that if what she wanted was to immediately work on reducing the phobia, a behavioral therapist might be her best choice, but if she wanted to understand the phobia and how it fit into her life, then we should continue to work but do so meeting more frequently.

Thus began a four-year intensive treatment in the course of which we found out that Jennifer had almost died as a four-year-old child. She and her mother had been standing at the edge of a cliff when the ground gave way and both fell, Jennifer sustaining injuries that would have killed her had not a physician been at the scene and given her immediate care. Jennifer did not remember the accident, only the look of helpless terror on her mother's face and the sense that her body was moving and out of control. Her father blamed her mother for the accident and there were endless angry fights between them. He had also wanted Jennifer to have been a boy and a tough one at that. His career required the family to move many times, and Jennifer lost her friends each time. Her father belittled her for her tears. Together, these consolidated in her phobia, a feeling of defectiveness, and her desire to marry a man who she saw as being able to supplement her functioning. In her treatment, the accident was reworked multiple times, its greatest significance being her loss of her sense of her mother's protective power and her feeling of being out of control. This loss and her terror merged with her father's view of her—that, as a woman, she was, like her mother, deficient, unreasonably emotional, and excessively fearful. Together, these contributed to her decision to make an early marriage to a man whom she idealized as her protector but could not allow herself to know as fully human. By the end of treatment, Jennifer better understood her fears and felt more compassionate toward herself. Her phobia had diminished enough that she could pursue her career more fully (with a Valium in her pocket that she never took but often touched, as a transitional object), she liked herself better as a woman, and she had a new relationship with a man that seemed more equal and intimate.

In Jennifer, compromised potential could be seen in her life choices prior to her seeking treatment—a limited work life and a very limited marriage. Here, though, is where our very ambitions in psychoanalytic treatment come into play as an ally of the plasticity of the brain. As Southwick has reported, because there is no single part of the brain in which "memory" is stored but rather multiple systems, some very enduring (the amygdala, for one), some more vulnerable to forgetting (cortex), and because sensory information is stored in the parts of the brain that received the stimulation (visual in visual, auditory in auditory, etc.), each act of remembering or bringing to mind involves a reconstruction of the memory. The reconstruction of the memory occurs in a particular circumstance. If a person has post-traumatic stress disorder, for example, each loud noise brings back the traumatic event, and if the individual can't avoid noises, he or she is retraumatized over and over, the neural pathways involved in the symptoms are strengthened, and the post-traumatic stress disorder worsens. In the therapist's office, the remembering should be with a person who has earned a degree of trust and who stays emotionally present to bear the affect and hold it with the patient in as much emotional safety as possible so that the memory is slightly transformed and becomes a new memory in which the experience is one of being less alone and less afraid than before. This transformation, this reduction of the level of fear of the memory, is in addition to all the dynamic work that also needs to go on—all the ways in which the patient made sense of what happened in the trauma as well as what he or she wished for, how the patient experienced himself or herself and those around him or her, what the patient felt responsible for, the patient's rage, the patient's desire, the patient's shame at his or her symptoms, and how these played out in the transference and countertransference.

In psychoanalytic treatment we need to hear with feeling and bear the experiences that the patient both expresses to us and evokes in us. Elvin Semrad, who was the teacher of many generations of us in Boston, used to say, "If you can't sit with the patient until you feel his feelings in your own body, you're in the wrong line of work." Although he didn't write, Semrad was describing what many have written of, notably Winnicott's "holding environment." Our ability to hear and bear the affect, reflecting, slightly changes the experience over time through a slight change in perspective, so that more of the experience is moved from a direct, physical, isolated, nonreflective repetition into a more bearable, flexible, thoughtful, known, and, finally, symbolized and shared experience that the patient knows the analyst/therapist carries and holds within him or her. This is a process of moving the experience from an unmodulated one to one that is increasingly integrated in higher structures of the brain, with more thoughts and more differentiated, bearable feelings. It is also moving away from the isolation of the experience toward an experience with another and with others. Perhaps at some point we will understand better how the attachment systems of the brain may underlie this process and interact with the fear systems. There is much to look forward to. But the process of reworking the emotions, what is remembered, what is lost to memory, what is recreated in the present, creating an underlying climate of safety and a coherent story, is the work of psychoanalytic treatment. And by this, "traumatic memory becomes narrative memory, and confused, wordless feelings and unhappiness become stories of trauma and loss" (Lindy, 1996, p. 526).

# References

Bowlby, J. (1982). *Attachment.* New York: Basic Books. (Originally published 1969.)

Brenner, I. (2004). *Psychic trauma: Dynamics, symptoms and treatment.* New York: Jason Aronson.

Breuer, J., & Freud, S. (1893–1895). Studies on hysteria. *Standard Edition* 2:1–251. London: Hogarth Press.

Damasio, A. (1999). *The feeling of what happens.* New York: Harcourt.

Fonagy, P., Gergely, G., Jurist, E. L., & Target, M. (2002). *Affect regulation, mentalization and the development of the self.* New York: Other Press.

Freud, A. (1973). Infants without families: Reports on the Hampstead Nurseries—Report 12. *The writings of Anna Freud* (Vol. 3, pp. 142–211). New York: International Universities Press.

Freud, S. (1895). Project for a scientific psychology. *Standard Edition* 1:295–397.

Freud, S. (1905). Three essays on the theory of sexuality. *Standard Edition* 7:135–243.

Freud, S. (1920). Beyond the pleasure principle. *Standard Edition* 18:7–64.

Freud, S. (1923). The ego and the id. *Standard Edition* 19:3–66.

Freud, S. (1939). Moses and monotheism. *Standard Edition* 23:1–137.

Huizenga, J. N. (1990). Incest as trauma: A psychoanalytic case. In H. G. Levine (Ed.), *Adult analysis and childhood sexual abuse* (pp. 117–135). Hillsdale, NJ: Analytic Press.

Kramer, S. (1990). Residues of incest. In H. G. Levine (Ed.), *Adult analysis and childhood sexual abuse* (pp. 149–170). Hillsdale, NJ: Analytic Press.

Kramer, S., & Akhtar, S. (Eds.). (1992). *When the body speaks.* Northvale, NJ: Jason Aronson.

Krystal, H. (1978). Trauma and affects. *Psychoanalytic Study of the Child, 33,* 81–116.

Laub, D., & Auerhahn, N. (1993). Knowing and not knowing massive psychic trauma: Forms of traumatic memory. *International Journal of Psychoanalysis, 74,* 287–302.

LeDoux, J. (1996). *The emotional brain: Mysterious underpinnings of emotional life.* New York: Simon & Schuster.

Lindy, J. D. (1996). Psychoanalytic psychotherapy of posttraumatic stress disorder: The nature of the therapeutic relationship. In B. A. van der Kolk, A. C. McFarlane, & L. Weisaeth (Eds.), *Traumatic stress: The effects of overwhelming experience on mind, body, and society* (pp. 525–536). New York: Guilford Press.

Massie, H., & Szajnberg, N. (2006). My life is a longing: Child abuse and its adult sequelae: Results from the Brody longitudinal study from birth to age 30. *International Journal of Psychoanalysis, 87,* 471–496.

Panksepp, J. (1998). *Affective neuroscience: The foundation of human and animal emotion.* Oxford: Oxford University Press.

Sandler, J. (1960). The background of safety. *International Journal of Psychoanalysis, 41,* 352–356.

Schore, A. N. (1997). A century after Freud's Project: Is a rapprochement between psychoanalysis and neurobiology at hand? *Journal of the American Psychoanalytic Association, 45,* 807–840.

Schore, A. N. (2003). The human unconscious: The development of the right brain and its role in early emotional life. In V. Green (Ed.), *Emotional development in psychoanalysis, attachment theory and neuroscience: Creating connections* (pp. 23–54). New York: Brunner-Routledge.

Solms, M., & Turnbull, O. (2002). *The brain and the inner world: An introduction to the neuroscience of subjective experience.* New York: Other Press.

Turnbull, O., & Solms, M. (2003). Memory, amnesia and intuition: A neuropsychoanalytic perspective. In V. Green (Ed.), *Emotional development in psychoanalysis, attachment theory and neuroscience: Creating connections* (pp. 55–85). New York: Brunner-Routledge.

Van der Kolk, B. A. (1996). Trauma and memory. In B. A. van der Kolk, A. C. McFarlane, & L. Weisaeth (Eds.), *Traumatic stress: The effects of overwhelming experience on mind, body, and society* (pp. 279–302). New York: Guilford Press.

Van der Kolk, B. A., & McFarlane, A. C. (1996). The black hole of trauma. In B. A. van der Kolk, A. C. McFarlane, & L. Weisaeth (Eds.), *Traumatic stress: The effects of overwhelming experience on mind, body, and society* (pp. 3–23). New York: Guilford Press.

Werner, E. E. (1989). High-risk children in young adulthood: A longitudinal study from birth to 32 years. *American Journal of Orthopsychiatry, 59,* 72–81.

Winnicott, D. W. (1971). *Playing and reality.* New York: Basic Books.

# 10

# RESILIENCE AND ITS CORRELATES

*Harold P. Blum, MD*

Psychoanalysts and psychotherapists have regularly encountered trauma in their clinical work. The focus of concern has typically been the pathological effects on the personality, both short-term and enduring long-term consequences and ramifications. However, it has long been known that some individuals, despite massive and protracted trauma, are able to manage much more than sheer physical and psychological survival. These individuals seem to have the ability and inner strength either to not succumb to the trauma in the first place or to overcome the trauma sufficiently to subsequently lead relatively normal lives with renewed vigor and efficacy. The study of resilience therefore takes us away from the traditional focus on traumatic psychopathology to theoretical and clinical considerations of resistance to being traumatized and recovery from trauma. Everyone has a breaking point at which the personality is overwhelmed and retreats into global regression if not chaotic disorganization. Some hardy individuals, both children and adults, are able to build and rebuild their lives, sometimes with surprising or even amazing achievement and accomplishment. Some survivors of the Holocaust and of other genocidal massacres, for example, in Cambodia, have been incredibly abused and traumatized; some suffered multiple losses of loved ones and/or witnessed horrific atrocities. Having physically survived the atrocities and associated pervasive, destructive violence, some of these individuals, children as well as adults, showed remarkable capacities to mobilize inner resources. Some were able to resourcefully assist others who were severely traumatized.

Resilience is a broad concept, and there is no consensual definition of the term. Although seemingly simple enough, it is a complicated notion, subject to different meanings in different contexts. First, how does resilience differ from the early analytic concept of ego strength, of resistance to regression, the

capacity to confine regression to selected areas of the personality, or the capacity to reverse regression? Many ego functions as well as the capacity to turn
passive into active and the capacity for mastery of trauma may all be regarded
as components of resilience. However resilience may be defined, it is a gestalt
that transcends its individual components and developmental origins. I
would distinguish two different forms of resilience. Resilience denotes both
resistance to traumatic decompensation and the capacity for recovery from
traumatic experience.

Within the traumatic situation, those individuals who may be considered
resilient are possibly rare, and certainly constitute a minority. They manage
to avert being traumatized or have only very mild transient disturbance.
Resilient individuals are better able to withstand trauma, are less severely traumatized, or recover more readily than others from traumatic experience. In
the case of children, resilience refers to the capacity to resume progressive
development and ego growth, rather than developmental retardation, devia-
tion, or arrest (Tedeschi, Park, & Calhoun, 1998). Resilience would also have
to take into account the possible deferred action of trauma. Resilient children
are those who remain asymptomatic, do not suffer from psychopathology in
later life, or resourcefully recover from trauma in later childhood. In this connection Anthony and Cohler (1987) describe the "invulnerables" who not
only survived but in many respects thrived despite appalling environments,
managing to maintain coherent personality organization and innovative
adaptations. However, this often occurred at the expense of a rich emotional
life and capacity for intimacy. Resilient individuals may bend or twist, but are
able to snap back into shape; they bounce back from trauma with remarkable
flexibility and elasticity. Neubauer and Neubauer (1990) describe three children of a paranoid schizophrenic mother. The older daughter also developed
paranoid schizophrenia, but a younger daughter was able to make a fairly
good adaptation in life, and the youngest son had a brilliant postcollege
career. This son was able to use his father as an alternate sustaining object and
to avoid ego damage or dominant identification with his psychotic mother.

Henri Parens represents resilient healing after massive trauma. He
assumed the moral and psychological burden of writing his own Holocaust
story, but waited until 2004. His brilliance and bravery are evident in his
accomplishments after a lacerating legacy of loss and trauma. Parens had
experienced losses before the Holocaust. His parents divorced when he was
four and his mother then took him to Belgium, leaving his father and older
brother in Poland, Henri's birthplace. He never saw his father and brother

again and for a long time could not inquire about their possible fate. Living in Brussels with his mother in close proximity to relatives, he was just 11 years old when he was caught in the diabolical maelstrom of the Nazi invasion. Henri and his mother escaped to France, where they sought asylum but were herded and sent to a detention camp and then to a concentration camp. Parens observed the primal animal scene of the mating of a bull and cow, noting that the cow survived what appeared to be hazardous copulation. Fortunately Henri Parens also survived the starvation and sadism of French concentration camps in Nazi-dominated southern France. He has conveyed the suffering in silence, the stifled crying of the anguished prisoners, and the bleak, numbed existence and bare subsistence that he and his mother endured. At age 11 to 12 his early exclusive relationship with his mother was now reinforced in their incarceration together. Following his mother's resourceful preparation and instructions, Henri escaped and fortunately lived to tell the tale. He was scared to death but avoided deportation to Auschwitz and being murdered there, his mother's fate. A Jewish organization arranged his safe transportation to America, where he found affectionate caregivers and a new Jewish foster family. Parens underscores the importance of considering each individual Holocaust survivor as a unique person with his or her own special endowment and life experiences. This has to be kept in mind even when significant generalizations can be made, for example about the prevalence of survivor guilt. Parens was not simply guilty because he survived while his mother was murdered. He wondered whether his escape somehow incriminated his mother as a conspirator and accomplice in the escape. He sensitively and touchingly informs us that his psychic survival has been greatly aided by a loving wife, children, and grandchildren. A source of delight, the children represent the continuity of the generations in triumph over the threat of genocidal extinction. Each person caught in the hell of the Holocaust has his or her own feelings about having survived and feelings about family and friends who didn't survive or whose fate is unknown. Moreover, affects and attitudes during the trauma and during the immediate posttraumatic period may undergo alteration in later years.

Machtlinger (in press) described six child survivors of the Shoah who appeared to have defied all the usual explanations for diminished vulnerability and demonstrated remarkable resilience. She reported,

> They had all lost their mothers at birth or in the very first few months of life and had experienced very little gratification of basic needs or stability

in their relationships to their caretakers. Under conditions of anxiety and terror they had been passed from hand to hand in their first year, lived not in a family but in a group situation (also characterized by severe restrictions, anxiety, deprivation and terror) in their second and third year and were again uprooted three times during their fourth year. They had all been sent to Terezin between the ages of six and twelve months. . . . They must have been kept alive by different caretakers at constantly changing locations. We must work on the assumption that their mothers and or parents were all deported and killed. . . . It is difficult to imagine that any of them had experienced even a short period of undisturbed mutual contact with one constant mothering person in the first year of life.

Thirty-two years later, five of the six children were living in stable, long-term marriages, and these five had become parents of their own children.

Machtlinger speculates on the possible factors leading to this unpredictable positive outcome. Could these children extract sufficient nurturance and the internalization of good enough objects to develop and maintain stable psychic structure and relationships in life (Burlingham & Freud, 1944; Freud & Dann, 1951)? This appeared to take place in the absence of anything that would allow for stable attachment and for a normal process of separation individuation with an affectionate, responsive caregiver. What qualities did the children possess that enabled their physical and psychic survival under conditions that would seem to preclude any infant's survival? Machtlinger proposes three main factors:

1. The child's active contribution in initiating and maintaining reciprocal interactions with available adults helped to avoid massive and malignant narcissistic withdrawal.
2. An extraordinary, highly unusual group structure provided for group cohesion as well as a gratification for individual wishes and needs. This structure helped to preserve psychological investment in the object world and may have also provided necessary narcissistic supplies.
3. The environment offered to the children in the safety of their residential treatment in England promoted by Anna Freud presumably enabled them to form adult attachments at their own pace and in their own style. Their new safety and security offered opportunities to receive emotional support from affectionate, thoughtful caregivers with whom they were identified. Since no babies or toddlers can survive without appropriate

care, it is postulated that there must have been fleeting, but lifesaving caregivers. Moreover, the caregivers, who were themselves on death row, may well have had a special investment in keeping the babies and toddlers alive. In this way they could hope to defeat Nazi extermination and continue their own lives through identification with the children's lives. Perhaps resilient adults were able to save these resilient children. These children were invulnerables who survived against all odds; they were able to withstand maltreatment, malnutrition, lack of a comforting, holding environment, inconsistent and insecure attachment, and inevitable periods of neglect.

Boris Cyrulnik (chapter 2) has been able to draw on his own experience as a child survivor as well as his clinical experience in working with survivors of World War II and the Holocaust. In the Holocaust, Jews survived by luck, by chance events, by their wits, by the wisdom of their families, and by making use of any opportunity to remain obscure, to hide in plain sight or out of sight, to escape, to befriend those who could provide assistance. Chance also played a role in encounters with kindly strangers and those obscure individuals who during the Holocaust provided shelter and protection from the murderers. Chance also favored the prepared mind, which could then better cope with emergency situations. Hiding in a house in southern France, Dr. Cyrulnik evaded the grasp of the Nazis by hanging from rafters above the ceiling as the house was being searched (personal communication, April 2007). An imperiled 12-year-old lad, he was able to cope with the situation with uncanny aptitude, thus saving his own life. It may be useful to note here that the term *cope* is closer to effective adaptation than to mechanisms of defense. Coping may involve defense mechanisms but also involves other ego resources such as the sense of reality, reality testing, judgment, discrimination among different choices or possible decisions, and the capacity to either postpone action or take emergency corrective action. The defenses used to survive the traumatic experience, for example in the Nazi concentration camps, might involve denial, dissociation, repression, and suppression of protest and rage. These defenses may be effective for psychic survival in the deprived and depraved conditions of the concentration camp but might be maladaptive for life after liberation and being able to adapt to the new and novel situations. Being able to cope under extremely adverse conditions will therefore not guarantee that the individual will be more resilient than others under distresses and strains of ordinary life. Under such a reign of terror, resilience implies the capacity to resist overwhelming panic and to flexibly and even innovatively utilize appropriate combinations of ego functions. This capacity for rapid effective action, especially when one has to decide what to do and when and how to act, may be a hallmark of resilience in the face of enormous external danger. To maintain signal anxiety, to not retreat from reality or regress into infantile helplessness, and to maintain a cohesive self in the traumatizing danger situation is indicative of the unusual resourcefulness that is associated with resilience. Furthermore, like many survivors of the Shoah, Cyrulnik was also actively helpful and altruistic in adult life. Like his good friend and fellow survivor, Dr. Henri Parens, he became a psychiatrist, specializing in child psychiatry and family therapy. He has been devoted to helping traumatized children and families, contributing his special skills, knowledge, and experience in the service of the disturbed child and his or her family. It is very gratifying to learn that despite all manner of traumatic abuse and deprivation, many Holocaust survivors are able to be fine therapists and devoted parents, as well as being dedicated to humanitarian causes.

Cyrulnik noticed that many French children were traumatized by watching the collapse of the twin towers of the World Trade Center on September 11, 2001. However, whether the child was traumatized depended on the reaction of the parents or caregiver, whom Cyrulnik refers to as the attachment figure. The child was shocked if the parent was shocked, conveying his or her shock and horror to the child. In this view the child was not traumatized by the destruction of the victims in the burning and collapsing towers, but responded to the profound emotional response of the parental figure. The parents' reaction is internalized in the inner world and psychic reality of the child. The child is not then primarily empathic with the victims but with the shocked parental authorities (Burlingham & Freud, 1944). The parent's responses are contagious, and the child subjectively resonates with and responds to the affective reactions of the parent. If the attachment figure or parental authority provides a secure base, the child is likely to feel secure. If there is no reassuring caregiver, the child may be traumatized twice, both by the frightening scenes and by the absence of caregiver support and comfort (Freud & Dann, 1951). The context, including secure attachment to an available caregiver, the level of the child's language and cognitive development, and the capacity of the caregivers to affectively communicate with the child, is a factor in promoting or impeding resilience. In the aftermath of trauma, the revival of basic trust and the emotional bond to a concerned caregiver in a safe setting is very important in helping the child (and also adult) to affectively assimilate the traumatic experience (Ornstein, 1985). Putting the associated thoughts and feelings into words helps to organize the disorganizing effect of trauma and to modulate and regulate the profoundly disturbing affects of anxiety, anger, grief, and so forth intrinsic to the traumatic situation.

The intersubjective response of child and caregiver in a potentially traumatic situation is reminiscent of the behavior of infants in the visual cliff experiment (Feinman, 1992). An apparent visual cliff was constructed. When the one-year-old infants started to cross the deep side of the visual cliff, they saw their mother's face either with a smile or with an expression of fear. The majority of infants whose mothers smiled crossed the deep side of the visual cliff, but none of the infants whose mothers were apprehensive were able to cross over. This form of social referencing in infants is more likely a form of maternal affective communication regarding the infant's response than the one-year-old infant's cognitive appraisal of danger. The social referencing response of the infant in the visual cliff situation is analogous to the child's contingent and contagious response to the parent's emotional expression. The child's reaction demonstrates introjection and identification with the parent's feelings and attitude.

Cyrulnik considered the effect of repeated and protracted trauma on the child's and adolescent's evolving identity. In general agreement with Cyrulnik, I regard the effect of trauma on the youngster's identity and ego development as dependent upon the child's innate dispositions, developmental phase, psychic reality, external reality, family, community, society, and culture. The social support is an important factor in resilience, but I am doubtful that it is the most important one. Cyrulnik, however, is correct that the family support can sometimes be stifling, "as protective as a jail" (chapter 2). This will depend on how the child's trauma is processed within the family, for example, whether in silence or expressive speech, and how well the family is able to function. (Of course, endless repetition can be another form of stifling spontaneous affective expression.) What may be decisive is whether the parents or caregivers have themselves been traumatized. Although not true in all cases, traumatization of parents may impair their parenting functions and skills so that they cannot provide the necessary security and safety net for the child. The child also identifies with the parental anxiety and dysphoric, unregulated affects. The resilient child is often able to develop alternative supportive relationships in the host culture and to identify with nurturing, healing, and protective extrafamilial objects (Blum, 1987). The abandoned child could find a secure base through adoption by new caregivers or possibly in a group of peer survivors (Kestenberg & Kahn, 1998). The group of young children described by Anna Freud and Sophie Dann (1951) was largely dependent on each other for basic human warmth and needs.

Cyrulnik referred to a group of Jewish children brought up in families composed of two or three survivors. The individuals in the families were not resilient but were depressed and relatively mute. The children had been indoctrinated to be silent and secretive, and to keep the lowest possible public profile. Their sadness, in my view, was probably also related to the guilt of the survivor. This was guilt transmitted within the surviving family through identification with each other. The surviving family was in mourning for murdered loved ones and a lost sense of community, security, and trust. Cyrulnik described a form of dissociation or split between those children depressed at home, yet happy at school. Children may be guilty about enjoying life outside their home when their bereaved parents agonize over their losses and injuries. Furthermore, these children were ambivalent and guilty about expressing complaints to parents who had suffered so much. These fragile caregivers may have been particularly threatened by a complaining, petulant child. The guilt of the survivor is not simply guilt because of ambivalent death wishes toward murdered loved ones. Survivor guilt may also be related to anger toward other grieving or dysfunctional members of the family as well as guilt over hostility engendered by feelings of abandonment by relatives and friends. The social surround has often been indifferent or downright hostile to Jewish survivors of the Shoah (Holocaust), reinforcing the need of the survivor to suppress thoughts and feelings, fostering the internalization of aggression against the self. Parents and children may enact disguised, modified repetitions of their past trauma with each other (Kogan, 2002). While it is true that survivors' children may have been overinvested in academic success in school where they might find some bit of happiness, other children were overinvested in school because such success was important to their parents to justify their own and their child's survival. Those survivor parents who demand that their children be problem free may promote resilience or contribute to regression.

Krystal (2004) has proposed that core infantile omnipotence provides an unshakable conviction of invulnerability. This invaluable psychological resource is grounded in the infant's secure relationship with an empathic, adoring mothering person. Accordingly, the person with such infantile narcissism can retain initiative, plan, and appropriately evaluate risks and solutions to dangers. However, I believe that infantile omnipotence may have the opposite effect of a person's taking excessive risk with the fantasy of magical protection, without acceptance of limitations. Furthermore, initial survival may appear to validate and bolster dangerous omnipotent fantasy. I agree that mourning may have to be postponed until after release from the traumatic situation. Self-caring and self-soothing may have been impaired. Krystal identifies splitting defenses that help to preserve the self and resilience. In addition to the splitting of good and bad self and object representations, there may be splitting of the observing and experiencing ego, past and present, victim and oppressor. Recovery after massive trauma requires a gradual reintegration of the polarized parts of the personality with their isolated and unregulated affects (Krystal & Krystal, 1988). Affect expression and control may have to be cultivated. A diminished capacity to symbolize and fantasy, a traumatic alexithymia, noted by Krystal and Krystal (1988), may be associated with demands for immediate gratification. With empathic sensitivity to the conflicts of these patients and their therapists, Krystal and Krystal underscore how interpretation without attention to affect intolerance may have no effect. After the war and the Holocaust, the resilient were able to rather resourcefully resume their lives without crippling obsession and identification with the dead. Having been loved, reexperiencing love, and being able to love are seen as vital to resilient recovery.

Issues of resilience are also relevant to the adaptation of children hidden during the war and Holocaust. These children, often separated from their parents, manifested complex problems and conflicts, depending upon each individual and the circumstances. The hidden child has been the subject of a number of studies, and I can only comment here on the extraordinary resilience shown by some children. Some remained with their foster parents, and some were adopted by them; some were reclaimed by surviving parents. Resilience was highly variable, related to the children's innate resources, ego development, and the form and extent of support they received in their particular surround. The Jewish children saved by Christians had split identities between Jewish and Christian, being a part of the foster family and the former biological, Jewish family. Some children only learned of their Jewish origins as adults. Split identities were also evident among other war orphans and refugees. Either family may be idealized or devalued, but internalization of an anti-Semitic surround often resulted in devaluation of the Jewish family as well as self-denigration. Children who were torn from their foster families after the war suffered a double loss. Having lost their original family, they then lost the foster family to whom they had become attached. Being able to mourn the losses and integrate the split identifications and identities was an arduous and essentially lifelong task for many of the survivors. The resilient individuals, favored by new, affectionate relationships in a safe surround, were able to rebuild their personalities and lives, confirming unconscious fantasies of rebirth.

Many survivors of massive trauma have posttraumatic disorders, some with relatively invisible scars. Even among the resilient survivors with minimal symptoms there are pathogenic residua and scars. Resilience may be confined to certain areas and periods of life. Primo Levi, extraordinarily creative after his Auschwitz trauma, was resilient within limits consequent to psychobiological damage and later life stress. He wrote of his irreversible damage and incurable injury, a harbinger of his probable suicide,

> It is interesting to examine the memories of our extreme experiences. . . .
> The memory of a trauma received or inflicted is itself traumatic because to recall it is painful . . . it is iniquitous that the victim himself should still suffer, decades later. . . . It is painful to observe that the offense is incurable. (Anissimov, 2006, p. 361)

The victim of severe trauma can indeed be a prisoner of the past, fixated on trauma, unable to move forward in life. The victim may be flooded by traumatic memories and tormented by anxiety, depression, and/or extremely distressing somatization. The adage holds true that the past is not even past. Terrifying memories, never a simple, precise reproduction of the actual traumatic events, appear in intrusive flashbacks, in nightmares, and in isolated images evoked, for example, by the sound of a siren or an alarm bell. At the other end of the memory spectrum are those whose traumatic memories are repressed, dissociated, and/or affectless, or whose significance is denied or minimized. The traumatic past may be only acknowledged in fragmentary form with isolation or displacement of painful affects. One group cannot get traumatic memories out of their minds, and another group will not let traumatic memories enter their conscious minds. Mired in past trauma, the survivor continually struggles to emerge from the traumatic situation and to expend immense effort in "damage control." Trauma may be recognized in an occupied zone of consciousness while in other aspects repressed, dissociated, and denied (Laub & Auerhahn, 1993). Traumatized individuals may be afraid to look back as noted in the biblical story of Lot; they will turn to salt from an ocean of tears. Like the Greek myth of Orpheus searching for Eurydice, if they look back the fantasy of finding the lost object will have to be relinquished. The loss of loved ones and one's own former self will have to be painfully acknowledged. Reviewing the past may not be possible or even psychologically desirable for some persons for a long time after the traumatic situation. Buried alive, the ghosts of the past may be frightfully revived. The reality is that even the resilient survivor cannot go home again; neither the survivor nor his or her world will ever be the same. What happened in the traumatic past may refer to factual history condensed with personal and familial myths about the past. On the other hand, the survivor may attempt to reconstruct his or her own life with subjective distortion despite dedication to historical and emotional truth. Resilience favors resistance to inner temptation and to external seduction or intimidation to evade or distort the past (Blum, 2007; Bohleber, 2007). The traumatic experience can then be put into personal as well as psychosocial and historical perspective, and assimilated with awareness of sequelae.

Traumatic events of the remote past could not be registered in declarative memory if the trauma occurred before this form of memory developed. Or the trauma could not be registered in the verbal and symbolic processes due to an incapacitated ego. Trauma might still be registered in implicit memory as well as in somatization. Implicit memory is presumed to be nonverbal and nonrepressed yet detectable in transference and behavior. Implicit memory refers to the attainment of automatic skills such as playing the piano or riding a bike. In current controversial propositions, attachment models have been internalized in infant life, persist in implicit memory, and can be recognized in treatment transference. Given the complexity of memory networks, different memory systems may interact with reciprocal influence. Isolated, unaltered implicit memory of trauma awaits confirmation, but clinical work with torture victims and war veterans validates the importance of conscious and unconscious autobiographical, declarative memory.

Social mythology and a social conspiracy of silence invite another form of splitting between the individual's sense and knowledge of historical reality and the distorted reality that has been socially constructed. This split between actual history and historical myth may also involve a splitting of attitude between the generations. The generation of perpetrators may have a strong investment in silent avoidance and amnesia; succeeding generations, with far less guilt and shame, have been able to confront and correct the historical record. This has involved a painful uncovering of the attitudes and activities of the grandparent and parent generations, accomplished in degree and with great difficulty regarding close relatives and friends. Parallel to the concept of group regression, might there be group resilience in the reconstruction and recovery from social and cultural trauma?

In the process of "Healing From the Holocaust" (chapter 6), Henri Parens's remarkable achievements were not magically bestowed or attained with ease. Parens notes that healing from the Holocaust has required lifelong conscious and unconscious efforts to cope with the pain and loss of family; reactive inner and rage; and the refugees' experience of being uprooted, disoriented, while ambivalently adapting to culture shock, change in language and customs, and a new life in a new home and homeland. Parens's experience in the Holocaust was very different from those who had been in death camps, in hiding, or in armed resistance to persecution. The memoir of Henri Parens is a testament and monument of the Holocaust by a very gifted, insightful survivor and psychoanalyst. Parens is aware of the laws of probability and that every survivor of attempted genocide has cheated death against the odds and is lucky to be alive. However, resilience greatly increases the probability, not only of survival, but of avoiding severe, irreversible psychological and physical damage. Resilience, which he agrees is based on internal resources and external support, is nevertheless a complex set of qualities emerging from genetic and developmental processes influenced by time, experience, and object relationships. Resilience is dependent upon a number of synergistic functions and their coordination under different conditions. In my view it is not resilience per se that is subject to regression and to growth, but rather the ego functions, and their stability and flexible coordination, may undergo global or selective regression. Resilience may be apparent in some ego functions but not necessarily in other or all ego functions in the same degree and at the same time. Identification with competent, devoted caregivers promotes cognitive skill, affect regulation, and positive self-esteem. In addition to such factors such as frustration tolerance and impulse and affect control, a number of authors have stressed the importance of agency, autonomy, and the feeling that one's efforts can have favorable effects and produce positive outcomes. These personality resources permit and promote successful achievement. Resilience may also apply to the tolerance of initial disappointment or failure and perseverance in the face of opposition and danger. Resilience seems to be related to the will to live and striving for active mastery rather than passive resignation to one's fate. The predominant attachment and identification appears to be with the mother of birth and life rather than with a rejecting mother or a dead mother. Modest degrees of stress are proposed to immunize the child against later, more severe stress and trauma. Conversely, severe stress and traumatization may have sequelae of ego damage and vulnerability, leaving the child sensitized and at greater risk for subsequent traumatization. The child can adapt to and develop coping skills for moderate degrees of stress, but excessive stress evokes excessive anxiety, regression, and impairment of ego functions necessary for a flexible and innovative adaptation. In general, repeated traumas increase vulnerability and diminish resilience. Trauma tends to activate past trauma, and added trauma undermines and weakens various ego functions such as the crucial differentiation between fantasy and reality. Most analysts, at least in North America, do not accept a death instinct or that humans are governed by life and death instincts, Eros and Thanatos. Resilience and recovery require a necessary strong endowment but also real assistance from the external world and the transmission of life-sustaining values. In order for the survivor to heal from the Holocaust, he or she needs help from helpers who provide needed parental functions. The internalized good object wants the survivor to live in contrast to the murderous bad object and despised self who desire death. Parental life wishes or death wishes communicated to the child may provide a saving grace or a suicidal goal for the child. The parent's caring and ego strengths are usually important for their child's resilience, but not necessarily for the exceptionally endowed child (Anthony & Cohler, 1987).

Are those who believe that nothing is left to chance, that everything is foreordained, less vulnerable to trauma and more resilient during and after a traumatic experience? It is possible, but not proved, that deeply spiritual persons who have great faith in supernatural protection that will save them from death, or believe they will have a rewarding life after death, have a better prognosis. Whether or not the individual is self-reliant and self-confident, or part of a support group with shared beliefs and goals, might be a very valuable sustaining asset. Positive expectations of oneself and the object world facilitate cooperative ventures rather than lonely alienation, passive resignation, or narcissistic withdrawal.

Those who have returned from the Nazi concentration camps or from the Soviet gulag may feel that they returned from another planet. The resilient are able to eventually use adversity to advantage. Parens's unique traumatic experience and personality have propelled him on a life trajectory in which assimilation of the past is used to create a better and brighter present and future. He has persistently labored to heal the wounds of others, with the particular objectives of understanding aggression and preventing violence toward

children. Parens has concluded that children subjected to malignant prejudice, persecution, and repeated traumatization are far more likely to manifest
uncontrolled destructive aggression than children with more normal life experience. Nondestructive aggression can be utilized and more readily integrated
into the personality for positive adaptive purposes. Parens's healing and self-
healing have given him a strong sense of civic duty and altruism, potentiated
by humanitarian and psychoanalytic values. With grace and humility he
understates his extraordinary achievements and his abiding commitment
toward making this a better world for the next generations.

Why did Parens and others write Holocaust memoirs (Bergmann, 1985)?
Why was so little written about the Holocaust in the immediate post–World
War II period? What was the price of the silence of the survivor versus the
reactivation of lacerating memories and the danger of reactivated traumatization? Parens's use of foreign phrases symbolizes his trail of dislocation and
adaptation, and contributes to affect expression and regulation. We know
from such authors as Elie Wiesel and Primo Levi of their need to record and
publish their experience. Denials of the Holocaust incurred outrage and
became illegal in many European countries. Denial attempted to obliterate
the catastrophic tragedy and the memory of all those who were martyred and
murdered. The inner injunction to write the Holocaust memoir is also closely
related to the need to bear witness to the incredible, the long forgotten, and
the unforgettable. Bearing witness breaches the wall of silence and denial. The
witness revives the memory of the murdered, and records the atrocities that
were committed. Capturing the attention of an audience may provide an
emotional catharsis as well as finding sustenance and support in the audience.
It is also a demand for justice that can never be obtained; so many of the perpetrators literally got away with murder.

Inevitably pained, Parens developed severe eczema while writing *Renewal
of Life: Healing From the Holocaust* (2004). Although he didn't want to expose
his patients to his traumatic narrative, he was aware of his unconscious conflict about self-disclosure. Not everything should be or can be publicly
exposed. Anna Freud and others have indicated that they would be taking
secrets to the grave. Why, when, and what should be disclosed is a decision
that is bound to be conflicted and ambivalent for each survivor. Historical
truth, with its intrinsic subjective limitations and variations, is important for
society as well as the individual. Aleksandr Solzhenitsyn bore witness to persecution and mass murder in the Soviet gulag, 1918–1956, in an Olympian
masterwork. He wrote, "I dedicate this to all those who did not live to tell it.

And may they please forgive me for not having seen it all nor remembered it all, for not having divined all of it" (1973, p. iii).

The qualities and components of resilience so apparent in the life and work of Drs. Cyrulnik, Krystal, and Parens are essentially congruent with their own conclusions. Optimism, flexibility, incisive appraisal, decision, and appropriate action are components and correlates of resilience. Coping rather than passive withdrawal are all identified by these authors, and by Steven Southwick, as promoting resilience to the effects of stress, and promoting recovery from trauma. Southwick notes the interaction among these factors, which can be mutually enhancing and synergistic. The capacity to imagine a better future may be a component of resilience, but, I may add, it could also be a consequence of resilience and effective posttraumatic adaptation. While usually very helpful, realistic appraisals of potentially traumatic situations may mobilize panic or denial. False optimism can be very dangerous. Denial and optimism that the Nazi regime would be transient led many to the foreclosure of escape. Southwick's very scholarly interdisciplinary contribution is at the research frontier of neurobiological aspects of stress and resilience. The ability to learn from stress and trauma, to find meaning in adversity, and to profit from knowledge gained while coping with stress facilitates a return to neurobiological homeostasis. Southwick pointedly notes that the converse may also be true, that delay or failure of neurobiological stress symptoms to recover after stress and trauma increases the risk of post-traumatic stress disorder and anxiety and mood disorders. The neurobiological correlates of resilience involve brain networks and regions, the sympathetic and parasympathetic nervous systems, the endocrine and cardiovascular systems, the immune system, and metabolism. Negative emotions theoretically increase autonomic nervous system activity while positive emotions such as pleasure and love decrease autonomic arousal. Positive emotions may imbue stressful experiences with positive meaning and expectations, minimizing feelings of helplessness and hopelessness. Resilient individuals may avoid being overwhelmed, with optimal neurochemical reactions to stress and trauma. Current research has shown that changes in the brain can be observed in the process of learning through repetition. Mature role models and mentors are highly important for the development of resilience. In this connection Southwick notes the repetition of innate primate imitation. From a psychoanalytic point of view, imitation has to be superseded by the internalization and identification with the role model's coping functions. The recent discovery of mirror neurons has led to the proposition that these neurons underlie empathy and identification, providing a genetic neurobiological basis for understanding affective and cognitive meanings of observed behavior (Gallese, Eagle, & Migone, 2007). The changes in the brain occur silently, and for the most part the psychosomatic reactions to stress and trauma occur outside of conscious awareness. Neuropeptides, including oxytocin released during lactation, appear to foster mammalian maternal caregiving and nurturance. Oxytocin also moderates the neurobiological effects of stress reported in postpartum lactating women. Similar responses have been observed in men who received oxytocin during a social stress test.

Unconscious, preconscious, and conscious processes interact in the determination of responses to danger and trauma. In the subcortical brain, the amygdala is primed for automatic anxiety responses consequent to past trauma. From an evolutionary viewpoint this may provide for alarm reactions and "fight or flight"; however, it may also result in uncontrolled immediate panic with impairment of resilience and appropriate decision and action. The benefit of psychoanalytic and psychotherapeutic treatment of panic disorder may be objectively validated, if panic disorder then subsides in conjunction with progressive transformation of amygdala function. The amygdala is necessary for recognizing fear in facial expression, for fear conditioning, and for anxiety regulation (Damasio, 1999). Child abuse may predispose to adult post-traumatic stress disorder, and such trauma has been correlated with diminished volume of the corpus callosum and hippocampus. The hippocampus shrinks as a result of severe trauma, and since declarative autobiographical memory is significantly based in the hippocampus, damage to the hippocampus may interfere with memory function. Giving meaning to new experience and constructing a future, so critical to posttraumatic resilience, seem to be a function of the right hippocampus. Subcortical structures associated with affect and memory communicate with the cerebral cortex and are biopsychologically related to resilience and self-repair (Damasio, 1999; Schore, 2003).

In conclusion, the concept of resilience is multidimensional. Intrapsychic, psychosocial, neurobiological, and biogenetic factors interact to impede or facilitate the developmental processes converging in resilience. Children who have been abused and traumatized are more vulnerable to personality as well as central nervous system damage if they have a biogenetic predisposition to be vulnerable to stress. The concept of resilience shifts attention from neurobiological damage and psychopathology to both the prevention of and recovery from trauma. Genes that fortify stress tolerance, and the presence of one or more resilient caregivers who provide external support and a sustaining relationship, are all important for the development and stability of resilience (Murphy & Moriarty, 1976). While I do not believe that resilience can be induced or indoctrinated, it can be modeled and potentiated. Conversely, resilience can be diminished or lost in states of regression and/or personality damage. Some survivors of severe, protracted, and recurrent traumatizations have, nevertheless, been able to rebuild posttraumatic rewarding lives. Not all those who survive manage to thrive, but resilience can make the difference between effective coping and chronic debility. There is also no simple relationship between resilience in childhood and the resilient adolescent and adult. Irreversible damage is not inevitable, and beneficial life experience as well as psychotherapy favor resilience and recovery. A critic of the concept of resilience might object that it is tautological to have a benign outcome following trauma dependent on resilience and then resilience confirmed by the benign outcome.

Drs. Cyrulnik, Krystal, and Parens have exemplified resilience and have all made very valuable contributions to the understanding and treatment of psychic trauma. Their powerful social conscience testifies to their capacity to assimilate trauma and sublimate impassioned aggressive reactions. Psychoanalysis, self-analysis, and subsequent benevolent life experience paved the way for Parens's poignant, trenchant account of his healing from the Holocaust. Altruism and responsibility are overdetermined and not reducible to the expiation of survivor guilt.

A brief commentary about analytic/therapeutic technique in clinical work with survivors may be permitted. Unanalyzed identification with the aggressor might lead to the abuse of others or masochistic self-torment as might happen with abused children who later become abusive parents. Caregivers can be assisted in helping children to control and resolve destructive aggression. Beyond repression and dissociation, where the trauma has been experienced in infancy or is so damaging that it cannot be represented or verbally communicated, the therapist has to help repair the damage and chaotic confusion. The analyst may have to reconstruct, in degree, missing areas of the survivor's experience and identity. An adult survivor may then come to know the hitherto unknown or bear what had been unbearable. Pharmacological intervention may help the patient deal with overwhelming anxiety, depression, and threats of disorganization. A cohesive self can hopefully be maintained or restored alongside motivation for recovery. This requires a listening and understanding therapist who is able to tolerate the terrible without undue countertransference responses or enactments. Attention to the nonverbal, affects, and somatic reactions may be as important as or initially more important than verbalized memories, fantasies, and associations. Working with survivors demands a sensitive responsiveness without joining the traumatized individual in a folie à deux. The analyst/therapist should be able to avoid being seduced or manipulated into the patient's victim-perpetrator fantasy system. The analyst/therapist has to be sufficiently attuned to transference-countertransference issues to withstand a particularly disturbing transference representation as a cruel perpetrator. This will also permit irrational survivor guilt to be related to the guilt, projected guilt, and lack of guilt of the perpetrator. It is important to interpret and work through internalized injunctions to not know and not speak of trauma and tragedy. Breaking the silence limits intergenerational transmission of trauma. The more the massive trauma can be understood and assimilated, reintegrated within the mature personality, the greater the likelihood that survival will lead to resilient revival and the building of a better tomorrow for one's self and society.

## References

Anissimov, M. (2006). *Primo Levi.* Woodstock, NY: Overlook Press.

Anthony, E., & Cohler, B. (Eds.). (1987). *The invulnerable child.* New York: Guilford Press.

Bergmann, M. (1985). Reflections on the psychological and social function of remembering the Holocaust. *Psychoanalytic Inquiry, 5,* 9–20.

Blum, H. (1987). The role of identification in the resolution of trauma. *Psychoanalytic Quarterly, 56,* 609–627.

Blum, H. (2007). Holocaust trauma reconstructed: Individual, familial, and social trauma. *Psychoanalytic Psychology, 245,* 63–93.

Bohleber, W. (2007). Remembrance, trauma, and collective memory. *International Journal of Psychoanalysis, 88,* 329–352.

Burlingham, D., & Freud. A. (1944). *Infants without families.* London: Allen & Unwin.

Damasio, A. (1999). *The feeling of what happens.* New York: Harcourt.

Feinman. S. (Ed.). (1992). *Social referencing and the social construction of reality in infancy.* New York: Plenum.

Freud, A., & Dann, S. (1951). An experiment in group upbringing. *Psychoanalytic Study of the Child, 6,* 127–168.

Gallese, V., Eagle, M., & Migone, P. (2007). Intentional attunement: Mirror neurons and the neural underpinning of interpersonal relations. *Journal of the American Psychoanalytic Association, 55,* 131–170.

Kestenberg, J., & Kahn, C. (Eds.). (1998). *Children surviving persecution: An international study of trauma and healing.* Westport, CT: Praeger.

Kogan, I. (2002). Enactment in the lives and treatment of Holocaust survivors' offspring. *Psychoanalytic Quarterly, 71*, 251–272.

Krystal, H. (2004). Resilience: Accomodation and recovery. In D. Knafo (Ed.), *Living with terror, working with trauma* (pp. 67–82). New York: Jason Aronson.

Krystal, H., & Krystal, J. (1988). *Integration and self-healing: Affect, trauma, alexithymia.* Hillsdale, NJ: Analytic Press.

Laub, D., & Auerhahn, N. (1993). Knowing and not knowing massive psychic trauma: Forms of traumatic memory. *International Journal of Psychoanalysis, 74*, 287–302.

Machtlinger, V. (in press). How can we understand the resilience shown by the children of Bulldogs Bank psychoanalytically. Paper, Berlin Freud Study Group.

Murphy, L., & Moriarty, A. (1976). *Vulnerability, coping, and growth.* New Haven, CT: Yale University Press.

Neubauer, P., & Neubauer, A. (1990). *Nature's thumbprint: The new genetics of personality.* Boston: Addison-Wesley.

Ornstein, A. (1985). Survival and recovery. *Psychoanalytic Inquiry, 5*, 99–130.

Parens, H. (2004). *Renewal of life: Healing from the Holocaust.* Rockville, MD: Schreiber.

Schore, A. (2003). *Affect regulation and the repair of the self.* New York: Norton.

Solzhenitsyn, A. (1973). *The Gulag Archipelago.* New York: Harper and Row.

Tedeschi, R., Park, C., & Calhoun, L. (1998). *Post-traumatic growth.* Hillsdale, NJ: Lawrence Erlbaum.

# INDEX

abuse: enacting/remembering/reflecting therapy for, 163. *See also* sexual abuse

aggression, 110

Alexander, Franz, 88

ALS. *See* amyotrophic lateral sclerosis

amygdala, 158, 188

amyotrophic lateral sclerosis (ALS), 7–8

anger: chronic, 3

Angier, Carole, 87–88

ANS. *See* autonomic nervous system

anxiety: modest v. excessive, 90; trauma and, 161

attachment: figure as shaken, 23–24; psychodynamic model of, 132–34; systems, 167; theory, 92

Auschwitz Resistance, 55

Auschwitz scrolls, 55–56

autonomic nervous system (ANS): stress responses of, 135

belonging: feeling of, 27

Bowlby, John, 156

brain: emotional systems of, 156; fear system's operation in, 155–56; memory systems in, 157; stress altering chemistry of, 134

Brenner, Ira, 160

*A Brief History of Time* (Hawking), 9

brooding: masochistic, 3

Burlingham, Dorothy, 156

Cannon, Walter B., 88

caregiver: relationship following trauma, 178–80. *See also* foster parents; parenting

chance, 185; humans as challenged by, 94–95; rules of governance, 94

chaos: making sense out of, 26–27

children: gratitude of, 125; Holocaust survivors, 30–31, 181–82; innate capabilities of traumatized, 42; measuring resilience of, 42; representation of time distorted by, 32; resilience capacity of, 39, 156–57, 174; role models/mentors for, 140–42; social network surrounding traumatized, 29; trauma during childhood, 165–67; trauma influencing identity of, 179–80; traumatizing event embedded in development of, 23; war's influence on, 24–25; World Trade Center attack traumatizing, 23–25. *See also* infants; orphans

Coates, Susan, 92

community: social support from, 28. *See also* social support

coping: strategy, 26; with stress, 139

creative arts, 13

creativity: fantasy play and, 123–24, 190; as source/consequence of resilience, 17

culture: EWM changed by, 32

curiosity, 133

Cyrulnik, Boris, 90

danger, 50–51

death: confrontation with, 75; Freud's preoccupation with, 91; instinct, 91–92; longing for, 43–44

defenses: deployment of manic, 78–79; dissociation, 41; resilience and, 134

self-representation: parasitic, 57; traumatic
   splitting of, 57
Selye, Hans, 88
Semrad, Elvin, 167
September 11, 2001, 178; PTSD of disaster
   relief workers following, 67–68
sexual abuse, 67
SNS. *See* sympathetic nervous system
socialization, 125; capacity for, 59
social relations: benefits of, 59
social support: as defined, 142; for developing resilience, 142–44; developmental
   stage and, 144; optimal source of, 144;
   poor, 142–43; strong, 143
Solzhenitsyn, Aleksandr, 186–87
somatic reactions, 157–58
startle reactions, 3
*Still Me* (Reeve), 9
stress: ANS response to, 135; brain chemistry altered by traumatic, 134; coping
   with, 139; heritability and, 136–37;
   HPA axis response to, 135–36; inoculation, 90, 139; optimism in situations of,
   50; reaction of individual to, 88; SNS
   activated by, 135. *See also* post-traumatic
   stress disorder
Suchomel, Franz, 52–53
suffering: rebound from, 4–5
surrender, 55
survivors: guilt of, 62, 88, 108, 180;
   Holocaust, 30–31, 49, 57, 177–78; of
   sexual abuse, 67; syndromes, 62
survivor testimonies: cognitive styles of,
   56–57
sympathetic nervous system (SNS): stress
   activated, 135

terrorism: behavior/emotional problems
   from traumas of, 40–41. *See also*
   September 11, 2001
time, 9; diachronic, 33–34; representation
   of, 32; war and, 32
torture, 74
transference, 167
trauma: anxiety and, 161; caregiver relationship following, 178–80; in childhood,

165–67; children and, 23–25, 29,
42, 179–80; clinical implications of,
155–60; destructive reactivation of, 161;
dissociation as defense in psychic, 41;
ego and, 3, 53; of family, 31–32; Freud
on, 159; identity influenced by, 179–80;
invisible scars following, 182; medication for patients with, 160; memory of,
34, 158, 168, 183; motivations to heal
from massive, 92–93; narrative identity
determined by, 28; neurobiology of,
155–60; oral history and, 56; posttrauma state/parameters, 94; pretrauma
state/parameters, 93; prevention and ego
functions, 53; process of, 52; psychoanalytic clinicians and patients with,
160–64, 173; psychoanalytic concepts
of, 159–60; recall/abreaction of, 44;
from representation/reality, 24–25;
resilience and, 164–68; resilient narrative of, 26–27, 45; severe, 44–45,
182–83; stages of process of, 69–81;
from terrorism, 40–41; transgenerational transmission of, 121–22;
transtrauma parameters, 94; traumatic
situation v. state of, 54; treatment of
severe, 44–45; understanding, 189; validating, 161; vicissitudes of massive psychic, 69; victims of severe, 182–83. *See
also* intrapsychic trauma; post-traumatic
stress disorder; psychological trauma;
traumatic events; war trauma
trauma preparation: cognitive/behavioral
   model of, 68; as new field, 68
traumatic events: becoming part of personality, 23; different meanings for same,
   25; feelings attributed to, 28–29; mas-
   tering meaning attributed to, 25–26;
   of remote past, 183
traumatism: stage of, 39

United Nations Children's Fund, 39–40
*The Universe in a Nutshell* (Hawking), 9

Vietnam War: veterans, 49, 136
Vrba, Rudolph, 55, 107

war: children as influenced by, 24–25; in
    Lebanon, 29–30; time's representation
    distorted for children of, 32. *See also*
    Vietnam War
Warsaw Ghetto uprising, 91
war trauma: reaction to, 41–44; symptoms
    arising directly from, 40

Wiesel, Elie, 107
Wilde, Jan, 8
World Trade Center: children traumatized by
    attack on, 23–25. *See also* September 11,
    2001

Ziering, Sigi, 79–80

# ABOUT THE EDITORS AND CONTRIBUTORS

Susan C. Adelman, PhD, Faculty, Psychoanalytic Center of Philadelphia; Clinical Associate, Department of Psychiatry, University of Pennsylvania Health System; Adjunct Medical Staff, Pennsylvania Hospital

Salman Akhtar, MD, Professor of Psychiatry, Jefferson Medical College; Training and Supervising Analyst, Psychoanalytic Center of Philadelphia, Philadelphia, PA

Harold P. Blum, MD, Clinical Professor of Psychiatry and Training Analyst, New York University School of Medicine, Department of Psychiatry

Ira Brenner, MD, Training and Supervising Analyst, Psychoanalytic Center of Philadelphia, Clinical Professor of Psychiatry, Jefferson Medical College

Boris Cyrulnik, PR.D., Dr. Hon. Causa, Neurologist, Psychiatrist, Director of Diploma of Attachment and Families Systems, University of Toulon, France

Henry Krystal, MD, Professor Emeritus of Psychiatry, Michigan State University, and Member of the Faculty, Michigan Psychoanalytic Institute and the Michigan Psychoanalytic Council

Linda C. Mayes, MD, Special Advisor to the Dean, Arnold Gesell Professor of Child Psychiatry, Pediatrics, and Psychology, Yale Child Study Center

Fatih Ozbay, MD, Assistant Professor of Psychiatry, Mount Sinai School of Medicine, New York

Henri Parens, MD, Professor of Psychiatry, Jefferson Medical College; Training and Supervising Analyst (Adult and Child), Psychoanalytic Center of Philadelphia, Philadelphia, PA

Barbara Shapiro, MD, Training and Supervising Analyst, Psychoanalytic Center of Philadelphia; Associate Professor of Pediatrics and Psychiatry, University of Pennsylvania School of Medicine

Melvin Singer, MD, Training and Supervising Analyst, Psychoanalytic Center of Philadelphia; Clinical Associate Professor, Department of Psychiatry, University of Pennsylvania School of Medicine

Steven M. Southwick, MD, Professor of Psychiatry, Yale School of Medicine; Deputy Director, National Center for PTSD, VA Connecticut HealthCare System

Glenda Wrenn, MD, Chief Resident in Psychiatry, University of Pennsylvania School of Medicine, Philadelphia, PA